美国建筑与文化

孙晓辉　主编
王婷婷　孙蒙蒙　彭瑞红　陈磊　副主编

山东大学出版社
·济南·

图书在版编目(CIP)数据

美国建筑与文化：汉、英/孙晓辉主编. —济南：山东大学出版社，2020.12

ISBN 978-7-5607-6978-3

Ⅰ. ①美… Ⅱ. ①孙… Ⅲ. ①英语—阅读教学—高等学校—教材②建筑物—介绍—美国 Ⅳ. ①H319.4：TU

中国版本图书馆 CIP 数据核字(2021)第 060225 号

Meiguo Jianzhu yu Wenhua

策划编辑 唐 棣

责任编辑 李 璐

封面设计 杜 婕

出版发行 山东大学出版社

社 址 山东省济南市山大南路 20 号

邮政编码 250100

发行热线 (0531)88363008

经 销 新华书店

印 刷 济南巨丰印刷有限公司

规 格 787 毫米×1092 毫米 1/16

16.75 印张 463 千字

版 次 2020 年 12 月第 1 版

印 次 2020 年 12 月第 1 次印刷

定 价 38.00 元

前　言

教材简介

根据《大学英语教学指南(2020版)》,大学英语教学的主要内容可分为通用英语、专门用途英语和跨文化交际三个部分,由此形成大学英语必修课、限定选修课和任意选修课三个类别的课程。本书作为专门用途英语在线开放课程"游美国,学英语"的配套教材,旨在赏析美国著名近现代建筑的同时介绍美国文化、全面提高学习者的英语能力。本书适合作为高等学校相关专业学生专门用途英语的选修课教材使用,也适合欲从事建筑业翻译的英语专业学生学习使用。

本书共11章,介绍了美国城市的地标建筑、著名历史建筑、名人故居、科技企业园区、好莱坞电影中的传奇建筑、著名大学建筑,以及能源、农业、交通等领域的各种基础设施建筑。书中每节配有背景文化讲解和中文导读,让学生轻松了解美国近现代建筑特色以及建筑背后的历史文化知识;同时,通过精心挑选的外刊阅读材料和难度递增的课后练习题,学生们可以逐步提高词汇、阅读、听力、口语和写作技能。

教材特色

· 建筑知识与英语能力共融

本书在讲解建筑背后的美国历史文化的同时,引导学生深入学习与建筑相关的英语知识,提高他们的口语表达和写作能力。本书使大学英语从"单一的语言学习"走向新文科所倡导的"学科交叉融合”，努力实现培养“国际化、创新型、懂外语的复合人才”这一特色目标。

• 文化素养与批判性思维共育

本书将美国历史文化融入经典的美国名师名家代表建筑作品中进行讲授，涵盖城市地标、国家公园、工业厂房、交通设施、农业生产、能源利用、城市街道等类型，同时使用新闻报道、文学作品等丰富学习资源，激发学生的学习兴趣。本书培养学生在中西方文化交流中的历史观，提升他们的视野和格局；同时，积极培育学生的思辨能力，启发学生运用批判性思维方法理性分析美国历史发展进程中的问题与矛盾。

• 全球视野与文化自信共建

本书从科技发展的全球视野分析美国在城市人居环境、绿色环保建筑、大型基础设施等方面的发展历程，引导学生深度讨论科技进步对国家发展的影响，激发学生的科学精神和民族责任感从而在跨文化交际中坚定中国文化自信和民族自豪感，更好应对新形势下的大国关系问题。

编者的话

“智慧树网”在线平台数据显示，在过去两年时间里，“游美国，学英语”这门课程得到了来自全国20个省、自治区、直辖市的59所高校两万余名在校大学生的认可。他们不仅认真完成了这门在线课程的学习，还就他们关心的问题跟我们进行了深入的探讨和交流。在师生思想碰撞中，我们发现了学生们的兴趣，也了解了他们的疑惑、困难和问题。我们基于网络教学中的这些数据丰富了本书的内容，因此这本书的部分内容要感谢那些积极参与我们课程的同学们——是你们对知识的孜孜以求、对未知的钩深索隐，让我们有了无限的动力把这本书编好。

语言是文化的载体，学习一门语言离不开对该语言背后的文化的学习。建筑不仅是一种工程技术，也是艺术、历史和文化的融合。正如我们设计课程时所畅想的那样——将语言、文化和建筑融合起来，依托建筑知识输入丰富英语语言学习，而不是以学习语言本身为主要目的，只有这样我们才能用英语传播知识、传递思想、交流文化。我们希望学生们借此书认识到用英语获取信息和交流信息的重要性，从而也提高英语学习的主动性和自觉性。

最后，由于编者教学压力大、编写时间仓促，教材中难免会有疏漏和错误，恳请您向我们提出宝贵的修改意见。

编　者

2020 年 12 月 18 日

目　　录

第一章　美国城市地标建筑

概　述

美国最大城市排行榜的前三名分别是：纽约、洛杉矶和芝加哥。大规模的城市并不是美国的传统，在美国建国后的最初 150 年中，城市人口比例非常低。即便到了今天，根据 2018 年的统计，人口超过 10 万的城市也仅有 310 个，居住在超过 5 万人的城镇中的人口仅占全国人口的 40%。本章所选择的美国城市中有些是人口和经济数据排位靠前的城市；有些城市则具有独特的历史地位和文化价值，它们同样是我们了解美国的一个重要窗口。本章所包含的城市有：代表国家权力的华盛顿特区，世界金融中心纽约，体现西部开发特色的西雅图，湖区城市发展的杰出之作芝加哥，充满传奇色彩的费城和美国历史文化名城波士顿。在这一章中，我们将从地标建筑的视角出发，探访这些城市发展背后的历史和文化特色。

第一节　美国首都——华盛顿特区

2019 年，美国首都华盛顿的人口仅 70 万，抵不过中国的一些县级市；它的实际生产总值为 1093 亿美元，居美国第 34 位，大概相当于中国的辽宁沈阳或者山东烟台。但华盛顿特区的影响力不可小觑。2019 年全球城市 500 强的排名中它位居第 20 名。[①] 它有这样的影响力靠的不是经济，而是它的政治、文化背景。它是美国唯一的一个直辖特区城市，是大多数美国联邦政府机关与各国驻美国大使馆的所在地，是世界银行、国际货币基金组织等国际组织总部的所在地。此外，它还拥有为数众多的博物馆与历史文化遗迹。

① "How Many Cities Are There in the United States", https://www.reference.com / geography / many-cities-united-states-cfb3be08284e6a62.

Culture Express

华盛顿特区的地标建筑(landmarks)可分为三类。第一类是与其政治中心地位相关联的,比如白宫和美国国会大厦(United States Capitol)。第二类是各种风格的纪念碑、纪念馆。它们大部分环绕在国家广场的周围,其中最耀眼的是矗立在全城中心位置的华盛顿纪念碑。它高 169 米,内部安装电梯,游客们可以在 70 秒内到达顶端,进行免费参观。其他有名的纪念场所有林肯纪念堂、杰弗逊纪念堂、越战纪念碑、马丁·路德·金纪念碑等。在华盛顿纪念碑和国家广场之间有十座博物馆或美术馆,它们构成了华盛顿特区的第三类地标性建筑。其中,史密森尼博物院是世界上最大的博物馆体系,位于国家广场旁的是它的主楼。

Reading Passage 1

导读

下文介绍了华盛顿特区的行政区划以及华盛顿纪念碑作为历史文化遗迹的基本信息。

Washington, D.C., formally the District of Columbia and commonly referred to as Washington, D.C., or the District, is the capital of the United States. Founded after the American Revolution as the **seat** of government of the newly independent country, Washington was named after George Washington, the first president of the United States and a **Founding Father.** As the seat of the United States federal government and several international organizations, Washington, D.C. is an important world political capital. The city, located on the Potomac River bordering Maryland and Virginia, is one of the most visited cities in the world, with more than 20 million tourists annually.

The geometric layout of Washington, D.C.'s streets and green spaces, originally designed by Pierre L'Enfant, reserved a **prominent** space for a monument to George Washington at the intersection of lines radiating south from the White House and west from the Capitol. In 1833, the Washington National Monument Society, a private organization, was formed to fund and build a monument to the first president that would be "**unparalleled** in the world." The Society **solicited** for donations and designs for a decade, settling on a design by Robert Mills in 1845. Mills' design called for a 600-foot Egyptian-style **obelisk** ringed by thirty 100-foot columns. The design was **audacious**, ambitious, and expensive, creating numerous complications during its construction.

(Adapted from *https://www.nps.gov / wamo / learn / historyculture / index.htm*)

注释:

1.seat (组织、活动的)中心地,所在地;(豪门的)宅邸
2.Funding Father 开国元勋
3.the geometric layout 几何结构

4.prominent 杰出的

5.unparalleled 史无前例的

6.solicit 恳求

7.obelisk 方尖碑，古埃及的杰作之一，是古埃及崇拜太阳的纪念碑，方尖碑外形呈尖顶方柱状，由下而上逐渐缩小，顶端形似金字塔尖

8.audacious 大胆创新的

Reading Passage 2

导读

自由广场(Freedom Plaza)距离白宫仅几个街区。这个广场的地面用大理石和花岗岩铺设了一幅地图，展示了华盛顿特区建城之初的街道，现在人们不仅能够看到这些最初的街道的布局，还能在上面行走。这是对华盛顿特区这个城市的历史非常好的纪念。2011 年，在阿富汗战争爆发 10 周年纪念日的前一天，自由广场曾经上演了一场“占领华盛顿”的抗议示威活动。示威者们高举标语，谴责大企业利用金钱影响政治，要求政府将更多资源投入保障民生的项目中，同时反对政府补贴大企业或在海外发动战争。下文摘自《华盛顿邮报》的报道。

Many of those who “occupied” Freedom Plaza on Thursday said they had never been to a protest before but were **inspired** to come to downtown Washington by the Occupy Wall Street movement that began last month in New York and has spread to cities across the country.

“This is the first time I’ve ever done anything like this,” said Tina Strobel, an unemployed medical transcriptionist from Kansas who had driven 1,100 miles with her husband and teenage son for Thursday’s event. She sat in the grass, clutching a sign that read, “Lost my job, found an occupation.”

Strobel said she had lost faith in the country’s political system during the past two years, but “when I read about this, I thought, well maybe this will be a beginning.”

Hundreds opened sleeping bags and raised tents in the public plaza near the White House, **vowing** to stay indefinitely—or until their voices were heard. (They only have National Park Service permits through Sunday.)

First-timers like Strobel stood side by side with veteran antiwar and anti-poverty activists, chanting, singing, and waving signs that said “Tax the rich.” They **derided corporate greed**, ineffective political leadership, and the growing inequity between the rich and poor. Many carried signs and identified themselves as part of the “99 percent”—a dig at the 1 percent of American earners who take in a quarter of the country’s income.

Christopher Bueker, 25, a paraprofessional in the Cincinnati public school system, set up a tent in Freedom Plaza with three friends who had traveled to Washington for the event. He said he was happy that a protest movement that he likened to those in Europe and the Middle East had finally been sparked in the United States.

"We're definitely influenced by movements happening all over the world," he said, "This isn't just happening in D.C. This is happening globally."

(Adapted from *https://www.washingtonpost.com / local / occupy-dc-protesters-rally-in-freedom-plaza* /2011/10/06/*gIQATeeLQL_story.html*)

注释：

1.inspire 激励，启发
2.vowing 宣誓
3.deride 嘲弄，嘲笑
4.corporate greed 企业的贪婪

Reading Passage 3

导读

华盛顿特区的纪念碑代表了人们对历史人物和历史事件的反思。位于国家广场西南部的马丁·路德·金纪念碑于2011年揭幕，以纪念1963年马丁·路德·金在国家广场的林肯纪念堂前发表的演讲"*I Have a Dream*"。那次集会有25万人参加，对美国的民权运动影响深远。这个雕塑出自中国雕塑家雷宜锌之手。同样留下中国人印记的还有华盛顿纪念碑。1848年，中国清政府为华盛顿纪念碑的建造捐献了一块花岗岩石碑并镌刻了碑文，它如今镶嵌在华盛顿纪念碑第十层内壁上。

下面这篇文章介绍了一位华裔美国人Maya Lin设计越战纪念碑的过程。

Vietnam Veterans Memorial, also called The Wall, is a national monument in Washington, D.C., honoring members of the U.S. armed forces who served and died in the Vietnam War (1955-75). The memorial, located near the western end of the Mall, is a black granite V-shaped wall inscribed with the names of the approximately 58,000 men and women who were killed or missing in action. It was designed by American architect Maya Lin.

As a senior at Yale University, Lin entered a nationwide competition sponsored by the Vietnam Veterans Memorial Fund, and her design was selected from the more than 1,400**submissions** that were received.

In 1981, Lin wore her hair down to her knees. She was a **myopic grind** so indifferent to the rest of the world that she often didn't bother to wear her glasses in class. "I grew up in a college town in the middle of Appalachia," she explained, "so I'm still wearing Frye boots, and wearing my hair really long, and everyone's thinking I'm some **sixties hippie.** I have no idea what that's about. I'm not cutting my hair because I'm a good Chinese daughter. I'm wearing Frye boots because I'm a fashion disaster. And they connected me with antiwar and sixties **radicals.**" She was also, of course, a woman, and her parents were Asian. The veterans decided that the best move would be to get her off the stage as fast as possible and let the grownups take over. They misjudged their designer. "I'm fairly **clueless**," Lin told me, "I'm also really stubborn."

(Adapted from *https://www.thehistoryreader.com/military-history/maya-lin-vietnam-veterans-memorial/*)

注释：

1.submission 提交
2.myopic 近视的
3.grind 美语中表示刻苦用功的学生
4.sixties hippie 美国20世纪60年代的嬉皮士，指代身着奇装异服、与社会格格不入的人
5.radical 激进分子
6.clueless 一无所知的

Word Power

1.*Adjectives are often used to describe a person or thing or give extra information. Which of these adjectives are positive (P)? Which are negative (N)? Which could be either (E)?*

stubborn ________
ineffective ________
prominent ________
unparalleled ________
audacious ________

2.*Fill in the blanks with an appropriate word from the above table. Change the form where necessary. Each word can be used only once.*

(1)He has an ________ plan to win the presidency.
(2)The country is facing a crisis ________ since the Second World War.
(3)This is the most ________ independent newspaper.
(4)He is a ________ character used to getting his own way.
(5)The train company is overstaffed and notoriously ________.

Summary

Fill in the blanks with words or phrases from Reading Passage 3.

Vietnam Veterans Memorial is a black granite V-shaped wall (1) ________ with the names of soldiers served and died in the Vietnam War. Its (2) ________ is an American architect Maya Lin, who was a senior at Yale University. Lin's design was (3) ________ from the more than 1,400 (4) ________. Maya Lin was (5) ________ by the veterans, but she counted herself as (6) ________ and (7) ________.

Listening

Scan the code and listen to a microlecture about the landmarks in Washington, D. C. Please choose the best answer to each of the following questions.

(1)Who gave Washington D.C. the name "A city of magnificent intentions"?

A.George Washington.　　B. Christopher Columbus.

C.Franklin Roosevelt.　　D. Charles John Huffam Dickens.

(2)Who is the main drafter and writer of *The Declaration of Independence*?

A.Thomas Jefferson.　　B. George Washington.

C.Franklin Roosevelt.　　D. Theodore Roosevelt.

(3)Which of the following building was designed by Maya Lin?

A. Vietnam Veterans Memorial.　　B. Second World War Memorial.

C. Jefferson Memorial.　　D. Martin Luther King, Jr. Memorial.

Speaking

Washington, D.C. is a city of magnificent intentions. Think about in what ways its architecture is different from the other American cities' and then discuss with your classmates. Refer to the following words and expressions if necessary.

monument / memorial / museum / commemoration / awe-inspiring / solemn / a feast for the eyes

Writing

1. Example Sentence

Washington, D.C., formally the District of Columbia and **commonly referred to as** Washington, D.C., or the District, is the capital of the United States.

2. Analysis

(1) Washington, D.C.的正式名称是 the District of Columbia。

(2)现在有人叫它 Washington, 或者 D.C. 或者 the District。

(3)它是美国的首都,即 it is the capital of the United States。

为了传递更丰富的信息,同时又保持句子主干部分简明清晰,(1)和(2)这两条信息被放在主语后,作同位语。这种写作方法值得我们学习借鉴。

3.Practice

使用同位语,用一句话表达下面的信息。

Lin graduated from Yale University.

Lin was a designer of the Vietnam Veterans Memorial.

Lin entered the competition and won again.

第二节 国际金融中心——纽约

纽约是美国第一大城市，"大都市"是它最鲜亮的名片。然而2001年的一场恐怖袭击暴露出这个庞然大物的脆弱之处。这一节中，我们既涉猎它曾纸醉金迷的历史，看看大财阀们的意气凌云，也阅览后现代设计师对以往种种的总结与反思。全球人类构成的是一个命运共同体，在构建新的全球价值的过程中，这些经验与理念的互通是一条必经之路。

Culture Express

纽约的世界贸易中心曾是两座高达110层的大厦，号称"双子星"，这两座高耸入云的大厦是当时纽约的标志性建筑。在2001年9月11日的恐怖袭击中，两架飞机分别撞向世贸中心北塔楼和南塔楼，随即发生爆炸，世界贸易中心所有建筑损毁殆尽、面目全非，"双子星"永远消失在人们的视野中。新闻界把纽约世贸中心的爆炸现场称为"ground zero"。"ground zero"最初用来指原子弹爆炸的地点，因为爆炸点附近的一切都被炸毁，荡然无存。后来人们不仅用"ground zero"表示一片狼藉的爆炸现场，而且也用来指任何威力强大的爆炸装置的攻击目标。如果把十几岁孩子的卧室比作"ground zero"，那大概是因为这些孩子的房间乱得一团糟。

Reading Passage 1

导读

位于纽约的克莱斯勒大厦被誉为纽约最美的摩天大楼，它是爵士乐时代装饰建筑的杰出代表作。它背后是一个美国汽车工业"飞黄腾达"的时代故事。它的缔造者们为它倾尽财力和智力。近百年来，它的珠光宝气、它的精美绝伦使它在纽约的天空下傲然绽放，"艳压群芳"。

The Chrysler Building is an example of a building caught up in the **quest** to become the tallest in the world, which it obtained briefly for 11 months before it was surpassed by the Empire State Building. But because of its **iconic** and beautiful design, the height of the building never really mattered.

Being a classic example of **Art Deco architecture**, the Chrysler Building is considered by many contemporary architects to be one of the finest buildings in the world. In 2005, New York's Skyscraper Museum asked one hundred architects, builders, critics, engineers and historians to choose their 10 favorite New York towers. The Chrysler Building came in first place with 90% of people ranking it number one.

The building was designed to represent the Chrysler automobile and the machine age of the 1920s. **Gargoyles** and eagles ornamented the building like the hood **ornaments** of the Plymouth automobile. The corner ornaments were made to look like the 1929 Chrysler **radiator** caps.

The quest for height **supremacy** continued in secret. Being built simultaneously, 40 Wall Street was also boasting of becoming the tallest building in the world. 40 Wall Street's **spire** was lengthened by 60 feet to push it to 925 feet, or 85 feet taller than the Chrysler Building's plan.

So, Chrysler and the designer of the building, Van Alen decided to add a surprise 186-foot spire. They **hoisted** 4 parts of the spire secretly to the top and **riveted** them together in 90 minutes. 40 Wall Street even held a celebration for being the tallest building in the world, without realizing that they had been surpassed.

But Chrysler's victory would only last for 11 months when the Empire State Building surpassed it as the tallest building in the world. But here we see that the quest for the world's tallest building didn't really matter, as buildings will always be built taller. In the end, it was Van Alen's design that is most iconic. It may not be the tallest building in New York, but it is the best looking.

(Adapted from *https://www.jamesmaherphotography.com / new-york-historical-articles / chrysler-building /*)

注释:

1.quest 探索,追求
2.iconic 图标的,偶像的
3.Art Deco architecture 装饰艺术建筑
4.gargoyles 滴水兽
5.ornaments 装饰物
6.radiator 散热器
7.supremacy 最高地位,霸权
8.spire 塔尖
9.hoist 吊起
10.rivet 铆接

Reading Passage 2

导读

“9·11”事件之后,纽约的建筑还能充分展现人们对天空的“征服欲”吗?一座座拔地而起的摩天大楼投向天空的剪影,构架出一片“真实”森林。在这片森林里,有风生水起的金融界的弄潮儿,也有迷茫的都市穿梭人。在一场恐怖袭击灾难后,建筑师们将对他们的作品做出怎样的反思?

New York's skyline is probably one of the best known in the world. Visitors and natives alike would undoubtedly be able to trace the **silhouettes** of its buildings with their eyes closed.

Less familiar, but no less striking, are the new constructions shaping up in the city.

The 21st century has brought some exciting new developments.

More than 15 years ago, *New York Times* architecture critic Herbert Muschamp wrote, "After the **catastrophe** of 9/11, who wanted to think about the **aesthetics** of architecture? For many people, it turned out, buildings were the targets of the terrorist attacks. Fantasies of new buildings became a form of recovery: signs of the city's **resilience** in the face of unprecedented enemy **assault.**"

Today, New York is experimenting with **scale**, form and texture, and is no longer just a city of tall, shiny buildings that reflect a desire to push engineering abilities, but a playground for architects who wish to innovate.

The High Line is one of the most successful and well-known spaces of this new urban makeup. **Teeming** with visitors, the project takes advantage of an abandoned railroad to build a public space at human scale.

Another addition to the city's **revamp** is Renzo Piano's sculptural new home for the Whitney Museum of American Art, a display of severe and exciting lines in his signature style.

(Adapted from *https://edition.cnn.com/style/article/new-york-contemporary-architecture/index.html*)

注释:

1.silhouettes 轮廓,剪影
2.catastrophe 灾难
3.aesthetics 美学
4.resilience 快速恢复的能力,回弹
5.assault 袭击,攻击
6.scale 规模
7.teem 充满,倾注
8.revamp 翻新,修改

Word Power

Fill in the blanks with the words given below. Change the form where necessary. Each word can be used only once.

revamp, rivet, hoist, radiate, ornament

(1)Decorations and patterns on a building or a piece of furniture can be referred to as ________.

(2)A ________ is a short metal pin with a flat head which is used to fasten flat pieces of metal together.

(3)If someone ________ something, they make changes to it in order to try and improve it.

(4)If something ________ heat or light, heat or light comes from it.

(5)If you ________ something heavy somewhere, you lift it or pull it up there.

Summary

Fill in the blanks with words or phrases from Reading Passage 2.

As a classic example of (1) ________ architecture, the Chrysler building was designed to represent the Chrysler (2) ________ and the (3) ________ age of the 1920s. Gargoyles and eagles (4) ________ the building like the hood ornaments of the Plymouth automobile. The corner ornaments were made to look like the 1929 Chrysler (5) ________ caps. After being the tallest building in the world for only 11 months, it was surpassed by the (6) ________ Building. But because of its (7) ________ and beautiful design, the height of the building never really mattered. It is considered by many (8) ________ architects to be one of the finest buildings in the world.

Listening

Scan the code and listen to a microlecture about New York City. Please choose the best answer to each of the following questions.

(1)Which of the following is the greenest Skyscraper in New York City?

A. George Washington. B. John Hancock Center.

C. The Empire State Building. D. Bank of America Tower.

(2) What was the name of the city before it was called New York City?

A. New Amsterdam. B. George Town.

C. Amsterdam. D. York.

(3) Which is the tallest building in New York City?

A. One World Trade Center. B. World Trade Center.

C. The Empire State Building. D. Chrysler Building.

Speaking

Can you briefly introduce the competition of buildings to be the tallest skyscraper in 1930s in New York City? Refer to the following words and phrases if necessary.

the Chrysler automobile / the machine age / ornaments / gargoyles / hoist / spire / rivet

Writing

1. Example Sentence

Less familiar, but no less striking, are the new constructions shaping up in the city.

2. Analysis

(1)less familiar 的意思是：不怎么熟悉。

(2)no less 的意思是：仍然，依旧。

(3)familiar 和 striking 都是作表语的形容词，被提前到句首时，后面的句子主谓倒装。

(4)使用 but 对比前后，作者想表达“虽然不那么熟悉，但引人瞩目”的意思。

这种倒装句的写作方法可以使句式富于变化，值得我们学习借鉴。

3. Practice

使用倒装句改写下面句子。

(1)Those who are contented are happy.

(2)The attack was so sudden that he had no time to escape.

第三节　风城——芝加哥

一如迈克尔·乔丹在全世界篮球迷心目中占据的重要位置，芝加哥在很多人看来，同样是一座有重要意义的城市。它曾是世界上发展最迅速的城市，是美国东西部水陆交通的枢纽；它曾经历了浴火重生的痛苦，也是孕育了工人福利的摇篮。作为“摩天大楼的故乡”，这里有万众瞩目的天际线；同样地，作为国际金融中心，它的地位与纽约相比也是不遑多让。

芝加哥是美国第三大城市，在伊利诺伊州，它可谓“一家独大”，因此，许多人想当然地把它当成了州首府，因此还闹了一个非常著名的乌龙。二战时为阻止德军的伪装渗透，美军宪兵以美国人众所周知的常识来问询甄别。一次，一名宪兵拦住布拉德利将军，问他伊州首府是哪里，将军正确地回答了是斯普林菲尔德，但这个宪兵竟认为将军答错而将其扣押，可见这个错误有多么普遍。当然，作为伊利诺伊州首府所在地的斯普林菲尔德并不是一个默默无闻的城市，那里曾出过一位律师，名叫亚伯拉罕·林肯。

Culture Express

1871 年芝加哥大火，2/3 的房屋被毁，重建工作吸引了来自全国各地的建筑师。为了在有限的城市中心区内建造更多房屋，现代高层建筑开始在芝加哥出现。在采用钢铁等新材料以及高层框架等新技术建造摩天大楼的过程中，芝加哥的建筑师们逐渐形成了趋向简洁独创的风格，芝加哥学派(Chicago School)由此诞生。这个学派突出了功能在建筑设计中的主导地位，明确了功能与形式的主从关系，力图摆脱折衷主义的羁绊，使之符合新时代工业化精神。芝加哥学派包括了众多建筑师，他们建筑设计的共同特点是：注重内部功能，强调结构的逻辑表现，立面简洁、明确，并采用了整齐排列的大片玻璃窗，突破了传统建筑的沉闷之感。

Reading Passage 1

导读

从密歇根湖远望芝加哥，一座座别具一格的摩天大楼拔地而起，你会恍惚觉得这里是纽约。芝加哥大火对芝加哥这座城市的许多建筑设计可谓影响巨大：街道变宽，楼房变高，自然元素融入外观设计，建材与科技进步结合等，处处显示出芝加哥人无坚不摧、大胆果敢的历史担当。

After the Great Chicago Fire of 1871, a bold commercial style of architecture emerged in the city. The buildings constructed immediately after the city's rapid rebuild became unsuited to supporting the **flourishing** downtown. The **Chicago School** was a **culmination** of timely and **groundbreaking** engineering techniques, such as the introduction of the **hydraulic** elevator, which made it possible to extend a building's height over six stories. Improved techniques in foundation construction also helped architects take building to new heights on the **swampy** Chicago ground, and steel frameworks replacing iron **skeleton construction** made the skyscraper possible—these steel and glass structures were flexible in terms of floor plan and virtually fireproof.

But it was the details and flourishes—the artistic consideration—of these tall buildings that made the Chicago School iconic. Architects like Daniel Burnham and John Wellborn Root and William Le Baron Jenney added delicate natural forms to the interiors, **adorning** the cornices and entrances with flowers, leaves, wreaths, and ribbons. Louis Sullivan took those same forms and upgraded them by adding geometric shapes, covering facades with lacy roulette curves.

Buildings of the Chicago School can be singled out by their stocky appearance, substantial height, masonry cladding, and decorative cornices. Many feature Chicago windows, fixed central glass panels flanked by two narrower glass sashes, filling bays that are often repeated horizontally and vertically.

(Adapted from *https://chicago.curbed.com / 2019/12/5/20976351/ chicago-architecture-guide*)

注释:

1.flourishing 繁荣的,茂盛的

2.Chicago School 芝加哥学派,指的是 19 世纪晚期芝加哥一群设计和建造摩天大楼的建筑师和工程师

3.culmination 定点,极盛期

4.groundbreaking 开创性的,突破性的

5.hydraulic 液压的,用水发动的

6.swampy 沼泽的,湿而软的

7.skeleton construction 骨架结构

8.adorn 装饰

Reading Passage 2

导读

雕塑是城市地标建筑的重要组成部分。芝加哥的一座叫作“云门”的雕塑位于密歇根湖畔,背靠广袤的平原,毗邻鳞次栉比的现代高楼。建筑师通过雕塑的曲线形镜面反射出

头顶的天空、脚下的土地，以及身处其中的自己。也许设计师就是想通过视觉创造，让参观者看到自然与自我的真实存在。

Chicago, with its elementary geography of an immense plain, lake and magnificent man-made urban landscape, is made for *Cloud Gate*. The sculpture, in a dialogue with the skyscrapers that create **verticality** in this flat space, is an instrument that allows everyone to play with light to propose all the mixtures, all the **distortions**, all the reconstructions of this landscape. It is a new scope, which, by distortion and **dilatation**, changes how we see us in the world. This sculpture processes the elements of the landscape around the viewer, and changes his or her perception. The Skyline is now in front of us. We are in immediate **proximity** with the massive buildings behind Michigan Avenue. This new kind of scale focuses our attention on what is immediately around us.

The contrast with Hannah Arendt's Analysis of Galileo's observation of the Moon and its **bezel** is **radical**:

"We always handle nature from a point in the universe outside the earth. Without actually standing where ***Archimedes*** *wished to stand, still bound to the earth through the human condition, we have found a way to act on the earth and within* ***terrestrial*** *nature as though we dispose of it from outside, from the Archimedean point. And even at the risk of endangering the natural life process we expose the earth to universal,* ***cosmic*** *forces alien to nature's household."*

In its simplicity, *Cloud Gate* is just a giant mirror, after all. Its curved shape provides all kinds of mirrors with different curves and viewing angles. This is how everyone builds their own image of Chicago. Unlike Galileo's telescope, the viewer sets up his or her own presence, choosing a place and that of others during the construction of the image. For a moment, we all become sculptors of our own environment and its **ephemeral** representation.

(Adapted from *http://theconversation.com / anish-kapoors-cloud-gate-playing-with-light-and-returning-to-earth-our-finite-world-102272*)

注释：

1.verticality 垂直度

2.distortions 失真，曲解

3.dilatation 膨胀，扩张

4.proximity 接近

5.bezel 边框，嵌槽

6.radical 根本的，彻底的

7.Archimedes 阿基米德(公元前287～前212年)，伟大的古希腊哲学家、科学家、数学家、物理学家

8.terrestrial 陆地的，地球的
9.cosmic 宇宙的，极广阔的
10.ephemeral 瞬息的、短暂的

Word Power

Fill in the blanks with the words given below. Change the form where necessary. Each word can be used only once.

flourishing, groundbreaking, terrestrial, radical, ephemeral

(1)What can the West's overly indebted and sluggish nations learn from a ________ Asia?

(2)These luxurious houses are in some ways a reminder that earthly pleasures are ________.

(3)Over the next two years they made their most ________ work, turning this poverty-stricken area into a modern town.

(4)The local Architects and Engineers Association has announced its proposals for a ________ reform of the way to reconstruct old building.

Summary

Fill in the blanks with words or phrases from Reading Passage 2.

In its simplicity, *Cloud Gate* is just a giant mirror, after all. Its (1) ________ shape provides all kinds of mirrors with different curves and viewing angles. This is how everyone builds their own (2) ________ of Chicago. It is a new scope, which, by (3) ________ and dilatation, changes how we see us in the world. This sculpture processes the elements of the (4) ________ around the viewer, and changes his or her (5)________. The Skyline is now in front of us. We are in immediate (6) ________ with the massive buildings behind Michigan Avenue.

Listening

Scan the code and listen to a microlecture about Chicago. Please choose the best answer to each of the following questions.

1.What building material made high buildings possible in Chicago?

A. Tower crane. B. Glass wall.

C. Structural steel. D. Light ceiling.

2. Which city is called the great city of winds and fire?

A. Seattle. B. Chicago.

C. Washington, D. C..

D. New York City.

3. Which of the following building used exoskeleton for the first time?

A. John Hancock Center.

B. Marina City.

C. Jefferson Memorial.

D. Lake Point Tower.

Speaking

Can you briefly introduce the modern sculpture named Cloud Gate in Chicago? Refer to the following words and expressions if necessary.

the curved shape / distortion and dilatation / skyline / massive buildings / proximity / the way we see us in the world

Writing

1. Example Sentence

The sculpture, in a dialogue with the skyscrapers that create verticality in this flat space, is an instrument that allows everyone to play with light to propose all the mixtures, all the distortions, all the reconstructions of this landscape.

2.Analysis

(1) in a dialogue with 的意思是"与……对话",该部分是介词词组作插入语。

(2) instrument 后面部分是定语从句。

(3) all the mixtures, all the distortions, all the reconstructions of this landscape 这三个部分为并列结构,即各种混在一起的事物、镜中各种扭曲的景象、各种通过镜像重构的景物。

写作中这种介词词组作插入语的句式,值得我们学习借鉴。

3. Practice

使用介词词组作插入语,合并下面句子。

He hoped to win the contest of designing eco-friendly homes.

He worked day and night for nearly three months.

He even consulted the professor working at his college.

第四节　翡翠之城——西雅图

西雅图是美国西北部非常重要的城市,仅从人们对这个城市的称呼就可以窥见她的背景。西雅图市的取名是为了纪念一位当地的印第安部落酋长西雅图。西雅图酋长在白人殖民者组织的一次集会上恳请他们善待并敬畏大自然中的一切,因为这片土地是神圣而有生命的,这段讲话被誉为在环境保护方面最动人心弦的语句。西雅图城市的兴起要从西部开发运动中的伐木业说起。伐木业一度是西雅图市的支柱产业。著名的波音公司在制造飞机之前就是依靠伐木产业积累了雄厚的资本。除了波音公司,位于西雅图的世界著名公司还有微软和星巴克。

Culture Express

西雅图属于温带海洋性气候，因其雨季持续较久，故而获得了“雨城”的称号。除此之外，西雅图另有三个别称，它们分别代表了它独特的地理位置、环境资源以及经济支柱产业。

西雅图位于华盛顿州的西北角，这里距离美加边境仅有161千米，其独特的地理位置使它获得了“阿拉斯加门户”的称呼，它是通往亚洲贸易路线的主要门户，是北美第四大港口城市。这里的森林和湖泊广布，因此也被称为“翡翠之城”。伐木业曾经是西雅图的第一支柱产业，19世纪末期，依托伐木业，它的商业和造船业开始兴起，经济发展获得了重要转型。波音公司使西雅图获得“喷气机之城”的称号，然而波音公司也正是从伐木业开始发家的。

Reading Passage 1

你知道西雅图最有特色的社区吗？它位于Lake Union，这里至今保存着500多所船屋。每隔一年，这个社区举行一次开放日活动，让人们有机会近距离参观这些属于私家住宅的“移动房屋”。这样的住宅形式体现了人类亲近自然的渴望，这里有在掩护严密的现代住宅中体会不到的自然乐趣。

Seattle's floating home community on Lake Union is the city's most distinctive neighborhood, where homes **erupt** with **exuberant** color, **quirky** details, and lavish gardens, and there's an attitude that nothing is to be taken too seriously.

Even though it's changing—prices are soaring, and the funky bohemian edge is in danger of **evaporating**—it still harbors more character and sheer delight than any **land-lubbing** neighborhood in the city.

Every other year the Floating Homes Association opens the doors to a dozen or so houseboats, offering a one-day public tour as a **fundraiser**. Since the docks are private property, there's no other way to see the nearly 500 houseboats from land.

Part of the fun of tooling around the community is the mixture of high and low architecture and design. The elaborate, architect-designed floating homes that you see today didn't come onto the scene until the last 40 years, when the Lake Union houseboats first became **sanctioned** in the eyes of the city. Before then, **sewage** had been a serious issue, and wealthy homeowners on the hills above the lake **abhorred** the tottery **shacks** at the fringe of their water view. In the 1960s, the city government labored mightily to get rid of them, and in fact managed to **evict** more than 200 owners.

The sewage problem disappeared with a pumping system, and the city zoned houseboat moorages as residential, requiring new moorages to provide parking. That prompted property values to **skyrocket**, and the design aesthetic shot up along with them. Yet some of that early spirit endures—there's still plenty of character and imagination on display here. Some of the newer houseboats feature porthole windows and bowed roofs, recalling the era when houseboats actually were boats, capable of moving under their own power. Some feature totem poles, and at least one has classical Doric columns, as majestic as an old bank. Container gardens are lavish, and several residents have created substantial gardens on rafts tethered to their houses. Every house has a boat, ranging from **battered** canoes to 30-foot sloops. Ask about disadvantages to houseboat living, and you'll usually get a joke in reply. "No lawn to mow," says one resident, a **pouty** look creasing his face. An advantage they cite surprisingly often is that living in a small space forces them to simplify their lives.

The common denominator of the entire Lake Union community, says Jeri Callahan, who published a book about it two years ago, is "very strong feelings about the value of the life we have here."

Callahan notes her theory on why people are so **enamored** with houseboats. Everyone has an innate need to be grounded in nature, she says, but most American homes today work hard to disconnect us — they're **insulated**, **double-glazed**, and air-conditioned so that the outside world hardly intrudes at all. Houseboats, in contrast, respond directly to nature, even rocking with the waves **nudged** by a modest breeze.

(Adapted from *https://www.sunset.com / travel / northwest / houseboat-hopping-seattle*)

注释:

1.erupt 喷发,突然冒出
2.exuberant 热情洋溢的,喜气洋洋的
3.quirky 离奇的,怪诞的
4.evaporating 消失,蒸发
5.land-lubbing 不习水性的,其反义词为 water-dwelling
6.fundraiser 资金筹款活动
7.sanctioned 被处罚,被制裁的
8.sewage 污水
9.abhor 憎恶
10.shacks 简陋的小屋
11.evict 驱逐
12.skyrocket 突升,猛涨
13.battered 破旧的
14.pouty 噘嘴的,容易生气的
15.enamored 倾心的,被迷住的
16.insulated 隔绝的,隔热的
17.double-glazed 镶双层玻璃的
18.nudge (用肘)轻推

Reading Passage 2

导读

本文介绍了西雅图两处古老的建筑，它们是这个地区百年沧桑的见证者，各自的命运也富有传奇色彩。

Nobody knows for sure which structure in Seattle is the oldest, but history **sleuths** have long **conferred** that **honor on** the Ward House at 520 E Denny Way.

Built in 1882 during Seattle's first big boom, the house is a rare example of the urbane Victorian style known as **Italianate**. Originally located on Boren Avenue between Union and Pike, the Ward House was threatened in the mid-1980s with **demolition** due to its location in the shadow of the new Washington State Convention and Trade Center. Happily, Historic Seattle had already saved the structure a decade earlier, and sold it to Seattle attorney David Leen, who moved it up the hill to its current location on the corner of East Denny and Belmont Avenue East, where it underwent a complete **restoration** in 1986. Today the Ward House is among the best **preserved** examples of high life in 19th century Seattle.

But an even older house still stands in greatly modified form in West Seattle—the original home of Seattle pioneer and promoter David "Doc" Maynard. Built in the 1860s, Doc Maynard's house near Alki Point is an example of an earlier Victorian style known as **Gothic Revival**, and while its architectural character is almost unrecognizable today, the simple, straight forward structure reminds us of the **sturdy** character that made Maynard and his colleagues the true **progenitors** of the Seattle Spirit.

(Adapted from *https://blog.seattlepi.com/thebigblog/2010/05/04/what-is-the-oldest-structure-in-seattle/*)

注释：

1.sleuths 侦探
2.confer the honor on... 将荣誉授予……
3.Italianate 意大利风格的
4.demolition 拆毁
5.restoration 修复
6.preserved 保存完好的
7.Gothic Revival 哥特复兴
8.sturdy 强壮的，坚定的
9.progenitors 祖先，前辈

Word Power

Fill in the blanks with the words given below. Change the form where necessary. Each word can be used only once.

abhor, sturdy, evict, erupt, quirky

(1)If you ________ something, you hate it very much, especially for moral reasons.

(2)You say that someone ________ when they suddenly have a change in mood, usually becoming quite noisy.

(3)If someone is ________ from the place where they are living, they are forced to leave it, usually because they have broken a law or contract.

(4) If you say someone is ________, you mean that he is rather odd in his appearance, character, or behavior.

(5)Someone or something that is ________ looks strong and is unlikely to be easily injured or damaged.

Summary

Fill in the blanks with words or phrases from Reading Passage 2.

Built in 1882 during Seattle's first big (1) ________, the Ward House is a rare example of the (2) ________ Victorian style known as Italianate. Originally located on Boren Avenue between Union and Pike, it was (3) ________ in the mid-1980s with demolition due to its location in the (4) ________ of the new Washington State Convention and Trade Center. David Leen, who moved the house up the hill to its current (5) ________ on the corner of East Denny and Belmont Avenue East, where it underwent a complete (6) ________ in 1986. Today the Ward House is among the best (7) ________ examples of high life in 19th century Seattle.

Listening

Scan the code and listen to a microlecture about Seattle. Please choose the best answer to each of the following questions.

(1) Which one of the following corporations didn't start its business in Seattle?

A. Amazon.　　B. Starbuck coffee shop.

C. Microsoft.　　D. Yahoo.

(2) Which of the following isn't the nickname for Seattle?

A. Jet City.　　B. Gateway to Alaska.

C. Rain City.　　D. City of Hope.

(3) Which industry contributed the most to Seattle's economy in 19th century?

A. Lumbering.　　B. Mining.

C. Planting.　　D. Textile.

Speaking

What are the features of houseboats in Seattle? Why would people like to live in houseboats in Lake Union according to reading passage 1? Refer to the following words and expressions if necessary.

close to nature / architect-designed floating homes / exuberant color / quirky details /lavish gardens / gentle breeze

Writing

1. Example Sentence

Houseboats, in contrast, respond directly to nature, even rocking with the waves nudged by a modest breeze.

2. Analysis

(1)Houseboats 作主语,respond 作句子的谓语。

(2)in contrast 是插入语,表示该句和上文之间的对照关系。

(3)even rocking 作状语。

厘清句子中的各种成分可以帮助我们正确使用标点符号。在英文中,逗号通常不能连接两个独立的句子。所以,英文写作中不可以随意根据语气停顿使用逗号。一个信息表述完了,应该使用句点。但是,插入语、状语前可以使用逗号,从而将它们与句子中的其他成分区分开来。

3. Practice

分析下面句子,并为它填上缺失的逗号。

Built in the 1860s Doc Maynard's house near Alki Point is an example of an earlier Victorian style known as Gothic Revival whose architectural character is almost unrecognizable today.

第五节　历史传奇——费城

费城(Philadelphia)得名于希腊语,意为兄弟之爱。费城是当之无愧的美国最重要的历史名城之一:它曾经是美国的第一个首都(1790～1800 年),这里诞生了第一部联邦宪法和第一面美国国旗,它举办了第一、第二次大陆会议。费城的城市布局和谐有序,处处透露着超凡的艺术气息;它是美国公共雕塑最多的城市;在建筑方面,它是以路易斯·康(Louis I. Kahn)为代表的费城学派的大本营。

Culture Express

费城建筑界曾有一个不成文的"君子协定",即全城建筑在高度上都不超越市政厅顶端的威廉·潘恩雕塑。在"威廉·潘恩"雄踞全城百年之后,因为城市发展的需要,才有一座高 288 米的大楼超过了它,此后费城又出现了为数众多的摩天大楼。不过可能是由于人们对这座城市的缔造者威廉·潘恩心怀崇敬,这些摩天大楼都建造在雕塑的身后。因为这一"君子协定"被打破,人们将费城主场球队的连续失利与此关联起来,认为是受到了诅咒。这就是在费城当地流传的约定、球赛和诅咒的故事。

Reading Passage 1

导读

在费城众多的摩天大楼中，One Liberty Place 并不是最高的，但它是第一座挑战费城"君子协定"的摩天大楼。"One man 's meat is another man's poison."这句英语谚语告诉我们对待相同事物人们可能有不同的看法。关于这"第一个吃螃蟹"的费城第一座摩天大楼，我们来看看当地报纸的评论是怎样的。

Liberty Place is a skyscraper complex in Philadelphia, Pennsylvania, United States. The **complex** is composed of a 61-story, 945-foot (288 m) skyscraper called One Liberty Place, a 58-story, 848-foot (258 m) skyscraper called Two Liberty Place, a two-story shopping mall called the Shops at Liberty Place, and the 14-story Westin Philadelphia Hotel. Prior to the construction of Liberty Place, there was a gentlemen's agreement not to build any structure in Center City higher than the statue of William Penn on top of Philadelphia City Hall. The tradition lasted until 1984 when developer Willard G. Rouse III of Rouse & Associates announced plans to build an office building complex that included two towers taller than City Hall. There was a great amount of opposition to the construction of the towers with critics believing breaking the height limit would lead to construction of many more tall skyscrapers, ruining the livability and charm of Center City. Despite the opposition, construction of One Liberty Place was approved and the first phase of the project began in 1985 and was completed in 1987. One Liberty Place became the city's first skyscraper.

On April 5, 1984, *The Philadelphia Inquirer* wrote: "It is a supremacy that must be maintained, for philosophical and aesthetic and, indeed, economic reasons—**density** caused by towering skyscrapers is one of the surest ways to **render** a downtown **ruinously** overbuilt while its **fringes wither.**" In 1990, the *Inquirer* took it all back, noting that Rouse transformed Philadelphia's skyline to near universal acclaim. In 1987, Paul Goldberger, an American architectural critic and educator, noted that: "The skyline of Philadelphia, far from being destroyed by One Liberty Place, is in fact given new life by this building. The skyline has been transformed from one of the flattest of any American city to one of the richest." He praised the shape which he said "strikes a remarkable balance between **dignity** and **verve.**"

(Adapted from *https://www.touristlink.com / united-states / one-liberty-place / overview.html*)

注释：

1.complex 建筑群

2.density 密度

3.render 造成
4.ruinously 毁灭地
5.fringe 边缘，穗
6.wither 衰弱，枯萎
7.dignity 尊严
8.verve 活力

Reading Passage 2

导读

一座城市如果能有众多精品建筑，那一定是建筑设计师和建造者们付出了很多努力。但仅有一座座辉煌的、独立的建筑还远远不够，城市规划能增添单栋建筑与环境的和谐统一。费城的城市发展史上有这么一位设计者，他使费城的城市发展走上有序、和谐的道路，因此被称为"现代费城之父"。

Heralded as the father of modern Philadelphia, famed city planner Edmund Bacon was the man behind many of the city's most notable post-WWII redevelopment projects, from Penn Center and Market East to Penn's Landing and Society Hill. While these projects are well-known and have become essential parts of the Philadelphia landscape, the plans and projects that never came to **fruition** are also a **compelling** part of Bacon's **legacy**. As outlined in his 1959 essay on urban planning and redevelopment, Bacon **envisioned** a new golden age for Philadelphia in the postwar years, one that would **reinvigorate** community investment and development to ensure "no part of Philadelphia is ugly or depressed" in fifty years' time. While some of Bacon's projects succeeded and others never came to pass, both outcomes provide a window into the evolution of city planning and the city itself in the post-industrial age as well as the ongoing struggles to navigate Philadelphia's future in a new era.

A Philadelphia native and Cornell-educated architect, Edmund Bacon served as Executive Director of the Philadelphia City Planning Commission from 1949 to 1970. Under Bacon's direction, the Planning Commission sought to **capitalize** on postwar optimism and looked to the future with coordinated, comprehensive plans to eliminate **blight** and liberate Philadelphia from its now **obsolete** industrial **clutter**. Whereas urban renewal projects in cities like New York and Chicago meant the **wholesale demolition** of **unsavory** neighborhoods, Bacon and his colleagues emphasized small-scale demolition and often restored older structures so that new features like shops and parks were **interwoven** with the existing landscape. Best exemplified in the redevelopment of Society Hill, these design principles were also publicly showcased at the Better Philadelphia Exhibition in 1947.

The Exhibition, which Bacon as a Planning Commission staff member co-designed with Oskar Stonorov and Louis Kahn, took up two floors of Gimbel's Department Store at 8th and Market Streets and attracted 385,000 visitors between September 8th and October 15th.

Following the theme "What City Planning Means to You and Your Children," the exhibition contained movies, murals, dioramas, and, most spectacularly, a 30-by-14 foot model of Center City that boasted 45,000 buildings, 25,000 cars and buses, and 12,000 trees. Notably, as a recorded narrator highlighted various parts of the model, segments flipped over to reveal the planners' future vision for the site, which frequently included open space, planning for pedestrians, and efforts to work within the original landscape.

(Adapted from *https://www.phillyhistory.org / blog / index.php* / 2010/10/ *the-city-that-might-have-been-edmund-bacons-philadelphia* /)

注释:

1.fruition 成就,结果实
2.compelling 引人入胜,扣人心弦的
3.legacy 遗产,遗赠
4.envision 设想,预想
5.reinvigorate 振兴,复兴
6.capitalize 资本化,估计价值
7.blight 损害,使枯萎
8.obsolete 废弃的
9.clutter 嘈杂
10.wholesale demolition 整体拆除(这里指与纽约和芝加哥的整体拆除不同,费城采用了小范围拆除和改建旧建筑的做法)
11.unsavory 臭不可闻的,名誉不好的
12.interwoven 交织的,关系密切的

Word Power

Match the word with its appropriate meaning in English.

reinvigorate, obsolete, wither, blight

(1)________ become weak
(2)________ cause great difficulties, and damages or spoils other things
(3)________ no longer used because something new has been invented
(4)________ give new energy or strength

Summary

Fill in the blanks with words or phrases from Reading Passage 2.

An urban plan often reveals the planners' future vision for the site. Edmund Bacon, a Philadelphia native and Cornell-educated architect, was the man behind many of the city's most notable post-WWII (1) ________ projects. He outlined in his essay on

(2) ________ planning and redevelopment, Bacon (3) ________ a new golden age for Philadelphia in the postwar years, one that would (4) ________ community investment and development to ensure "no part of Philadelphia is ugly or depressed" in fifty years' time. Under Bacon's direction, the Planning Commission sought to capitalize on postwar optimism and looked to the future with, (5) ________ comprehensive plans to (6)________ blight and (7) ________ Philadelphia from its now obsoleteindustrial (8)________.

Listening

Scan the code and listen to a microlecture about Philadelphia. Please choose the best answer to each of the following questions.

(1)Who is the founder of Pennsylvania and planner of the city of Philadelphia?

A. Thomas Jefferson. B. George Washington.

C. William Penn. D. Theodore Roosevelt.

(2) Which is the most historic building in Philadelphia?

A. Independence Hall. B. One Liberty Place.

C. William Penn's Statue. D. City Hall.

(3) Where was the *Declaration of Independence* approved?

A. Boston. B. Washington D.C..

C. Philadelphia. D. New York City.

Speaking

Can you briefly introduce the One Liberty Place in Philadelphia? Refer to the following words and expressions if necessary.

the gentlemen's agreement / complex / opposition / transformed the skyline / strikes a remarkable balance between dignity and verve

Writing

1. Example Sentence

The complex is composed of a 61-story, 945-foot (288 m) skyscraper called One Liberty Place, a 58-story, 848-foot (258 m) skyscraper called Two Liberty Place, a two-story shopping mall called the Shops at Liberty Place, and the 14-story Westin Philadelphia Hotel.

2. Analysis

(1)complex 的意思是"建筑群",该句的谓语是 is composed of。

(2)61-story 是一个前置定语。

(3)长度单位 foot 是一个西方惯用单位,英文一般将 foot 作为主要描述单位,将国际通用单位——米作为解释,放在括号里。

(4)called 引导的是后置定语。

在写作中需要注意前置定语和后置定语的搭配使用。另外,涉及英制单位和国际单位的句子在英文中往往优先或仅使用英制单位。

3. Practice

使用前置定语合并下面的句子。

The Empire State Building has a steel frame.

The Empire State Building rise 102 stories and when it was completed in 1931, it was the tallest building in the world until 1971.

Its height is 1250 feet (381 meters).

第六节 老城新貌——波士顿

波士顿是一座历史与现代交融的城市。它的古老、静谧,它的热闹、喧嚣,都让人流连。同时,它既是美国最早独立的十三个州之一的马萨诸塞州的首府,也是数所世界最著名大学的所在地。在这一节,我们将侧重介绍波士顿的现代城市地标建筑。对于这座城市中那些与美国历史密切相关的古老建筑,我们将其放到第八章(改变美国的建筑)介绍。而它著名的校园建筑将被放到本书最后一章中,和其他著名大学建筑一起介绍。

Culture Express

波士顿有座叫 Berkeley Building 的大楼,其也曾被称为 Old John Hancock Tower,是约翰汉考克保险公司所建。大楼顶部有用于播报天气的桅杆和灯塔。怎么用其播报天气呢?当地流传着这样一首儿歌"Steady blue, clear view / Flashing blue, clouds due / Steady red, rain ahead / Flashing red, snow instead!"。原来它是靠颜色播报天气:亮起蓝灯就代表天气晴朗,蓝灯闪烁就代表多云,红灯亮起就代表下雨,红灯闪烁代表下雪。

在棒球赛季,这座预报天气的灯塔如果闪起红灯,那就说明本地的红袜队(Red Sox)因天气原因取消比赛。而在 2004 年 10 月,这座灯塔第一次红灯和蓝灯间隔闪烁,这是为了庆祝时隔 80 多年,红袜队终于再一次取得了世界系列赛的冠军。[①]

Reading Passage 1

导读

波士顿的汉考克大厦外墙由蓝色玻璃构成,如一面通天的明镜将它身旁有着三百年历史的三一教堂投映在身上,它的设计者是著名华裔设计师贝聿铭。它线条简洁、笔直,全身一色。它的出现,宛如闹市中的蜃景,给人以无限如梦幻般的遐想。在波士顿人心尖

① "Berkeley Weather Beacon", http://www.celebrateboston.com / strange / weather-beacon.htm.

上建现代摩天大厦不是一件容易的事情，只有艺高人胆大的世界顶级高手才敢出手。但大厦在建成之时却饱受争议，这是怎么回事呢？

When plans were announced for the new John Hancock Tower in the late 1960s, public protests demanded that the new skyscraper be redesigned so as not to **cast** a **permanent** shadow over the Trinity Church in Copley Square.

Although the construction of a modern skyscraper at Copley Square **sparked** an intense debate, the architecture firm of **I.M. Pei** and partners proposed a **sleek** 60-story tower with a **glass curtain wall**, a **stark contrast** with the nineteenth-century Romanesque Trinity Church across from the street. The combination turns out to work well: the glass wall of the sixty story John Hancock Tower reflects its surroundings and does not interfere with it. The blue windows of Boston's tallest building provide an interesting reflection of the neighboring church that was built 99 years before. I.M. Pei would later **implement** a similar solution in Paris, where a glass pyramid is set in the middle of historic **Louvre**.

The John Hancock Tower was built in 1976 and at 790ft (241 meters), and it is still the tallest building in Boston. **Adjacent** to the modern John Hancock Tower is the 1947 Old John Hancock Tower. This building has a pyramid-shaped roof topped with a weather **beacon**. The beacon has a different color depending on the weather.

(Adapted from *https://encirclephotos.com / image / trinity-church-reflection-in-johu-hancock-tower-in-boston-massachusetts*)

注释：

1.cast 投，掷

2.permanent 永久的

3.spark 引发

4.I.M. Pei 贝聿铭(1917～2019 年)，出生于广东广州，祖籍江苏苏州，是苏州望族之后，美籍华人建筑师，美国艺术与科学院院士、中国工程院外籍院士，土木专家。

5.sleek 有光泽的

6.glass curtain wall 玻璃幕墙

7.a stark contrast 一个鲜明的对照

8.implement 实施

9.Louvre 卢浮宫

10.adjacent 毗邻的

11.beacon 灯塔

Reading Passage 2

导读

在波士顿有三座叫 John Hancock Building 的建筑物。这三座建筑物都是由约翰·

汉考克保险公司出资修建的。你知道约翰·汉考克吗？了解他对波士顿做出了哪些贡献吗？

John Hancock was an American merchant, statesman, and prominent **Patriot** of the American Revolution.

Before the American Revolution, Hancock was one of the wealthiest men in the Thirteen Colonies, having inherited a profitable **mercantile** business from his uncle. Hancock used his wealth to support the colonial cause as tensions increased between colonists and Great Britain in the 1760s.

Hancock was one of the most popular leaders in Massachusetts during the crisis that led to the **outbreak** of the American Revolutionary War in 1775. He then served as president of the Second Continental Congress. He was the first to sign the ***Declaration of Independence*** , and because his large and stylish **signature**, his name is so well remembered that the term "John Hancock" has become a **synonym** in the United States for one's signature. After working for the Continental Congress in Philadelphia for more than two years, he returned to Massachusetts and was elected governor of the Commonwealth, serving in that role for most of his remaining years. In January 1788, he was elected president of the Massachusetts **ratifying** convention. He gave a speech in favor of ratification. He used his influence to gain support from Samuel Adams, and together with whom he ensured that Massachusetts successfully ratified the United States Constitution in 1788.

When his health failing, Hancock spent his final few years as a **figurehead** governor. In 1793, he died at 56 years of age. By order of acting governor Samuel Adams, the day of Hancock's burial was a state holiday.

(Adapted from *https://www.revwartalk.com / john-hancock -2/*)

注释：

1.patriot 爱国主义者
2.mercantile 贸易的，商业的
3.outbreak 爆发
4.*Declaration of Independence*《独立宣言》
5.signature 签名
6.synonym 同义词
7.ratifying 签署，批准
8.figurehead 挂名的首脑

Word Power

Please put an appropriate preposition in the blank.

(1)All visitors have cast doubt ________ the statue's authenticity.

(2)The combination of modern and old architectures turns ________ to work well in this district.

(3)________ order of the mayor, the collapsing bridge was removed.

(4)The house adjacent ________ ours is under repair.

(5)Glass and steel are synonyms ________ modern architecture.

Summary

Fill in the blanks with words or phrases from Reading Passage 1.

There are two John Hancock Towers in Boston, the old one and the modern one. The old John Hancock Tower has a (1) ________ roof topped with a weather (2)________. (3)________ to the old John Hancock Tower is the Modern John Hancock Tower, which is a modern (4) ________ designed by I.M. Pei. The combination turns out to work well: the glass wall of the sixty story John Hancock Tower (5) ________ its surroundings and does not (6)________ with it. The blue windows of Boston's tallest building provide an interesting (7)________ of the neighboring church that was built 99 years before.

Listening

Scan the code and listen to a microlecture about Boston. Please choose the best answer to each of the following questions.

(1)Which was a key event that helped spur the American revolution?

A.Boston Tea Party. B. Old South Meeting House Party.

C. Refusing to pay tea tax. D. Tea Tax Debate.

(2) Which one of the following buildings isn't in Boston?

A. Independence Hall. B. Massachusetts State House.

C. Old State House. D. Old South Meeting House.

(3) Which of the following is a famous Irish community in Boston?

A. Back Bay. B. Little Irish.

C. Southie. D. Beacon Hill.

Speaking

What are the features of the modern John Hancock Tower in Boston? Refer to the following words and expressions if necessary.

blue glass / a glass curtain wall / a stark contrast of / cast shadows on / reflect

Writing

1.Example Sentence

Although the construction of a modern skyscraper at Copley Square sparked an intense debate, the architecture firm of I.M. Pei and partners proposed a sleek 60-story tower with a glass curtain wall, a stark contrast with the nineteenth-century Romanesque Trinity Church across from the street.

2. Analysis

(1)Although 引导让步状语从句,意思为"虽然在科普利广场建一栋摩天大楼引起了很大争议"。

(2)a stark contrast with 意即"与……的鲜明对比",对前一部分起到解释说明作用。

3.Practice

使用对比句型将下列句子组合成一句话。

In this heated debate, most people agree to demolish the old shopping center.

This professor thinks its unique style in architecture makes it valuable in research.

第二章　美国国家公园建筑

概　述

1872年，美国第十八位总统尤利西斯·辛普森·格兰特签署法案，成立了世界上第一个国家公园——黄石国家公园。1916年，美国国会通过《国家公园组织构成法》，建立国家公园管理局(National Park Service)，用以“保护自然风光、历史遗迹及其中的野生动植物，为人们提供休闲享受，同时保持它们不受损伤，留给子孙后代”。但是汽车工业在美国的发展给自然保护带来了一个挑战：当数以千万计的人们不计路途，渴望亲近这些旷世美景时，他们的需求将如何被满足？经过近一百五十年的摸索，历史告诉我们，任何人类活动都会打破原有的自然平衡，对自然资源的攫取要慎重又慎重。

如何在国家公园内兴修土木，如何平衡保护自然资源和开发旅游资源之间的关系，解决这些难题不是一朝一夕的事情。在这一章，我们将一起寻访四个美国国家公园的基础设施建设，并且透过它们了解国家公园面临的挑战：如何修路才能最大限度地保护其他生物的栖息地？要不要开发公园内的水电资源？是否应该在国家公园内修建娱乐设施？

第一节　黄石国家公园

黄石国家公园位于黄石河的源头，该公园以其地理位置而命名。早期环保运动的领袖约翰·缪尔在《我们的国家公园》(*Our National Parks*)一书中这样描写黄石公园：“间歇泉的悲歌与地震的轰鸣交相呼应，仿佛到了末日。然而乌云散去，又是晴空万里……水乌鸫在河水中惬意地歌唱，消除了所有恐惧，使一切都化为了爱。”作为世界上第一个国家公园，黄石无疑给全球6000多个国家公园树立了保护自然、合理开发旅游资源的典范。它在景区内选择在生态系统相对稳定的地方集中建立人类活动的社区(包括酒店、餐馆、加油站等)，并将之与其他地方隔离，以最大限度地保护资源和环境，给这里种类丰富的生命提供最好的栖息地。黄石是一个满是精灵的乐园，是有着奇幻感召力的地方，是朝圣自然的绝佳去处。我们敬畏黄石的力量，赞叹黄石的美丽，但是我们首先要学会克制人类的贪婪，合理地开发和利用自然。

Culture Express

20 世纪 50 年代初美国国家公园管理局因忽视公园体系建设而广受批评。1955 年，该部门的负责人 Conrad Wirth 提出了一个"十年计划"——计划在 1966 年，即国家公园管理局建成 50 周年之际，大规模地提高景区的服务能力以接纳更多的游客。该计划被称为 Mission 66，它主要涉及国家公园内的基础设施项目，比如修(扩)建公园内道路、员工居住区、游客中心等。除此之外，这项计划还注重提高环保宣教方面的服务水平。该计划抓住了二战后汽车工业蓬勃发展给旅游业带来的发展机遇，推动了美国国家公园的发展和壮大。

Reading Passage 1

导读

杰克逊湖畔木屋(Jackson Lake Lodge)是一处修建于 20 世纪 50 年代的酒店，它打破了传统的美式乡村建筑风格，使用大组的落地观景窗，使游客在酒店内也能将国家公园的美景尽收眼前。它的设计和修建，幕后推动人是美国实业家、超级资本家、美孚石油公司创办人约翰·洛克菲勒。

Jackson Lake Lodge was completed in 1955, and its modern design marked a sharp departure from earlier buildings in Teton and Yellowstone parks. To feature a **panoramic** view of the lake and the Tetons, architect Gilbert Underwood used large **banks of picture windows.**

John D. Rockefeller Jr., a driving force behind the 1950 creation of **Grand Teton National Park**, also wanted that park to appeal to modern tourists. He **commissioned** renowned architect Gilbert Stanley Underwood, who had designed several previous national park lodges, to design a new complex that broke with traditional **rustic** style.

For lower costs, Underwood used modern building methods such as **concrete** walls and a flat roof. Modern materials and **prefabricated** components made these buildings relatively inexpensive to construct quickly, and kept maintenance costs low. Contemporary stylings generally featured **asymmetrical** roofs and picture windows. An intentional lack of ornamentation kept the focus on the surrounding wonders rather than the buildings themselves.

Large blocks of windows allowed visitors inside to see the natural features they were learning about. In one sense this architectural style could bring people closer to the parks' science, spurring an intellectual appreciation of nature. Yet in another sense, a glass wall removed the tourist from **immersion** in nature. Lost were the spiritual benefits perceived by activists such as photographer Ansel Adams and Sierra Club director David Brower, both of whom condemned the trend.

The Jackson Lake Lodge had little of the log-and-stone character of previous "**parkitecture**"—and critics complained that it was "a concrete monstrosity," "a steamship without **smokestacks**," and a "**slab** sided concrete **abomination.**" But buildings in the rustic style were not only labor-intensive to build and **incompatible** with modern conveniences—they also couldn't handle large crowds. Ever-rising tourist volumes needed to be addressed by better-functioning buildings, even if that meant sacrificing some romanticism.

Rockefeller intended the Jackson Lake Lodge as an example for future Park Service development. NPS director Conrad Wirth, who attended its 1955 opening, was impressed. Trained as an architect, Wirth decided to embrace these principles to guide Mission 66.

(Adapted from *https://www.wyohistory.org/encyclopedia/modernizing-national-park-facilities-mission-66wyoming*)

注释:

1.panoramic 全景的,全貌的

2.large banks of picture windows 一组组的玻璃观景窗

3.Grand Teton National Park 大提顿国家公园,位于美国怀俄明州西北部壮观的冰川山区,1929 年建立,占地 1256 平方千米。

4.commission 委任

5.rustic 乡村的,朴素的

6.concrete 混凝土制的

7.prefabricated 预制的

8.asymmetrical 不对称的

9.immersion 沉浸,洗礼

10.parkitecture 公园建筑

11.smokestack 大烟囱

12.slab 厚板

13.abomination 嫌恶

14.incompatible 不匹配的

Reading Passage 2

导读

在旅游热持续升温的今天如何保护国家公园内自然奇观的完整性,使其独特的地貌不受到各种景点设施和建筑的冲击和伤害?本文提供了一个解决办法:分割使用。

To tourists, "overcrowding" often meant a line for the toilet, but to management, a bigger issue was how to keep sensitive natural wonders from being **trampled**. If visitation continued to grow, how could landscapes **retain** their natural **integrity**? One answer was **segregation** of uses. Then-popular suburban land planning techniques created, for example, separate zones for industry, residences, and retail—could national parks be similarly zoned?

Modern conveniences would be segregated from nature, which would remain "picturesque," "unspoiled," "wilderness"—separate from the masses of people. You could enjoy the view of the canyon, and then go eat dinner or gas up the car in a less scenic, less **fragile** landscape. In this way the canyon wilderness could be enjoyed by larger numbers of people.

By zoning human activity away from natural beauty, Mission 66 **initiatives** created "villages" with hotels, restaurants, shops, gas stations, and visitor centers. Yellowstone's Canyon Village and Grant Village were built along these principles, as was Colter Bay Village in Grand Teton.

The village philosophy also influenced the Park Service's relationships with surrounding communities. In-park villages were necessary only for vast expanses such as the Yellowstone-Teton complex; a better solution put human-centered development, especially hotels, outside the parks and their **pristine** nature. Eventually, even some park administrative facilities and visitor centers themselves were located in gateway communities.

A major Mission 66 innovation was the "visitor center." The idea was modeled on 1950s "shopping centers," in part because tourists who needed to learn how to appreciate a park resisted going to museums or education centers. Visitor centers across the nation have often been admired, both for function and modernist architectural uniqueness.

(Adapted from *https://www.wyohistory.org/encyclopedia/modernizing-national-park-facilities-mission-66-wyoming*)

注释:

1.trample 践踏,伤害
2.retain 保持,保留
3.integrity 完整
4.segregation 分割
5.fragile 易碎的,脆弱的
6.initiatives 倡议
7.pristine 原始状态的

Word Power

Fill in the blanks with the words given below. Change the form where necessary. Each word can be used only once.

commission, segregation, fragile, integrity, trample

(1)She was a musician, and a woman who, I think, had courage, ________ and determination.

(2)Many Muslim immigrants suffer from relative poverty, high levels of crime and social ________.

(3)It makes our life ________, ephemeral, and as a result of that, more precious.

(4)Some tourists ________ the grass, pitch tents and build campfires in the park.

(5)The Minister of Social Security quickly has ________ a study to determine the causes of and possible cures for this disturbing stale affairs.

Summary

Fill in the blanks with words or phrases from Reading Passage 2.

If visitation continued to grow, segregation is one possible way to retain the (1) ________ of natural beauties. Modern conveniences would be (2) ________ from nature. Tourists could enjoy the (3) ________ of the national park, and then go eat dinner or gas up the car in a less (4) ________, less (5) ________ landscape. Mission 66 initiatives created the concept of "villages" in national parks, which means having hotels and other facilities such as hotels, restaurants, shops, gas stations and visitor centers outside the parks and their (6) ________ nature. The village philosophy also influenced the Park Service's relationships with (7) ________ communities.

Listening

Scan the code and listen to a microlecture about Yellowstone National Park. Please choose the best answer to each of the following questions.

1.Where is most part of Yellowstone National Park located?

A.Wyoming. B. Montana.

C.Idaho. D. Utah.

2.Which president signed the law to establish Yellowstone National Park in 1872?

A.Theodore Roosevelt. B. Franklin Delano Roosevelt.

C.Ulysses Simpson Grant. D. Thomas Jefferson.

Speaking

Please specify how the concept of segregation in Yellowstone National Park works. You may find the following words and expressions useful.

land planning / zone / segregated / scenic / fragile / surrounding communities

Writing

1. Example Sentence

Yellowstone's Canyon Village and Grant Village were built along these principles, as was Colter Bay Village in Grand Teton.

2. Analysis

(1)句子的主干在前半部分，黄石的 Canyon Village 和 Grant Village 就是照这些原则来修建的。

(2)as 引导非限制性定语从句，指代整个主句内容，as 引导的定语从句可置于句首、句中或句尾。

3. Practice

使用 as 引导的非限定性定语从句翻译下列句子。

(1)我们要保护这些濒危的物种，这是众所周知的事情。

(2)这个材料具有弹性，如数据所示。

第二节　约塞米蒂国家公园

约塞米蒂与黄石，可谓美国国家公园双璧。不同于黄石的广袤瑰丽，约塞米蒂国家公园以它的史诗气质冠绝美国所有国家公园。约塞米蒂国家公园的缔造者，著名环保运动先驱约翰·缪尔奠定了这首气势恢宏的史诗的主旋律。不论是他朝圣于荒野的非凡经历，还是他赢得了与学术权威关于这里地质成因的争论，抑或是他令老罗斯福总统亲历其境，成功说服总统建立国家公园，都是深深渗入公园骨血的传奇。在缪尔的描述中，这里“总是像阳光一般，在岩石与空间交构的广大建筑中，闪耀着绿色与金色的神奇光辉”，“没有任何人造的殿堂可与之相提并论”。自约翰·缪尔始，如何同时欣赏与保护这所自然圣殿就一直是人们关注的重中之重。

Culture Express

景区管理是一门大学问，仅仅修筑好公路，建好观景平台，设置好景点服务区，乃是远远不够的。经人工改造的自然景观，在性质和功能上都与真正的自然相去甚远，有时，保护反会带来破坏性的结果。约塞米蒂也走过这样的弯路。严格的防火措施使得植被过于茂密，灌丛、草原被树林替代，使得巨杉等许多特有植物无法生长；同时茂盛的树木也遮挡了观景点的视线，影响了游客的游览体验；游客造成的生物扰动又使得外来物种泛滥。20世纪七八十年代，公园启动了“景区管理计划”研究，为景区的改造和保护提供了科学的指导。具体的措施包括：监控而不是扑灭山火，让自然的改造力量得以贯彻；适当间伐和清除乔木、灌木，使约塞米蒂山谷恢复橡树林生境；修剪一些遮挡视线的枝干，让游客看到更好的景色。约塞米蒂国家公园用系统的管理计划替代了原先散乱随意的维护，为世界上其他地区公园、景区的管理树立了范本。

Reading Passage 1

导读

约塞米蒂国家公园内道路由联邦公路局负责维护和重建。修建园区内的道路绝非易事,除了要使道路能承载一定的交通运输压力外,设计和施工者需考虑的首要问题是道路怎么修建才能与园区的旷世美景融为一体。

In 1925, the National Park Service signed an agreement with the Bureau of Public Roads, U.S. Department of Agriculture, under which the BPR (later, the Public Roads Administration) would be responsible for upgrading and reconstructing roads within the National Park System. The BPR immediately **commenced** road work in Yosemite National Park, beginning with the **paving** of the Valley road system in 1926 to eliminate the choking dust that irritated so many visitors.

The BPR then planned a new "**high gear**" highway to replace the 1875 Wawona Road between the park's south entrance and Yosemite Valley. Construction began in 1932. The National Park Service insisted that the new road should not adversely affect the park's scenic qualities. To preserve the beauty of the Valley landscape, a tunnel was **bored** below Turtleback Dome. The new \$2 million Wawona Road was completed in 1933, and in 1934-35 the spur road to Glacier Point was rebuilt. Motorists could now enjoy some of the park's most outstanding views.

The National Park Service and the Bureau of Public Roads showed great care in constructing a modern road network through the incomparable scenery of Yosemite. Preservation of the park's natural beauty was the planners' chief concern, and every **modification** of the landscape was subjected to careful scrutiny. The roads were designed not only to carry heavy traffic loads, but to integrate into their natural settings.

To minimize the effect of roads through the landscape, tunnels were bored to avoid unsightly **scarring** of the **granite** cliffs. Stone retaining walls were employed to conceal road cuts, and bridges faced in natural materials were used at highly visible stream crossings. Telephone and power lines were located away from the roadside and out of the visitors' view. **Road margins** were **reseeded** with native plants by the park's landscape division, and in some cases by the Civilian Conservation Corps. The special Rustic Style designs and landscaping help the roads blend into their natural surroundings and make a drive through the park a wondrous experience.

(Adapted from *http://npshistory.com/publications/highways/yosemite/yosemite 4.htm*)

注释:

1.commence 开始

2.pave 铺设,硬化路面

3.high gear 高速的
4.bore 钻孔
5.modification 修正
6.scarring 结疤痕
7.granite 花岗岩
8.road margins 路边空地
9.reseeded 重新播种

Reading Passage 2

导读：

在美国，反坝运动的历史基本上是伴随现代水坝工程的建设实践而同步书写的。本篇文章向我们讲述了在约塞米蒂国家公园内修建一座水库所引发的对环保问题的讨论。美国国家公园的先驱人物约翰·缪尔曾极力反对修建将淹没约塞米蒂国家公园内的赫奇赫奇山谷(Hetch Hetchy Valley)的大坝。缪尔甚至写信给罗斯福总统，请他阻止该工程。经过12年的争论，罗斯福的继任者伍德罗·威尔逊总统于1913年12月19日签署了大坝修建法案。这场论战的结果是山谷被毁，缪尔对此感到极为失落，不久便郁郁而终。

Between 1908 and 1913, Congress debated whether to make a water resource available or preserve a wilderness when the growing city of San Francisco, California proposed building a **dam** in the Hetch Hetchy Valley to provide a steady water supply. The Hetch Hetchy Valley was within Yosemite National Park and protected by the federal government, leaving it up to Congress to decide the valley's fate. National opinion was divided between giving San Francisco the right to dam the valley and preserving the valley from development.

At the heart of the debate was the conflict between **conservationists**, who held that the environment should be used in a conscientious manner to benefit society, and **preservationists**, who believed that nature should be protected, saved from human interference. Siding with the conservationists, San Francisco citizens argued that the **reservoir** was necessary for the health of their city. On the other side, preservationists, led by John Muir, argued that Congress should protect the Hetch Hetchy Valley from destruction. Muir and his **allies** believed that nature should be enjoyed for its beauty, and not merely used for its resources.

Hundreds of individuals and organizations from across the country submitted **petitions** to Congress regarding the valley. These petitions, some of which are included below, bear witness to the birth of environmental activism as citizens weighed in, expressing multiple opinions about the proper use of National Park land and the relationship between local interests and national values.

In the end, Congress passed **legislation** that enabled the creation of a dam in the Hetch Hetchy Valley. President Woodrow Wilson signed the bill into law on December

19, 1913. Although the preservationists lost this battle, the damming of the Hetch Hetchy Valley raised public awareness about the importance of preserving nature, and helped justify the creation of the National Park Service in 1916.

(Adapted from *https://www.archives.gov / legislative / features / hetch-hetchy*)

注释：

1.dam 水坝
2.conservationists 生态环境保护者
3.preservationists(古建筑或乡村地区等的)保护主义者
4.reservoir 水库
5.ally 同盟，助手
6.petitions 请愿，祈求
7.legislation 法规，立法

Word Power

Fill in the blanks with the words given below. Change the form where necessary. Each word can be used only once.

petition, preservationist, pavement, conservationists, legislation

(1)________ consists of a law or laws passed by a government.

(2)A ________ is a document signed by a lot of people which asks a government or other official group to do a particular thing.

(3)A ________ is someone who takes action to preserve something such as old buildings or an area of countryside.

(4)A ________ is someone who cares very much about the conservation of the environment and who works to protect it.

(5)A ________ is a path with a hard surface, usually by the side of a road.

Summary

Fill in the blanks with words or phrases from Reading Passage 1.

The roads in Yosemite National Park were designed not only to carry heavy traffic loads, but to (1) ________ into their natural settings. The National Park Service and the Bureau of Public Roads showed great care in constructing a modern road network through the (2) ________ scenery of Yosemite.(3) ________ of the park's natural beauty was the planners' chief concern, and every (4) ________ of the landscape was subjected to careful scrutiny. The National Park Service insisted that the new road should not (5) ________ affect the park's scenic qualities. The special (6) ________ Style designs and landscaping help the roads (7) ________ into their natural surroundings and make a drive through the park a wondrous experience.

Listening

Scan the code and listen to a microlecture about Yosemite National Park. Please choose the best answer to each of the following questions.

(1) Which is the highest waterfall in North America?

A. Yosemite Falls. B. Iguazu falls.

C. Niagara Falls. D. Angle Falls.

(2) Which president signed the bill to set up Yosemite National Park in 1906?

A. Theodore Roosevelt. B. Franklin Delano Roosevelt.

C. Ulysses Simpson Grant. D. Thomas Jefferson.

Speaking

Please specify what considerations were given to upgrading and reconstructing roads in Yosemite National Park. Refer to the following words and expressions if necessary.

upgrade / reconstruct / bore a tunnel / road margins / blend with the natural surroundings

Writing

1. Example Sentence

National opinion was divided between giving San Francisco the right to dam the valley and preserving the valley from development.

2. Analysis

(1) 这句话的主干部分是 opinion was divided between... and...，意思是“观点分为……和……两派”。

(2) between 为介词，后面的宾语是 giving...和 preserving...。

3. Practice

翻译下面的句子。

美国人的观点分为两派：支持普通人持有枪支的权利和支持严控枪支。

第三节　大峡谷国家公园

到过科罗拉多大峡谷的人都有一个共同的认知：自然的伟力如此令人惊叹！这里并没有山，如果不看脚下，人们眼前是一望无际的平原。然而就是一条河，流淌了千万年的科罗拉多河，生生地向下切出了一道道深沟——最深处达 1600 米，将偌大的平原切得支离破碎。在游客眼中,大峡谷是一幅画卷,处处雄奇壮美;而在科学家眼中,大峡谷是记录了几十亿年地质史的连续档案:被河水切开的崖壁上,二十几亿年来的岩层历历在目,地球近半生的经历被清楚呈现。美国科罗拉多大峡谷,是世界自然遗产,是地球上最壮丽的自然风景,是美国西部游客最多的国家公园。

Culture Express

一如兰福德之于黄石,缪尔之于约塞米蒂,大峡谷国家公园也同样与一位传奇人物的名字永远联系在一起,他就是探险家约翰·鲍威尔(John Wesley Powell)。鲍威尔年轻时候就热衷于河流探险,曾划船沿密西西比河做深入探索。在他壮年时期,美国内战爆发,他加入联邦军,发挥自己在科学、地理方面的特长成为炮兵指挥,但不幸在战斗中失去右臂(所以关于鲍威尔的介绍中往往有"独臂少校""独臂漂流家"等称呼)。他于1869年和1871年两次组织了在科罗拉多河的地理探险,之后又投入大量的精力对探险结果进行科学研究,发表了许多研究大峡谷的论文和专著。鲍威尔独臂漂流科罗拉多河的英雄事迹极大地鼓舞了美国人开发西部的热情,大峡谷也在他的宣传下变得非常有名。1919年,大峡谷国家公园成立。虽然在公众印象中,鲍威尔是无畏的探险家和西部精神的代表,但他更真实的角色是学者和管理者,他长时间担任美国地质调查局局长和史密森学会民族学研究局局长,他对当时美国西部开发的狂热持保留态度。

Reading Passage 1

导读

美国大峡谷国家公园的空中走廊是一座马蹄形的透明玻璃桥。只要游客们有足够的胆量,就可以站在这座透明的空中天桥上,将脚下1200多米的峡谷谷底风光尽收眼底。是心惊胆战还是荡气回肠?这个问题还是留待你去亲自体验吧。

Do you **crave** adventure? Then you can't miss the Skywalk, a U-shaped **cantilevered** glass bridge extending 70 feet from the edge of the Rim at Grand Canyon West on the Hualapai Indian **reservation.** It offers **unparalleled** views—literally—straight down to the Canyon floor 4,000 feet below.

The Skywalk is a structure that projects horizontally into space, supported only on one end. Large cantilevered bridges like the Skywalk are supported using beams and **trusses** built using strong, heavy materials like structural steel or concrete box **girders.** The Skywalk rests on a foundation of 8 columns that support **box beams** that are 6 feet high, 32 inches wide, with 2-inch-thick walls. The foundations for the box beams are 45 feet deep, and are anchored into the limestone bedrock to act as counterweights for the Skywalk's cantilever design. The Skywalk itself is supported on **tuned mass dampers** designed to reduce normal **vibrations** caused by wind and people.

David Jin, a Las Vegas businessperson, first **envisioned** the Skywalk when he visited the Grand Canyon in 1996. In partnership with Lochsa Engineering, MRJ Architects, and Executive Construction Management, Jin designed and built the

Skywalk, and when it opened in March of 2007, the first people to step onto the Skywalk were lead by Buzz Aldrin and Jon Herrington, the first native American astronaut.

(Adapted from *https://www.canyonotours.com / guides / 8-questions-grand-canyon-skywalk /*)

注释:

1.crave 渴求,恳求
2.cantilevered 悬臂式的
3.reservation 保护区
4.unparalleled 前所未有的
5.trusses [建]桁架
6.girders 大梁,主梁
7.box beams [建]箱形梁,盒形梁
8.tuned mass dampers 调谐质量阻尼器
9.vibrations 振动,共鸣
10.envision 预期,展望

Reading Passage 2

导读

位于大峡谷国家公园内的沙漠观景塔(The Desert View Watchtower)和它所在的自然环境融为一体,即使走近了看,游客也很难分辨哪里是塔的墙基,哪里是峡谷的岩壁。本篇文章为我们讲述了它的设计者玛丽·柯尔特(Mary Elizabeth Jane Colter)的设计和构思。

The Desert View Watchtower (1932) **dominates** the near view. This structure was designed by Mary Elizabeth Jane Colter who is often referred to as the architect of the southwest. She traveled throughout the southwest to find **inspiration** and authenticity for her buildings. The architecture of the ancestral Puebloan people of the Colorado Plateau served as her model. Colter indicated that it was not a copy of any that she had seen, but rather modeled from several.

As you get closer to the building you might see how well it blends into the environment. It is difficult to tell where the rock of the canyon walls ends, and the tower begins. She said: "First and most important, was to design a building that would become part of its surroundings; one that would create no **discordant** note against the time eroded walls of this **promontory.**"

To obtain this result she insisted that the rocks not be cut or worked, so they would not lose the "weathered surfaces so essential to blend it with the canyon walls."

Note, too, some of the **intricate** designs she had built into the tower. For example, look for the white decorative stones near the top, which fade out as the eye goes around the tower. She had seen this pattern at Chaco Canyon and thought it would break the **monotony** of this Watchtower. The built-in cracks which are patterned from some of the ancient towers she had seen are deliberately designed. There are **petroglyphs** on some of the stones which were brought here from near Ash Fork.

The internal steel framework of the Watchtower was designed and supervised by the bridge builders of the Santa Fe Railway company. Upon this framework, each exterior stone was selected and carefully placed to ensure exactly the look Mary Colter was hoping to obtain for she was a **stickler** for detail. At one point she had to leave for a day and the workmen continued to put on stone, completing two layers. When she returned, she was not satisfied with one stone on the newly laid layers, and the men had to take the whole thing down and re-do it to her exacting specifications. Her attention to accuracy of detail was amazing.

The Kiva Room, which for years was used as retail space, in 2015 was returned to the open area that Mary Colter had intended, since the room was originally designed to be a rest area. It was here that visitors to the canyon in the 1930s could sit in comfort and have outstanding views of the canyon. The fireplace is unique in that it does not block the view for visitors. Gaze into one of the **reflectoscopes** and see a different perspective of the canyon.

As you climb the stairs, there are many stories imbedded in the paintings and artwork which decorate the walls. The first gallery, on the first landing, was done by Fred Kabotie, a Hopi from second Mesa. These represent the physical and spiritual origins of Hopi life. The ceiling images, painted by Fred Geary, are recreations of images from Abo Rockshelter, now part of Salinas National Monument in New Mexico.

(Adapted from *https://www.nps.gov / grca / learn / photosmultimedia / mary-colter——indian-watchtower.htm*)

注释：

1.dominate 主导，支配
2.inspiration 灵感
3.discordant 不和谐的
4.promontory 岬，凸起
5.intricate 精细复杂的
6.monotony 单调
7.petroglyphs 岩石画
8.stickler 坚持细节的人
9.reflectoscope 超声波探测仪

Word Power

Fill in the blanks with the words given below. Change the form where necessary. Each word can be used only once.

discordant, intricate, unparalleled, monotonous, dominating

(1) Something that is ________ is very boring because it has a regular, repeated pattern which never changes.

(2) A ________ person has a very strong personality and influence.

(3) You use ________ to describe something that has many small parts or details.

(4) If you describe something as ________, you are emphasizing that it is, for example, bigger, better, or worse than anything else of its kind, or anything that has happened before.

(5) Something that is ________ is strange or unpleasant because it does not fit in with other things.

Summary

Fill in the blanks with words or phrases from Reading Passage 2.

The Desert View Watchtower was designed by Mary Elizabeth Jane Colter who is often referred to as the (1) ________ of the southwest. She thinks the most important thing was to design a building that would become part of its surroundings; one that would create no (2) ________ note against the time eroded walls of this (3) ________. This tower was built with (4) ________ designs. For example, the (5) ________ white stones were used near the top of the tower, which fade out as the eye goes around the tower. As you climb the stairs, there are many (6) ________ stories in the paintings and artwork which decorate the walls. These represent the physical and (7) ________ origins of Hopi life.

Listening

Scan the code and listen to a microlecture about Grand Canyon National Park. Please choose the best answer to each of the following questions.

(1) Who was the first white man to traverse the Grand Canyon?

A. John Powell.　　B. John Stuart.

C. John Muir.　　D. John Mill.

(2) What are the two main reasons for shaping of Grand Canyon?

A. Seismic upheaval and glacial erosion.

B. Gravel grinding and glacial erosion.

C.Seismic upheaval and gravel grinding.

D.Gravel grinding and earthquake.

Speaking

What are the features of the Desert View Watchtower in Grand Canyon National Park? Refer to the following words and expressions if necessary.

discordant / promontory / petroglyphs on some of the stones / intricate / decorative / a stickler for detail / physical and spiritual origin

Writing

1. Example Sentence

The Skywalk rests on a foundation of 8 columns that support box beams that are 6 feet high, 32 inches wide, with 2-inch-thick walls.

2. Analysis

(1)rest on 的意思是"基于"。

(2)columns 和 beams 后面分别有一个定语从句。

(3)with 结构作状语，描述了箱形梁(box beam)上墙体的厚度。

3. Practice

使用"with"结构将下面的句子组合成一句。

(1)In 1990, chicken was the most popular meat in this city.

(2)Each person consumed about 285 grams of chicken every week.

第四节　红杉树国家公园

红杉树国家公园位于旧金山以北太平洋沿岸的群山中，公园中生长着大量北美红杉，这些可达 110 米以上、树龄可超 2000 岁的庞然大物，是世界上最高最壮观的树种。根据化石证据，红杉家族的各种巨大树木在 2000 万年前曾遍布北半球；但在第四纪冰川的影响下，不适应寒冷气候的巨木被压缩到极有限的区域之内，故而今天我们能看到如此高大的红杉林实属不易。同样的原因，红杉家族遗存至今的成员也已经不多，仅有北美红杉、巨杉和水杉三种。北美红杉和巨杉基本都生长在加利福尼亚州境内，其中北美红杉因为生境靠近海岸，故又有"海岸红杉"之称；而巨杉则分布在更靠内陆的内华达山脉之中，例如约塞米蒂国家公园里生长的就是巨杉，二者在生境上并无交叠，易于区分。由于人类对这些参天巨木的大量砍伐，19 世纪以来，北美红杉和巨杉的数量和生境缩减了 95%以上，濒临灭绝，红杉树国家公园及周边几个州立公园的设立就是为了保护北美红杉。

Culture Express

巨大的身躯、优质的木材，这些便于人类利用的优点，给红杉带来了灭顶之灾。它们挺过了第四纪冰川时代的冰天雪地，却抵挡不住文明的油锯，万难再次守住这最后的避难所。当意识到自己的过错并试着挽回时，人类发现生态系统的重塑并不如想象中一样顺利。在伐木业中，除了相当于剃光头一样的“全伐”，还会采取“间伐”的方式，即有选择地伐倒一片森林中小部分的树木，这是一种被认为是兼顾开发与保护的方法，在北美红杉的保护中也被广泛采用。然而，后来的研究表明，间伐后的林间空地被其他生长更迅速的树木占据，无法恢复成原有的红杉林，被保留的红杉，则因为彼此间空隙过大，而更易被大风吹倒。比起这些自以为是的办法，最好的保护措施就是彻底退出它们的家园。

Reading Passage 1

导读

相较于二百年前遍布美国西海岸的北美红杉林，现存于红杉树国家公园里的原生红杉的数量已十不存一。本文提到了 19 世纪人们疯狂砍伐红杉的三个原因。所幸，人们终于觉醒，建立了多个国家公园以保护这种地球上的最高树木。

When Euro-Americans swept westward in the 1800s, they needed **raw material** for their homes and lives. Commercial **logging** followed the expansion of America as companies struggled to keep up with the furious pace of progress. **Timber** harvesting quickly became the top manufacturing industry in the west.

When gold was discovered in north-western California in 1850, thousands crowded into the remote redwood region in search of riches and new lives. Failing in efforts to strike it rich in gold, these men turned toward harvesting the giant trees for **booming** development in San Francisco and other places on the West Coast. These trees are the tallest and one of the most **massive** tree species on Earth. The size of the huge trees made them **prized** timber, as redwood became known for its **durability** and workability. By 1853, nine **sawmills** were at work in Eureka, a gold boom town established three years prior due to the gold boom. At that period of time, redwood forest covered more than 2,000,000 acres (8,100 km^2) of the California coast.

The loggers used axes, saws, and other early methods of bringing the trees down. Rapidly improving technology in the 20th century allowed more trees to be harvested in less time. Transportation also caught up to the task of moving the massive logs. Railways started replacing horses and oxen. Land fraud was common, as acres of prime redwood forests were transferred from the public **domain** to private industry. Although some of the **perpetrators** were caught, many thousands of acres of land were lost in land **swindles**.

After many decades of **unobstructed** clear-cut logging, serious efforts toward conservation began. In 1918, the Save-the-Redwoods League was founded to preserve remaining old-growth redwoods, and their work resulted in the establishment of Prairie Creek, Del Norte Coast, and Jedediah Smith Redwoods State Parks among others. By the time Redwood National Park was created in 1968, nearly 90% of the original redwood trees had been logged.

(Adapted from *https://www.nps.gov/redw/learn/historyculture/area-history.htm*)

注释：

1.raw material 原材料
2.logging 伐木业
3.timber 木材
4.booming 繁荣的，飞速发展的
5.massive 大量的
6.prized 珍贵的
7.durability 持久性
8.sawmills 锯木厂
9.domain 领域，产业
10.perpetrator 犯罪者，作恶者
11.swindles 诈骗
12.unobstructed 畅通无阻的

Reading Passage 2

导读

在红杉树国家公园，为保护那些参天大树，公园管理者们既需要留心人类活动给树木带来的伤害，也需要采取有效措施积极修缮公园设施。对游客来说，学会正确的游览方式，比学会打开手机的美颜功能更重要。

Entering the redwood forest is like stepping back in time. Among all the towering trees, the exact location of the tallest, named the Grove of Titans, has long been kept secret—to help preserve them.

A few years ago, someone posted the GPS **coordinates** of the redwood on social media. Images online **lured** thousands of tourists to the area in search of the secret grove. They **criss-crossed** the park, creating unofficial trails (known as "social trails").

Calling it the Grove of Titans or the Secret Grove just enhanced the hunt. "Yeah, it **piqued** people's interest," Silver said, "People got **intrigued**—like, the big tree hunt, almost like **trophy** hunters." And like trophy hunters, people posed for pictures with the "Titans" sharing them online as proof of their conquest.

Forest ecologist Lathrop Leonard pointed out the damage to trees caused by the visitors' foot traffic. Along with destroying native plants, the soil compaction caused by standing next to a redwood harms the roots. Most of the roots of a redwood tree are in the first three feet or so. They need to be up right near the surface. Damage is also caused by people stepping directly onto the tree. Broken bark leaves the redwoods vulnerable.

Now the Redwood Parks Conservancy is raising money to protect the Titans. Raised walkways would be built for **selfies** without endangering the health of the trees. This three-year project needs about $1.4 million. In the meantime, people are being asked to stay on official trails. By staying on the trails, visitors can still see the forest and save the trees.

(Adapted from *https://www.cbsnews.com / news / trying-to-protect-california-redwoods-from-too-much-love /*)

注释:

1.coordinate 坐标
2.lure 引诱
3.criss-crossed 多次往返于,(在……内)纵横交错
4.piqued 激起,使愤恨
5.intrigued 好奇的,入迷的
6.trophy 奖品,战利品
7.selfie 自拍

Word Power

Fill in the blanks with the words given below. Change the form where necessary. Each word can be used only once.

booming, prized, unobstructed, piqued, intrigued

(1) The retractable design allows for boats to cruise through the canal ________, and the bridge rolls up every Friday.

(2) If someone is ________, they are offended or annoyed, often by something that is not very important.

(3) Torrey says he was also ________ by the history of Machu Picchu.

(4) If the economy or a business is ________, the number of things being bought or sold is increasing.

(5) Something that is ________ is wanted and admired because it is considered to be very valuable or have very good quality.

Summary

Fill in the blanks with words or phrases from Reading Passage 1.

There are three main reasons which contributed to the massive (1) ________ of coast redwoods in California. First of all, after Euro-Americans (2) ________ this area, they needed (3) ________ material for their homes and lives. (4) ________ harvesting quickly became the top manufacturing industry in the west. Second, when gold was (5) ________ in north-western California in 1850, thousands crowded into this area looking for gold mine. Disappointed at finding no gold, they turned to set up (6)________ to harvest the giant trees and made them (7)________ timber. Modern technology and transportation allowed harvesting more trees in less time.

Listening

Scan the code and listen to a microlecture about Redwood National Park. Please choose the best answer to each of the following questions.

(1) When was a national park created to protect the remaining of old-growth redwoods in California?

A. In 1968.　　B. In 1978.

C. In 1906.　　D. In 1898.

(2) Where is Redwood National Park?

A. In Wyoming.　　B. In Montana.

C. In California.　　D. In Washington.

Speaking

Please specify the measures taken by the Redwood Parks Conservancy to preserve the Grove of Titans in the Redwood National Park. Refer to the following words and expressions if necessary.

raising money / build raised walkways / stay on official trails

Writing

1. Example Sentence

Failing in efforts to strike it rich in gold, these men turned toward harvesting the giant trees for booming development in San Francisco and other places on the West Coast.

2. Analysis

(1)开头部分的 failing in efforts to 是分词短语作句子的状语,意为“没有做成”。

(2)strike it rich 是“走运”“发财”的意思。

(3)for 表示目的,booming development 意为“蓬勃发展”。

3. Practice

使用现在分词短语翻译下面的句子。

考研没有成功,她转而开始找工作,希望在工作中继续提高自己的专业技能。

第三章　美国先驱人物的故居

概　述

以建筑为引，本章撷取了美国历史上几位先驱人物加以介绍。他们中有才华横溢的开国元勋，也有为民请命的民权领袖；有兢兢业业的发明家，也有崇尚自然的思考者；有蜚声全球的大文豪，也有个性迥然的音乐人。他们是美国多元文化中举足轻重的特征符号，他们的居所和遗迹，是我们深入了解美国的指路牌。

第一节　托马斯·杰弗逊

在美国的开国元勋中，托马斯·杰弗逊的生平极富传奇色彩。除在政治上的成功外，一如本杰明·富兰克林是著名的科学家、发明家，杰弗逊也建树颇丰，他爱好考古、园艺、数学、文学，而他最为自豪并为后人所称道的是在建筑方面的成就。他将欧洲新古典主义建筑模式引入新独立的美利坚，是美国建筑史上的一代宗师。

Culture Express

有这样一栋建筑，它无关于美国历史上的各个政治事件，也不是某个繁华都市的地标建筑，但它出现在 2 美元纸币（1976 年以前版）以及 5 美分硬币的背面，可以说是美国人最为熟悉的一栋建筑。这栋"自传体"式建筑杰作已成为世界文化遗产，它就是第三任美国总统托马斯·杰弗逊亲自设计建造的庄园——蒙蒂塞洛（Monticello），也是杰弗逊总统极为钟爱、身后入葬的地方。Monticello 是意大利语，意为"小山"。杰弗逊受文艺复兴影响，钟爱与意大利有关的事物，从该建筑的名字和建筑风格就可见一斑。蒙蒂塞洛位于弗吉尼亚州夏洛茨维尔（Charlottesville）市内的山顶上，这里拥有绝佳的视野，可以眺望很远的地方。"Ville"在法语中是"村庄，市镇"的意思，这在弗吉尼亚州和马里兰州的地名中很常见。

Reading Passage 1

导读

按照杰弗逊自己的说法，他最喜欢的事情就是“拆了盖，盖了拆”，所以从杰弗逊壮年时期开始设计建造，直到他临终之前，蒙蒂塞洛的建设一直在持续。这座庄园是他毕生建筑设计理念的集成。2001年，有建筑界“诺贝尔奖”之称的普利兹克奖将颁奖典礼会址选在蒙蒂塞洛，这充分体现了现代人对这座修建于200多年前的庄园的欣赏和喜爱。

Construction on Monticello began around 1768 or 1769 when Jefferson was just 25 or 26 years old. As the site for his home, Jefferson chose a round hill overlooking the Charlottesville area. The first portion of Monticello was finished in 1772, but the home was a continual work-in-progress. Up until his death in 1826, Jefferson was always making improvements, additions, and remodeling.

Monticello is constructed in a**neo-classical architectural style.** Neo-classical architecture draws from classical Greek and Roman architecture. Columns, pillars, **arches**, and **domes** are common elements of neo-classical architecture.

In his construction of Monticello, Jefferson was highly influenced by Italian architecture. The word "Monticello" itself is an Italian word meaning "small mountain" and Jefferson considered his home a sort of Italian villa. Italian influences were strong in the first construction of Monticello. Jefferson was also influenced by French architecture. Jefferson lived in France during 1784-1789, and upon his return to Monticello, he **remodeled** the house to reflect some of the influences of French neo-classical architecture.

Since his death, Jefferson's contributions to American architecture have grown in **estimation**. In 1993, on the occasion of the 250th anniversary of Jefferson's birth, the American Institute of Architects **posthumously** granted him its Gold Medal for "a lifetime of distinguished achievement and significant contributions to architecture and the human environment." And, in 2001, Monticello was chosen to host the presentation of the Pritzker Architecture Award, which is widely regarding as architecture's highest award.

(Adapted from *https://study.com / academy / lesson / monticello-jeffersons-home-architecture-garden.html*)

注释：

1.neo-classical architectural style 新古典建筑风格(1750～1880年)

2.arch 弓形，拱门

3.dome 穹顶

4.remodel 改变结构

5.estimation 判断，尊敬

6.posthumously 死后地

Reading Passage 2

导读

坐落在弗吉尼亚州贝德福德的杨树林庄园是杰弗逊的妻子继承的家族遗产，在担任美国总统期间，杰弗逊坐镇华盛顿，遥控着这里的建设。他将此地改造成为繁忙政治生活之后的退隐之所。这座现在已是美国国家历史性地标的建筑与蒙蒂塞洛一样，很好地诠释了杰弗逊式建筑的风格特色。

One characteristic which **typifies** Jefferson's architecture is the use of the octagon and octagonal forms in his designs. Jefferson employed them as a design **motif** —**halving** them, **elongating** them, and employing them in whole as with the entire house at Poplar Forest, which was once Jefferson's personal **retreat**, and is now a historic house museum seeking to inspire visitors to explore Jefferson's legacy.

When construction began at Poplar Forest in 1806, Jefferson was still President of the United States. He supervised the construction from Washington, D. C. Thomas Jefferson was a self-taught architect known for his work at Monticello and the Virginia State Capitol; he frequently borrowed designs from classical sources, and was attracted to Palladio's classical architecture in Rome as well as designs from 16th century France. Jefferson designed Poplar Forest as his personal retreat house and selected the property because of its distance from his public life.

The octagonal house may have been the first of its kind to have been built in the United States. The house at Poplar Forest is made of brick and has an octagonal floor plan; it consists of a central square space and three sides made of elongated octagon rooms. There is an entry hall on the remaining side of the house, which is two smaller rooms divided by a short entry hall. Jefferson also elected to add **pedimented porticoes** on low **arcades** that were attached to both the northern and southern **facades** as well as the east and west stairwells. Scholars agree that the retreat house at Poplar Forest is an excellent example of octagonal symmetry; Jefferson's design for the building reflects a consistent **geometric** approach likely made possible by his well-known proficiency in algebra, geometry, trigonometry, and Newtonian calculus.

(Adapted from *https://archipaedia.wordpress.com/category/jeffersonian-classicism/*)

注释：

1.typify 作为典型，代表，象征
2.octagon 八角形
3.motif 作为装饰的图形，图示
4.halve 二等分
5.elongate 延长

6.retreat 隐退，休息寓所
7.pedimented 人字形的
8.portico 柱廊
9.arcade 连拱廊
10.facade（房屋的）正面
11.geometric 几何的

Word Power

Fill in the blanks with the words given below. Change the form where necessary. Each word can be used only once.

typify, halve, remodel, estimate, elongate

(1)If you exercise regularly and have a healthy diet, you can ________ the risk of having the flu.

(2)If you ________ something such as a building or a room, you give it a different form or shape.

(3)If you ________ something, you stretch it so that it becomes longer.

(4) If you ________ a quantity or value, you make an approximate judgment or calculation of it.

(5) If something or someone ________ a situation, they have all the usual characteristics of it and are a typical example of it.

Summary

Fill in the blanks with words or phrases from Reading Passage 1.

Monticello is constructed in a (1) ________ architectural style. The word "Monticello"itself is an Italian word meaning (2) ________ and Jefferson considered his home a sort of Italian (3) ________. It's a (4) ________ work-in-progress. Up until his death in 1826, Jefferson was always making improvements, additions, and (5) ________. Jefferson frequently borrowed designs from classical Greek and Roman architecture: columns, pillars, arches, and (6) ________. He was also attracted to designs from 16th century France.

Listening

Scan the code and listen to a microlecture about Thomas Jefferson. Please choose the best answer to each of the following questions.

(1)Which of the following is not the identity for Thomas Jefferson?

A.The father of University of Virginia.

B. The third president of the United States.

C. A philologist.

D. An Astronomer.

(2) Who once served as the rectors of University of Virginia?

A. Theodore Roosevelt and James Madison.

B. Thomas Jefferson and Franklin Roosevelt.

C. James Madison and Thomas Jefferson.

D. Franklin Roosevelt and James Madison.

(3) The building of Jefferson's home in Virginia is named ________, which is an Italian word.

A. Virginia House　　B. Palladio

C. Monticello　　D. Statehouse of Virginia

Speaking

Please briefly introduce Monticello, a house with great significance in American architecture history. Refer to the following words and expressions if necessary.

neo-classical architecture / forty-year construction period / remodel / Italian influence / columns / pillars / arches / domes

Writing

1. Example Sentence

Jefferson employed them as a design motif—halving them, elongating them, and employing them in whole as with the entire house at Poplar Forest, which was once Jefferson's personal retreat, and is now a historic house museum seeking to inspire visitors to explore Jefferson's legacy.

2. Analysis

(1)这句话很长，它的主干在开头部分。Jefferson 作句子的主语，employed 作谓语。

(2)which 引导了一个非限定性定语从句，目的在于解释 Poplar Forest 过去和现在的区别。

(3)which 引导的非限定性定语从句用于提供解释信息，又不打破原有句子的语序，值得我们在写作中借鉴。同样可以引导非限定性定语从句的还有 when、where、who、whom 或者 as。

3. Practice

使用非限定性定语从句合并下列句子。

(1) Empire State Building imbued New York City with a deep sense of pride. This sense of pride was desperately needed in the depths of the Great Depression.

(2) The Great Depression is the time when many city residents were unemployed and prospects looked bleak.

第二节 马丁·路德·金

如果更名换姓能够改变一个人的成就，那么佐治亚州亚特兰大市的老马丁·路德·金绝对做了他一生中最正确的选择：在一次欧洲之行后，这位原名迈克尔·金的牧师将他与他的儿子小迈克尔·金的名字都改成了马丁·路德·金，借以致敬那位著名的宗教改革家。而他的儿子，后来成为美国最著名的非裔民权领袖、世人心目中最伟大的美国人之一。神职人员世家的背景对马丁·路德·金的影响无疑是巨大的，他成年后就读于神学院并成了一名牧师。金一直宣扬心怀全人类，他甘愿服务他人，并为之贡献一生，即使成为民权运动领袖后也是如此。本节所介绍的，就是位于亚特兰大的马丁·路德·金一家三代神职人员的居所。

Culture Express

为了纪念马丁·路德·金，1980 年，美国内政部将他少年时期位于亚特兰大的居所和附近的几座建筑物指定为国家历史遗迹，然而，人们对这位伟大的民权运动领袖的纪念远不止于此。在美国，有超过 700 条道路以他的名字命名；他的纪念碑矗立在华盛顿特区的独立大道；每年 1 月的第三个星期一是美国的“马丁·路德·金纪念日”，也是美国唯一一个纪念个人的公众假日。2005 年美国选出的“最伟大的美国人”中，马丁·路德·金高居第三，位于乔治·华盛顿之上。可以说，美国人对他的崇拜和赞赏达到了无以复加的程度。

Reading Passage 1

导读

马丁·路德·金的外祖父是当地浸礼会的牧师。他的女儿嫁给了教会中的助理牧师——老马丁·路德·金；小夫妇跟老牧师住在一起，并在那栋房子里生下了小马丁·路德·金。老牧师去世后，他的女婿接替了他的职位，并把自己的儿子也培养成了牧师。这原本很正常的世代生活，因为一个不凡的人物，而成为万众瞩目的历史；他们生活的那栋房子，也成了美国国家历史遗迹。

Martin Luther King, Jr. was born in Atlanta at this home of his maternal grandparents, Adam Daniel Williams and Jennie Williams, on January 15, 1929. Adam Daniel Williams, then the **pastor** of Ebenezer Baptist Church purchased the house at the cost of $3,500 in 1909. When Martin Luther King, Jr.'s parents got married, the King family moved into the house on Auburn Avenue where they lived until 1941.

The birth home of Martin Luther King, Jr. is located in the residential section of the Auburn Avenue Historic District. It is a modest two-story frame house built in the Queen Anne style with a front **porch**, **parlor**, study, kitchen, dining room, bedroom, and bathroom on the first level. The second floor includes four bedrooms and a bathroom.

Since the early 1980s, decades after King had helped birth the civil rights movement, and about 14 years after his **assassination**, his birth home began hosting free tours for the public. It's since been a **cherished** monument to the **iconic** leader who helped shape not just Atlanta, but the United States at large. And the home was finally sold to the National Park Service.

The National Park Service, of course, did not come out of left field to make the buy. For three decades, the federal agency has **curated** the house-turned-museum, where droves of people flock each year—especially around Martin Luther King, Jr. Day, in January—to see where the late civil rights hero spent the first 12 years of his life, before moving a few blocks north on Boulevard.

In 1980, King's birth home was **designated** a national historic site by the National Park Service.

(Adapted from *https://www.ajc.com / news / martin-luther-king-birth-home-sold-national-park-service/Hcai18MhNHeWNp0N374KFM/*, *https://atlanta.curbed.com* / 2018/12/18/18144013/*martin-luther-king-jr-birth-home-national-park-service*)

注释：

1.pastor 牧师
2.porch 门廊
3.parlor 客厅，休息室
4.assassination 暗杀
5.cherished 真爱的
6.iconic 偶像的
7.curate 组织
8.designate 定名，指派

Reading Passage 2

导读

马丁·路德·金的故居，以及他祖孙三代所供职的教堂，都坐落在亚特兰大一条名为奥本大街的路边。这里是美国南部重要的非裔美国人聚居区，当地人称它为"甜蜜的奥本"。为何会有这样的叫法呢？它到底"甜"在哪里？

Extending less than two miles eastward from Peachtree Street, Auburn Avenue was the commercial, cultural, and spiritual center of African American life in Atlanta **prior** to the civil rights movement. Because Auburn Avenue's financial institutions **amounted** to a **consolidation** of African American wealth unique for its time, black Atlantans referred to the street as "Sweet Auburn." **Coined** by John Wesley Dobbs, a civic leader and the neighborhood's unofficial "mayor," the name reflected the avenue's prominence as a national center of black commerce.

"Sweet Auburn" boasted a concentration of black-owned businesses, entertainment venues, and churches that was **unrivaled** elsewhere in the South. Its **bustling** retail trade and wealthy business owners earned the street a national reputation for African American finance and **entrepreneurial zeal.**

Auburn Avenue was not simply a place to do business. Black Atlantans worshipped at Auburn's many churches, including Ebenezer Baptist Church, where three generations of Martin Luther King Jr.'s family were pastors. Whether for work or play, Auburn Avenue was the center of African American life in Atlanta.

Ironically, Auburn's civic activism led to its undoing. As the National Association for the Advancement for Colored People (NAACP) and local voting-rights organizations, from their Sweet Auburn offices, **lobbied** state and local governments for an end to **segregation**, and as native son Martin Luther King, Jr. led the crusade for civil rights before a national audience, the street began its steep decline. With the legal barriers to integration removed, many Auburn shopkeepers moved their businesses to other areas of the city, and residents began migrating to Atlanta's west side. At the same time, the street was **bisected** by the construction of the Downtown Connector. Once vital and vibrant, the community's fabric began to tear as Sweet Auburn fell victim to disinvestment and neglect. "It turned into a **decaying** memorial to a bygone era," observes Gary Pomerantz, "a necessary though regrettable price for freedom."

(Adapted from *https://www.georgiaencyclopedia.org / articles / counties-cities-neighborhoods / auburn-avenue-sweet-auburn*)

注释:

1.prior 优先的,在……之前的
2.amount 合计
3.consolidation 合并,团结
4.coin 创造
5.unrivaled 无敌的,无比的
6.bustling 繁忙的,熙熙攘攘的
7.entrepreneurial 创业的
8.zeal 热心,奋发
9.lobby 游说,陈情
10.segregation 分隔,隔离
11.bisect 平分
12.decaying 衰落的

Word Power

Fill in the blanks with the words given below. Change the form where necessary. Each word can be used only once.

decaying, assassination, consolidate, segregation, bustling

(1) The leader's ________ led to a political unrest against the government.

(2) To ________ a number of small groups or firms means to make them into one large organization.

(3) Shops on this street are getting more and more prosperous and ________.

(4) Hospitals provided a ________ between the patients with symptoms and those without symptoms.

(5) If something such as a society, system, or institution is ________, it's gradually becoming weaker or worse.

Summary

Fill in the blanks with words or phrases from Reading Passage 1.

The birth home of Martin Luther King, Jr. is located in the (1) ________ section of the Auburn Avenue Historic District which was the commercial, cultural, and (2) ________ center of African American life in Atlanta (3) ________ the civil rights movement. Since the early 1980s, decades after King had helped (4) ________ the civil rights movement, and about 14 years after his (5) ________, his birth home began hosting free tours for the public. It's since been a (6) ________ monument to the (7) ________ leader who helped shape not just Atlanta, but the United States at large.

Listening

Scan the code and listen to a microlecture about Martin Luther King, Jr. Please choose the best answer to each of the following questions.

(1) When was the first national holiday named after Martin Luther King, Jr. officially observed in all fifty U.S. states?

A. In 1964.　　B. In 1981.

C. In 2000.　　D. In 2008.

(2) Which city is Martin Luther King, Jr.'s birthplace and burial place?

A. Atlanta　　B. Philadelphia

C. Boston　　D. Austin

Speaking

Please briefly introduce Sweet Auburn Avenue, where Martin Luther King Jr.once lived in Atlanta. Refer to the following words and expressions if necessary.

commercial, cultural, and spiritual center / black commerce / civic activities / segregation / legal barriers to integration / decaying

Writing

1. Example Sentence

Once vital and vibrant, the community's fabric began to tear as Sweet Auburn fell victim to disinvestment and neglect.

2. Analysis

(1)once vital and vibrant 作句子的状语。形容词主要用作定语和表语,但有时也可用作状语(也称为主语补足语,因为它们是用来补充说明主语的)。

(2)fell victim to"成为牺牲者",to 后面接名词。

(3)形容词作状语,可以放在句子开头,也可以放在主语和谓语之间。

3. Practice

请将下面句子中的形容词改写成状语。

The little girl was cold and hungry, so she kept crying.

第三节　马克·吐温

马克·吐温是美国文学史上独树一帜的人物,他幽默而犀利的文字开创了批判现实主义文学。他的笔名过于耀眼,以至萨缪尔·兰亨·克莱门斯(Samuel Langhorne Clemens)这个本名很少被人提起。他青少年时期在美国南部密西西比河畔的生活经历无疑对他的几部最出名的小说有深刻的影响;当然,这些作品都是他居住在离纽约不远的哈特福德时著就的,那里的马克·吐温故居博物馆已经成了全世界文学爱好者的朝圣地。

Culture Express

1868 年马克·吐温第一次来到哈特福德时,就喜欢上了这个城市,他在写给当时还是未婚妻的奥利维亚的信中将这里描述成"所有美丽城市之冠"。之后不久,他们就在这里定居下来,并且倾力建起了一座独具特色的楼房。房屋的设计者爱德华·波特以设计教堂而知名,也正因此,这座维多利亚哥特式房屋在周边方方正正的住宅之间显得格格不入。不过马克·吐温夫妇对房屋和内部陈设显然很满意,作家先生甚至会抱怨家里太舒服、窗外风景太好,这些大大分散了他的注意力,让他什么都写不了,最后他只好把自己关到三楼的台球室去写作。而作为一个台球爱好者,他在关起门来的时间里是玩球更多些还是写作更多些,我们不得而知,反正结果是那些年里一些不朽的文字相继面世了。1891

年，因为投资失败，经济负担过重，马克·吐温一家搬去了欧洲；在哈特福德的日子是他生命中最欢乐幸福的一段时光。

Reading Passage 1

导读

1871～1891 年，马克·吐温在哈特福德居住了 21 年，这里是当时美国出版业的中心。在这里，马克·吐温从声名鹊起到享誉全球，他的家庭也历经了兴旺和衰落。

The Mark Twain House and Museum in Hartford, Connecticut, was the home of Samuel Langhorne Clemens (Mark Twain) and his family from 1874 to 1891. It was designed by Edward Tuckerman Potter and built in the American High Gothic style. Clemens **biographer** Justin Kaplan has called it "part steamboat, part **medieval fortress** and part cuckoo clock".

The Clemens family moved into the home in 1874 after its completion. The top floor was the **billiards room** and his private study where he would write late at night; the room was strictly off limits to all but the cleaning staff. It was also used for entertaining male guests with cigars and liquor. Twain had said, "There ought to be a room in this house to swear in. It's dangerous to have to **repress** an emotion like that."

The children had their own area with a nursery and a playroom / classroom. Mrs. Clemens tutored her daughters in the large school room on the second floor. Clemens played with his children in the **conservatory**, pretending to be an elephant in an imaginary safari. He noted that the house "was of us, and we were in its confidence and lived in its grace and in the peace of its **benediction**."

Clemens worked on many of his most notable books in this home, including *The Adventures of Tom Sawyer* (1876) and *Life on the Mississippi* (1883). The success of *The Adventures of Tom Sawyer* inspired him to **renovate** the house, and he had Louis Comfort Tiffany **supervise** the interior decoration in 1881. He also was fascinated with new technologies, leading to the installation of an early telephone.

Clemens formed the firm Charles L. Webster & Company which published his writings. But this company went bankrupt in 1894, leaving Twain with a large amount of debt. The losses from these investments as well as several bank panics led the Clemens family to move to Europe in 1891 where the cost of living was more affordable. He began lecturing across the continent to recoup some money for their family. Unable to afford living in the house, Twain rented it out, returning only once in 1895. "As soon as I entered this front door I was seized with a furious desire to have us all in this house again & right away," he wrote, "never go outside the grounds any more forever. It is the loveliest home that ever was."

(Adapted from *https://ctweekender.com / things-to-do-in-connecticut / buildings-architecture-ct / mark-twain-house-and-museum /*)

注释：

1. biographer 传记作家
2. medieval 中世纪的
3. fortress 堡垒
4. billiards room 台球室
5. repress 压抑
6. conservatory 温室，暖房
7. benediction 赐福祈祷
8. renovate 翻新
9. supervise 监督

Reading Passage 2

导读

1870年，盛名初就的马克·吐温同奥利维亚·兰登结婚，她的父亲是一名富商，所以遗产丰厚。克莱门斯一家于是就延请了著名的建筑师爱德华·波特(Edward Tuckerman Potter)设计建造了这栋维多利亚哥特式房屋。

The Mark Twain House was designed by Edward Tuckerman Potter, an architect from New York City. When it was being built, the *Hartford Daily Times* noted, "The **novelty** displayed in the architecture of the building, the **oddity** of its internal arrangement and the fame of its owner will all conspire to make it a house of note for a long time to come." The cost of the house was paid out of Mrs. Clemens' **inheritance.**

The home is in the style of **Victorian Gothic Revival architecture**, including the typical **steeply-pitched** roof and an **asymmetrical bay window** layout. Legend says the home was designed to look like a riverboat. According to *A Field Guide to American Houses* the house was built in the **Stick style** of Victorian architecture.

In 1881, an **adjoining strip** of land was purchased, the grounds re-landscaped, and the home was renovated. The driveway was redrawn, the kitchen rebuilt and its size doubled, and the front hall was enlarged. The family also installed new plumbing and heating and a burglar alarm. After its renovations, the total cost of the home amounted to ＄70,000, ＄22,000 were spent on **furnishings**, and the initial purchase of land cost ＄31,000.

(Adapted from *https://www.kronenbergersons.com/portfolio/the — mark — twain — house/*)

注释：

1.novelty 新颖
2.oddity 奇怪，怪异
3.inheritance 遗产，继承

4.Victorian Gothic Revival architecture 维多利亚哥特复兴式建筑
5.steeply-pitched 陡峭的屋顶
6.asymmetrical 不对称的
7.bay window 飘窗
8.Stick style 美国 19 世纪晚期的建筑形式,外墙有大量的条形木格架装饰
9.adjoining 毗邻的
10.strip 狭长的带状土地
11.furnishing 装饰

Word Power

Fill in the blanks with the words given below. Change the form where necessary. Each word can be used only once.

novelty, oddity, furnishings, renovation, inheritance

(1)Many assembly line workers did home ________ and other skilled work in their off-hours in order to regain their dignity.

(2)In addition to new windows and mechanical components, the interior received a fresh mix of ________, and new coats of paint throughout.

(3)She began her own business with the ________ she got from her grandfather.

(4)To wear vest, short pants, mini-skirt, and other ________ dress is prohibited in the working period.

(5)In the contemporary western world, rapidly changing styles cater to a desire for ________ and individualism.

Summary

Fill in the blanks with words or phrases from Reading Passage 1.

The Mark Twain House and Museum in Hartford, Connecticut, was built in the American High (1) ________ style. Clemens biographer Justin Kaplan has called it "part steamboat, part medieval (2) ________ and part cuckoo clock." The Clemens family moved into the home in 1874 after its (3) ________. Clemens worked on many of his most (4) ________ books in this home, the success of one of which inspired him to (5) ________ the house, including (6) ________ an early telephone. Unable to afford living in the house, Twain (7)________ it out, (8) ________ only once in 1895. Later in his life, he wrote: "It is the loveliest home that ever was."

Listening

Scan the code and listen to a microlecture about Mark Twain. Please choose the best answer to each of the following questions.

(1)Who was once called the greatest humorist and the father of American literature?

A.Mark Twain. B. Ralph Waldo Emerson.

C.Walt Whitman. D. Henry David Thoreau.

(2)Many of the works of Mark Twain deal with or take place near ________.

A. the Mississippi River B. St. Petersburg

C. Hannibal, Missouri D. Walden Pond

(3)How did Mark Twain revolutionize prose?

A.By writing in a conversational tone. B. By writing in a formal tone.

C.By using sarcasm. D. By using humorous expressions.

Speaking

Please briefly introduce the architecture of Mark Twain's house in Hartford, Connecticut. Refer to the following expressions if necessary.

medieval fortress / Gothic style / bay window / Stick style / steeply-pitched

Writing

1. Example Sentence

The driveway was redrawn, the kitchen rebuilt and its size doubled, and the front hall was enlarged.

2. Analysis

(1)该句使用被动语态强调动作,而忽略动作的发出者。

(2)Kitchen 和 size 的后面都省略了 was。

(3)多组被动结构并列时,可以省略相同部分,以使表达简练。

3. Practice

请将下面句子改写成省略句。

(1)Some are laughing, and some are crying.

(2)Sam won the first match, and John won the second match.

第四节 亨利·戴维·梭罗

作为一名超验主义者,亨利·戴维·梭罗(1817～1862 年)关心的都是接近本质的东西,生命、精神、政治乃至文字一应如是。他是一位散文家、诗人、哲学家、思想家,他的声名无人不知,他的《瓦尔登湖》是美国文学中最受欢迎的非虚构著作,然而他身后所留下的,除了这些指引后人思想的文字,再没有什么了。在他常年生活的康科德镇,因为秉行质朴的生活方式,他并没有置办什么产业,所以也未留存一栋真正意义上的“故居”,后人只能在他多年寄宿的爱默生故居和小镇的博物馆里寻到他生活的蛛丝马迹;瓦尔登湖边倒是有间小屋的复制品供游人凭吊——他亲力亲为的那间简陋的林间小屋，早就为密林所毁匿了。也许这正是顺应了梭罗极力摒弃冗余的自愿简朴哲学吧。

Culture Express

在瓦尔登湖边生活期间，梭罗因为反对黑奴制，拒交"人头税"而被捕。这段经历促使他写成了著名的政论《论公民的不服从》。梭罗的"公民不服从"指非暴力地拒绝遵守不合理的法令，他既不支持对不公正的默认，也不赞成以暴力对抗不公。他所宣传的这种依靠个人的力量、"非暴力抵抗"的斗争形式对印度的甘地和美国的民权运动领袖马丁·路德·金产生了很大的影响，在后世许多和平抗议运动中都有所运用。梭罗是一个有责任感的社会批评家，他的目的是揭露时代的弊端。选择隐居湖畔，并不是他借以晋身上流社会的"终南捷径"，而完全是他个人的志趣；他离开瓦尔登湖畔以后，也一再反对别人模仿他的行为，认为人们施行的应当是"自愿简朴"(voluntary simplicity)，而不是刻意的苦行。梭罗并不排斥现代科技文明给人们带来的物质享受，他只是批评我们没有很好地利用它，他指出人们正将生活变得越来越复杂，最终会导致生命的"衰落"。在经济飞速发展的今天，物质文明水平日新月异，与此同时，人们的欲望也随之膨胀，梭罗当年的忧虑成了严峻的现实。对此，阅读并领悟梭罗"自愿简朴"的思想，改变一些我们的生活态度，对现实生活是很有指导意义的。

Reading Passage 1

导读

1845～1847年，梭罗在瓦尔登湖畔独自生活，进行了一场他称为俭朴生活的实验。在某些关于梭罗在瓦尔登湖畔隐居的肤浅传说中，好像是他借了把斧子就去隐居了两年两个月又两天；事实上，他还是经过了一番准备和投资的。美国的土地大多私有，在别人的土地上营建并生活是要交钱的；梭罗在瓦尔登湖边的住所位于爱默生的私产之内，这位亦师亦友的长者允许他免费使用，这才让家境不好的梭罗完成这场实验。至于建屋的各种材料，梭罗曾列出了一个清单，共计花费了28.125美元。购买建屋用的木板一项中出现了半美分的零头，梭罗并未在书中做出解释，仅是很精确地记录了下来。算上通货膨胀，这个金额大约相当于现在的900美元。

In 1845, Henry David Thoreau, who was then 28, began what would be a 2-year experiment in living simply and **retreating from** society and its **materialistic** ills. He moved to the shores of Walden Pond, and built himself a tiny house.

Not opposed to getting a helping hand, this **rugged** individualist camped out on the property of his friend Ralph Waldo Emerson, where he constructed a rugged one-room cabin from materials that cost him 28 dollars and 12 1/2 cents, including a thousand bricks for four dollars and **two casks of lime** for $2.40, which he felt to be too expensive. (Adjusted for inflation, this comes out to $878.52 in 2018 dollars.)

Many of the boards used to build the house came from an old workman's **shanty**, which Thoreau purchased for $4.25 and **carted** to his building site. Others came from felling trees on the site.

The design of the cabin was very simple: just one room, 10 feet wide and 15 feet long, with a hearth at one side. Thoreau did all his cooking there, or outside, and **presumably** answered the call of nature while communing with nature. The outside of the house was **clad** in **shingles**, to keep it **weathertight**, and the inside **plastered**.

Like a lot of modern tiny house dwellers, Thoreau moved on from his experiment in small-space living: he abandoned the house after two years. Also like a lot of modern tiny house dwellers, he wrote an account detailing his experiences, which became *Walden*, Thoreau's enduring **paean** to simple living and self-reliance.

After he left it, Thoreau's little house presumably fell victim to the **ravages** of nature and time, although if you visit Walden Pond, you can still see the site where the cabin once stood, surrounded by stone markers. Walk inside them and you can see Thoreau's original hearthstone. There's also, in a slightly different location, a recreation of the original cabin, furnished as it would have been while Thoreau lived there. It's a neat little piece of history, and also a reminder of the timeless appeal of the simple life.

(Adapted from *https://www.apartmenttherapy.com / first-tiny-house-henry-david-thoreau*-255479)

注释:

1.retreat from 隐退
2.materialistic 唯物论的
3.rugged 崎岖不平的,起伏的
4.two casks of lime 两箱石灰
5.shanty 简陋的木屋
6.cart 费力搬运
7.presumably 据推测,很可能
8.clad 被……覆盖的
9.shingles 木瓦,屋顶板
10.weathertight 防风雨的,不透风的
11.plaster 涂满
12.paean 赞歌,凯歌
13.ravage 破坏,蹂躏

Reading Passage 2

导读

在旁人看来,梭罗不仅是自然主义和超验主义的实践者。在文学上,他是自然随笔这一文学类型的开创者;在社会活动方面,他的《论公民的不服从》启迪了圣雄甘地、马丁·路德·金等诸多民权运动领袖;在学术上,他留下了极有价值的生物学和物候学记

录。他所展示于人的，是一段不长但多彩的人生，是一个真挚的、充满哲思的灵魂。

It was a happy thought of Thoreau's friend William Ellery Channing, himself a poet, to **style** Thoreau, a Concord **hermit**, the "poet-naturalist"; for there seemed to be no year of his life, and no hour of his day when Nature did not whisper some secret in his ear. In another connection, speaking of natural beauty, Channing said, " Give him sunshine and a handful of nuts, and he has enough." He was also a naturalist in the more **customary** sense—one who studied and arranged methodically in his mind the facts of outward nature; a good **botanist** and **ornithologist** , a wise student of insects and fishes; an observer of the winds, the clouds, the seasons, and all that goes to make up what we call "weather" and "climate." Yet he was in heart a poet, and held all the accumulated knowledge of more than forty years not so much for use as for delight.

He kept detailed observations on Concord's nature **lore**, recording everything from how the fruit ripened over time to the fluctuating depths of Walden Pond and the days certain birds migrated. The point of this task was to "anticipate" the seasons of nature, in his word.

He became a land surveyor and continued to write increasingly detailed observations on the natural history of the town, covering an area of 26 square miles, in his journal, a two-million-word document he kept for 24 years. He also kept a series of notebooks, and these observations became the source of his late writings on natural history.

With the rise of environmental history and ecocriticism as academic disciplines, several new readings of Thoreau began to emerge, showing him to have been both a philosopher and an analyst of ecological patterns in fields and woodlots. For instance, he used experimentation and analysis to explain how forests **regenerate** after fire or human destruction, through the **dispersal** of seeds by winds or animals.

(Adapted from *https://books.google.com/books/about/The_Greatest_Works_of_Henry_David_Thorea.html*)

注释：

1.style 称呼
2.hermit 隐士
3.customary 依照惯例的
4.botanist 植物学家
5.ornithologist 鸟类学家
6.lore 传说，典故
7.regenerate 再生
8.dispersal 分散，驱散

Word Power

Fill in the blanks with the words given below. Change the form where necessary.

Each word can be used only once.

botanist, hermit, shanty, ravage, cart

(1) A ________ is a person who lives alone, away from people and society.

(2) A ________ is the scientist who studies plants and can differentiate varieties of plants.

(3) A ________ is a small rough hut which poor people live in, built from tin, cardboard, or other materials that are not very strong.

(4) We should not put the ________ before the horse.

(5) The rape of the countryside had a profound ________ on them.

Summary

Fill in the blanks with words or phrases from Reading Passage 2.

Thoreau retreated from the societies and became a Concord (1) ________. He is a poet-naturalist in the more customary sense—one who studied and arranged methodically in his mind the facts of outward nature: a good (2) ________ who studies plants, an (3) ________ who knows about birds, a wise student of insects and fishes; an (4) ________ of the winds, the clouds and the seasons. Yet he was in heart a poet, and held all the accumulated knowledge of more than forty years not so much for (5) ________ as for (6) ________. He became a land (7) ________ and continued to write increasingly detailed observations on the natural history of Concord.

Listening

Scan the code and listen to a microlecture about Henry David Thoreau. Please choose the best answer to each of the following questions.

(1) Where is Walden Pond?

A. Atlanta. B. Philadelphia.

C. Concord. D. Austin.

(2) Whose work is regarded as the most popular American non-fiction?

A. Mark Twain. B. Henry David Thoreau.

C. Edgar Allan Poe. D. Henry James.

Speaking

Please briefly introduce how voluntary simplicity and being a naturalist affect Henry David Thoreau's writing. Refer to the following words and expressions if necessary.

retreat from societies / solitude / hermit / observer / detailed description of nature

Writing

1. Example Sentence

Like a lot of modern tiny house dwellers, Thoreau moved on from his experiment in small-space living: he abandoned the house after two years. Also like a lot of modern tiny house dwellers, he wrote an account detailing his experiences, which became *Walden*, Thoreau's enduring paean to simple living and self-reliance.

2. Analysis

(1)这两句话是排比句式,并列了两个相同之处。Like a lot of modern tiny house dwellers 后面的部分是第一个相同之处。Also like a lot of modern tiny house dwellers 后面的部分是第二个相同之处。

(2)用 Also 连接排比句中两个并列的部分。

3. Practice

使用排比句结构翻译下面的句子。

礼貌是一种习惯,展现你对人生的态度。礼貌是一种尊重,传达你对他人的关爱。

第五节 托马斯·爱迪生

毫无疑问,提到发明家这个词,大多数人立刻就会想到爱迪生;一个又一个耳熟能详的关于他的故事,不论真假,在我们成长的过程中曾不断地跳出来。托马斯·阿尔瓦·爱迪生(Thomas Alva Edison,1847~1931 年)是人类历史上第一个利用工业化实验室从事专利发明而对世界产生深远影响的人。他将"发明"这个原先带有个人主义色彩的词语,变成了一种产业。他的名下有专利 1000 多项,其中留声机、电影摄影机和改进的电灯对世界产生了极大影响。这一节中,我们将走入爱迪生的工业化实验室和他的故居,从另一个方面来了解这位大发明家。

Culture Express

1876 年,爱迪生用他出售专利的收入建立了自己的家和研究实验室。实验室位于新泽西州拉瑞坦镇一个不成功的房地产开发项目"门罗公园"(Menlo Park)内。门罗公园实验室的重大意义在于它是最早进行实际商业应用研究的实验室之一。在这个以创新和改进技术为目的的机构里,爱迪生雇用年轻有为的科研人员在他的指导下进行研究和开发,并以自己的名义申请保护期较短的实用新型专利(utility model patent)。10 年里,爱迪生获得了包括留声机、白炽灯等在内的许多改变了世界的发明专利,这里的一条名为克里斯蒂的街道是世界上第一条使用电灯照明的街道。1954 年,拉瑞坦镇改名为爱迪生镇以纪念这位伟大的发明家。

以实验室的科研输出为基础,爱迪生成立了"爱迪生灯具公司"(Edison Lamp Company)、"爱迪生机械厂"(Edison Machine Works)、"爱迪生电灯公司"(Edison

Electric Light Company)等许多电力相关公司，1889 年，这些公司被整合成了“爱迪生通用电气公司”(Edison General Electric Company)，这就是著名的“美国通用电气公司”(GE)的前身。

Reading Passage 1

导读

米娜·米勒是爱迪生的第二任妻子，也是他的终身伴侣。他们结婚之后，爱迪生在新泽西州的西奥兰治买下了一栋名为格伦蒙特的豪宅，并在住宅附近重建了他的工业实验室。这所实验室可同时进行多个方向的科学实验，最多曾聘用了上万名科研工作人员，它正是后来各企业研究院的鼻祖。

In 1886, Thomas Alva Edison married Mina Miller and purchased an **estate**, Glenmont, for his bride. Thomas Edison lived here with Mina until his death.

When Edison moved to West Orange, he was doing experimental work in **makeshift facilities** in his electric lamp factory in nearby Harrison, New Jersey. A few months after his marriage, however, Edison decided to build a new laboratory in West Orange itself, less than a mile from his home. Edison possessed both the resources and experience by this time to build "the best equipped and largest laboratory extant and the facilities **superior** to any other for rapid and cheap development of an invention". The new laboratory **complex** consisting of five buildings opened in November 1887. A three-story main laboratory building contained a power plant, machine shops, **stock rooms**, experimental rooms and a large library. Four smaller one-story buildings built **perpendicular** to the main building contained a physics lab, chemistry lab, **metallurgy lab**, **pattern shop**, and chemical storage. The large size of the laboratory not only allowed Edison to work on any sort of project, but also allowed him to work on as many as ten or twenty projects at once. Facilities were added to the laboratory or modified to meet Edison's changing needs as he continued to work in this complex until his death in 1931. Over the years, factories to manufacture Edison inventions were built around the laboratory. The entire laboratory and factory complex eventually covered more than twenty acres and employed 10,000 people at its peak during World War One (1914-1918).

(Adapted from *https://www.nps.gov / edis / learn / historyculture / edison-biography.htm*)

注释：

1.estate 房产
2.makeshift facilities 临时设施
3.superior 优于……的，较好的
4.complex 建筑群
5.stock rooms 储藏室

6.perpendicular 垂直的

7.metallurgy lab 冶金实验室

8.pattern shop 制模车间

Reading Passage 2

导读

一位发明家的住宅理应是充满创意和各种便利设施的，爱迪生的格伦蒙特正是如此。他给这栋本来就设施先进的豪宅增设了供电线路、供暖和冷却系统，而且还使之相当环保。

When originally built, Glenmont was a **marvel** of modern living. It had many modern household facilities, such as a central heating system, hot and cold running indoor water, indoor flush toilets and even a refrigerator room in the kitchen. Glenmont was designed by famed architect Henry Hudson Holly.

Soon after buying Glenmont, Edison had it wired for electricity. Power for the mansion was provided by a dedicated line run from his nearby West Orange Laboratories, probably using underground cables very similar to the ones he was using to demonstrate his now **legendary** Pearl Street electric generating station and distribution system concept in New York City.

Glenmont was originally built using more than 157,000 bricks, and more than 10,000 pounds of iron and steel framing. It has 91 windows and 7 chimneys; and employs about 40 window **awnings.** It took two years to build (1880 – 1882). This massive and elegant building contains 20,000 square feet of living area. It has a 23-foot square open porch at its top (a widow's walk), from which New York City can be seen. It has a magnificent **conservatory** that dominates its southern face.

Glenmont is now heated and cooled using a natural earth energy system called **geothermal heating.** In the summer, heat from the house is **extracted** and stored down twelve 350-foot-deep wells, about 200 feet away from the house. In the winter, this heat is retrieved and used to heat the house. It all works on the same principle as the refrigerator. Six heat pumps do all the work in capturing and moving the heat between the house and its storage wells. A geothermal alternate energy system was chosen for installation during the home's massive renovation in 2004 – 05 as a way to recognize the Edison's respect and love for nature, he being an ardent environmentalist, **horticulturist,** and **conservationist;** and he using many natural materials in his inventions, as well as enjoying camping and nature tours.

(Adapted from *https://www.edisonmuckers.org / thomas-edison-historic-home /*)

注释：

1.marvel 奇迹

2.legendary 传奇的
3.awnings 雨棚
4.conservatory 温室，暖房
5.geothermal heating 地热采暖
6.extract 提取，提炼
7.horticulturist 园艺学家
8.conservationist 环保人士

Word Power

Fill in the blanks with the words given below. Change the form where necessary. Each word can be used only once.

makeshift, superior, marvel, extract

(1) A new technological ________ was invented at Cambridge University in England, the scanning electron microscope.

(2) They need to ________ as much information as possible from the first or second reading.

(3) The latest patients were admitted to ________ hospitals.

(4) We have to decide whether we are ________ or inferior to others on certain dimensions, such as attractiveness, intelligence, popularity, etc.

Summary

Fill in the blanks with words or phrases from Reading Passage 1.

Edison's laboratory in West Orange was the best (1) ________. And it was the largest laboratory extant and the facilities were (2) ________ to any other. The new laboratory complex (3) ________ of five buildings opened in November 1887. A three-story main laboratory building (4) ________ a power plant, machine shops, stock rooms, experimental rooms and a large library. Four smaller one story buildings built (5) ________ to the main building contained a physics lab, chemistry lab, metallurgy lab, pattern shop, and chemical storage. This laboratory allowed him to work on as many as ten or twenty projects at once. He continued to work in this (6) ________ until his death in 1931.

Listening

Scan the code and listen to a microlecture about Thomas Alva Edison. Please choose the best answer to each of the following questions.

1.What is the name of the first movie studio in the world?

A.Black house. B. West Orange.

C.Black Maria.　　D. Fort Lee.

2. Which of the following became the motion picture capital of America because of Thomas Alva Edison?

A.Hollywood.　　B.West Orange.

C.New York City.　　D.Fort Lee.

Speaking

Please briefly introduce Thomas Alva Edison's house called Glenmont in West Orange. Refer to the following words and expressions if necessary.

modern household facilities / awnings / conservatory / geothermal heating

Writing

1. Example Sentence

A geothermal alternate energy system was chosen for installation during the home's massive renovation in 2004 - 05 as a way to recognize the Edison's respect and love for nature, he being an ardent environmentalist, horticulturist , and conservationist ; and he using many natural materials in his inventions, as well as enjoying camping and nature tours.

2. Analysis

(1)这句话的主干部分在开头部分。"地热交替能量系统被安装"是这句话要表达的主要意思。

(2)as a way to recognize 是句子的状语,意为"目的在于纪念爱迪生对自然的尊重和热爱"。

(3)he being 和 he using 这两个部分是独立主格结构。

3. Practice

使用独立主格结构改写下面的句子。

Heavy fog enshrouded the earth in the evening. Nobody could make out what the dark mass was from a distance.

第六节　鲍勃·迪伦

1961～2020 年,鲍勃·迪伦这位流行乐坛的常青树已经活跃了整整 60 年了。他是美国最具代表性的歌手、音乐制作人,也是 2016 年诺贝尔文学奖的获得者。鲍勃·迪伦本名罗伯特·艾伦·齐默曼,生长于明尼苏达州,1959 年开始以"鲍勃·迪伦"为艺名演唱民谣。他的部分早期作品,如《答案在风中飘》和《时代在变》,成为当时美国民权反战运动的旗帜,他也被认为是美国新兴的反叛文化的代言人,尽管他本人一直否认这一观点。1965 年他从发行单曲《像一块滚石》开始转型演唱摇滚乐,在此后的职业生涯中,迪伦又尝试了很多种音乐风格,探索、个性和受争议是跟随了他一生的标签。他创作的歌曲在很大程度上塑造了美国精神，他也因此多次获得格莱美奖、金球奖，甚至多次获得诺贝尔文学奖提名。最终，2016 年的诺贝尔文学奖选择了这位以诗歌升华生活之美好的吟游诗人。

Culture Express

在流行音乐史上，鲍勃·迪伦的《像一块滚石》无疑具有举足轻重的地位，它甚至在著名的《滚石》杂志在 2004 年排出的"史上最伟大的 500 首歌"中高列榜首。这首歌曲的发行，正式标志着鲍勃·迪伦由民谣转入摇滚。根据当时美国的大众审美，民谣是有情调有品位的，而摇滚是粗俗的，所以迪伦原先的听众有的甚至蔑称迪伦为"犹大"。当然，历史为这块不合作的"滚石"正了名。"滚石"这一兼具叛逆、流浪、震撼的意象，也通过迪伦的助力，成为摇滚乐的化身。迪伦并不是开创这一意象的人，在 20 世纪 60 年代摇滚乐兴起的那段时间里，除了这首单曲，还先后出现了英国的"滚石"乐队（1962 年组建）以及美国的《滚石》杂志（1967 年创办），他们的取名都来自著名蓝调歌手穆迪·沃特斯 1950 年演唱的单曲《滚石》。滚石乐队是摇滚史上最成功的组合之一，他们也曾在 1985 年翻唱了迪伦的《像一块滚石》，一时传为佳话。

Reading Passage 1

导读

作为 20 世纪美国最有影响力的音乐人，鲍勃·迪伦自然拥有无数狂热的拥趸。他的唱片、图书，与他有关的物品、家具乃至住过的房屋，都成了人们收藏的对象。他的一位最忠实的歌迷已经买下了迪伦童年时期先后住过的两栋房屋，并在高价收购其他歌迷拥有的当时屋内的家具，以求建成迪伦故居博物馆供人参观。

Dylan has been described as one of the most influential figures of the 20th century, musically and culturally. He was included in *the Time* 100: The Most Important People of the Century, where he was called "master poet, **caustic** social critic and **intrepid**, guiding spirit of the **counterculture** generation".

There are many ways of remembering him as a genius. In 2005, 7th Avenue East in Hibbing, Minnesota, the street on which Dylan lived from ages 6 to 18, received the honorary name Bob Dylan Drive. In the town Hibbing, a walk of fame-styled "star" is embedded in a sidewalk with the words "Bob Dylan"as well as a cursive-*Z* for Dylan's nickname Zimmy in youth.

His fans collect his CDs, works, and even the house he used to live in. Bob Dylan's super-fan Bill Pagel has purchased the ultimate rock collectible: the Hibbing, Minnesota house where Dylan lived in his childhood from 1948 to 1959. According to the *Minneapolis Star Tribune*, he bought the 1,600 square foot home from Gregg and Donna French, who have lived there since 1990.

Pagel plans on restoring the home to its appearance during Dylan's childhood in the 1950s. "I'm trying to locate another collector who purchased many pieces of the original furniture, including Bob Dylan's bedroom set, from the Hibbing home in 1988," Pagel said in a statement. "I would appreciate hearing from anyone who may have a **lead** in locating this person."

Pagel, a pharmacist in his late seventies, has run the Bob Dylan essential fan website boblinks.com since 1995. Among many other things, it houses Bob Dylan's setlist from every night of the Never Ending Tour. They often go up minutes after a show ends, regardless of where they take place around the globe, making it an invaluable resource for Dylan fans.

In 2001, Pagel purchased Dylan's first childhood home—a **duplex** in Duluth Minnesota. It was the centerpiece of his Dylan collection, at least until his recent purchase of the Hibbing home. He hopes to turn both homes into Dylan museums.

(Adapted from *https://www.rollingstone.com / music / music-news / bob-dylan-superfan-hibbing-minnesota*-858270 /)

注释:

1.caustic 尖刻的，讥讽的
2.intrepid 无谓的，勇敢的
3.counterculture 反传统文化
4.lead 线索
5.duplex 连栋式住宅，复式住宅

Reading Passage 2

导读

2016年的诺贝尔文学奖颁给了一位音乐家——鲍勃·迪伦，这在当年的文化界引起了轩然大波，可以说是评委会有史以来最激进的选择了。不过迪伦似乎并不是很买账，他不但没有亲身出席颁奖仪式，而且连正式的获奖感言也拖延到截止日期之前几天才发表，一度闹出了"拒领诺贝尔奖"的传闻。不过，在获奖感言中，迪伦还是很真诚地向全世界关心文学与音乐的人们分享了他获得诺奖的激动心情和人生感悟。

The Nobel Prize committee announced on October 13, 2016, that it would be awarding Dylan the Nobel Prize in Literature "for having created new poetic expressions within the great American song tradition". *The New York Times* reported: "Mr. Dylan, 75, is the first musician to win the award, and his selection on Thursday is perhaps the most radical choice in a history stretching back to 1901."

Dylan's Nobel Lecture was posted on the Nobel prize website on June 5, 2017. *The New York Times* pointed out that, in order to collect the prize's eight million Swedish krona ($900,000), the Swedish Academy's rules **stipulate** the **laureate** "must deliver a lecture within six months of the official ceremony, which would have made Mr. Dylan's deadline June 10." Academy secretary Danius commented: "The speech is extraordinary and, as one might expect, **eloquent**. Now that the lecture has been delivered, the Dylan adventure is coming to a close."

In his essay, Dylan writes about the impact that three important books made on him: Herman Melville's *Moby-Dick*, Erich Maria Remarque's *All Quiet on the Western Front* and Homer's *Odyssey*. He concludes: "Our songs are alive in the land of the living. But songs are unlike literature. They're meant to be sung, not read. The words in Shakespeare's plays were meant to be acted on the stage. Just as lyrics in songs are meant to be sung, not read on a page. And I hope some of you get the chance to listen to these lyrics the way they were intended to be heard: in concert or on record or however people are listening to songs these days. I return once again to Homer, who says, 'Sing in me, oh Muse, and through me tell the story'."

(Adapted from https://pop-cuture.fandom.com / Bob_Dycan)

注释:

1.stipulate 规定

2.laureate 获得者

3.eloquent 雄辩的,有口才的

Word Power

Fill in the blanks with the words given below. Change the form where necessary. Each word can be used only once.

eloquent, caustic, intrepid, stipulate, laureate

(1) A ________ is someone honored for great achievements; figuratively someone crowned with a laurel wreath.

(2) The contract ________ the dates of the rest payments must be made before the accomplishment of the work.

(3) His abrasive wit and ________ comments were his students' nightmare.

(4) Some ________ ones were still prepared to make the last try.

(5) He was ________ about his love of old buildings in this city.

Summary

Fill in the blanks with words or phrases from Reading Passages 1and 2.

Dylan has been described as one of the most (1) ________ figures of the 20th century, musically and culturally. He was called master poet, (2) ________ social critic and (3) ________ guiding spirit of the counterculture generation. Dylan won Nobel Prize in Literature "for having created new (4) ________ expressions within the great American song tradition." He is loved by so many people. The street on which Dylan lived received the (5)________ name Bob Dylan Drive. The houses he once lived as a child were (6)________ by one of his super-fans, who hopes to turn Dylan's homes into Dylan museums.

Listening

Scan the code and listen to a microlecture about Bob Dylan. Please choose the best answer to each of the following questions.

(1) What prize was Bob Dylan awarded in 2008?

A. Nobel Prize in Literature.　　B. Presidential Medal of Freedom.

C. Nobel Prize in Music.　　D. Pulitzer Prize.

(2) Why was Bob Dylan awarded Nobel Prize?

A. For his great talents in music.　　B. For creating poetic expressions.

C. For his concern for peace.　　D. For his influence on literature.

Speaking

Please specify the reasons why Bob Dylan was awarded Nobel Prize in Literature. Refer to the following words and expressions if necessary.

poetic / lyrics / the impact of literature / social critic / guiding spirit

Writing

1. Example Sentence

They often go up minutes after a show ends, regardless of where they take place around the globe, making it an invaluable resource for Dylan fans.

2. Analysis

(1)这句话的主干部分在句子的开头。"它们经常在一个演出结束后的几分钟内就被上传到网站"是这句话要表达的主要意思。

(2)regardless of where... 是非限定性定语从句，目的在于解释演唱会发生的地点。

(3)making 后面的部分作状语。

3. Practice

使用非限定性定语从句写出下面的句子。

The southern states wanted to set up a country of their own. In this new country, they would be free to keep black slaves.

第四章　科技巨头的奇幻建筑

第一节　硅　谷

硅谷位于美国加利福尼亚州北部湾区(Bay area)的南面,是高科技企业云集的圣塔克拉拉谷(Santa Clara Valley)的别称。硅谷最早是研究和生产以硅为基础的半导体芯片的地方,因此得名。作为高新技术产业的摇篮,硅谷的内涵早已超越了从帕罗奥多市到圣何塞的那40千米谷地,已然成为各国各地高新科技聚集区的代名词,以至于为了不产生歧义,真正工作生活在那里的相关从业人员都自称是在湾区,而不是在硅谷。这一节,我们将寻访硅谷里的那些建筑奇迹,看看那些富于创新的硅谷人如何设计建造自己的梦想家园。

Culture Express

硅谷拥有超过100万名常住人口,同时也是许多世界科技巨头的总部所在地,称之为科技圣地一点也不为过。一个个科技巨头动辄斥资数十亿美元兴建豪华气派的新总部,并且拔高薪酬、招贤纳士。它是世界上最富有的地区之一,这里的平均工资是全美的两倍,年收入达到六位数的人只能勉强算是中产。但另一方面,贫富差距一直是困扰城市管理者的大麻烦。世代生活在这里的普通民众负担着天价房屋,承担着物价攀升的巨大压力,苦不堪言。同时这里也是美国流浪者聚集人数最大的地区。硅谷是美国贫富差距问题的缩影。

Reading Passage 1

导读

硅谷50年的发展史见证了苹果、谷歌、英特尔、脸书这些超级公司的发展壮大,同时这也使该地区成为世界上城市经济竞争力最强的地区之一。当年初创时租用的破屋旧舍如今换成了代表公司文化与形象的摩登大楼。我们来看看科技巨头们是如何设计自己的新总部的。

"For years, people came to Silicon Valley and asked where's the architecture? All these high tech companies and you tell me that's the building they're working in," said David Regester, president of the American Institute of Architects' Santa Clara Valley chapter. "It's been **paradoxical** to a lot of people. Now that's changing."

In a place known for **out-of-the-box thinking** and risk taking, tech firms have historically **played it safe** when it comes to their work spaces, opting for functional garages and **tilt-up** buildings over **futuristic** architecture that mirrors the innovation happening inside.

Not anymore. Apple hired prominent British architect Norman Foster to design a spaceshiplike headquarters that features the world's largest piece of curved glass. Google proposed building a **translucent canopy** with interior structures that can be rearranged like furniture, challenging the idea of immovable concrete buildings. A more recent plan shows a design that is more tent-like instead of a massive dome. And Facebook, which **tapped** Frank Gehry to design an office building with a 9-acre green roof, hired the world renowned architect again for two more office buildings.

The movement away from renting space in **banal** tilt-up buildings partly reflects a fast-paced tech industry that has evolved from manufacturing computer chips to writing code for computer software, Regester and other architects in the area say. Now tech firms are not only looking for **utilitarian** spaces but environments that reflect their workplace culture and foster creativity and better teamwork.

Some experts say Silicon Valley's tech construction boom is also part of a pattern that has happened throughout history in areas **infused** with wealth.

Companies such as Google and Apple are using their headquarters to project their image throughout the world, and as the competition to attract the best and brightest workers intensifies, they're all stepping up their games when it comes to building the most innovative office space.

(Adapted from *https://www.mercurynews.com / 2016/09/02/silicon-valley-architecture-apple-google-facebook-lead-the-way /*)

注释：

1.paradoxical　矛盾的
2.out-of-the-box thinking（打破传统的）创新思维
3.play it safe 求稳，谨慎行事
4.tilt-up 立墙平浇建筑法
5.futuristic 未来主义的
6.translucent 半透明的
7.canopy 华盖，顶棚
8.tap 发掘，利用
9.banal 陈腐的，平庸的

10.utilitarian 功利的，实用的

11.infuse 灌输，充满

Reading Passage 2

导读

在硅谷，最不缺的就是敢于创新的头脑和将创意变为现实的行动。当建筑师们因为加州频繁的地震、洪水而大伤脑筋时，这里就有人发明了浮在水坑里的住宅，确切地说，是在浮桥上建的房屋。这样的结构可以减震、防洪，一举两得。那么，住在里面的人会晕船吗？

A "floating village" project is being eyed in north San Jose's Alviso **hamlet** by tech company Arx Pax, using a technology that would **deploy** a group of **pontoons** beneath the buildings to protect the development from floods and earthquakes.

Los Gatos-based Arx Pax invented the technology, which uses principles similar to the 1.5-mile-long Hood Canal Bridge that traverses Washington state's Puget Sound.

Arx Pax, the creator of the SAFE Foundation, or **Self-Adjusting** Floating Environment, wants to construct in Alviso a mixed-use village of homes, offices and retail atop a system of concrete pontoons.

The system could also help coastal communities deal with rising sea levels should that become a long-term challenge.

Here's how the SAFE Foundation would work, according to information obtained from the Arx Pax website. First, a site would be **excavated.** Then, water would fill the site to a shallow depth. Next, a series of platforms consisting of concrete pontoons would be **interlocked** and laid over the water. Finally, the development would be constructed atop the interlocked floating pontoons.

"The mixed-use development proposal is consistent with the community vision outlined in the Alviso Specific Plan," said Erik Schoennauer, a San Jose-based land-use and planning consultant. "The patented foundation system is **indicative** of the innovation that San Jose and Silicon Valley are known for."

Much like a boat, if flooding were to occur, the buildings and the pontoons beneath would rise with the **influx** of waters. By being disconnected from direct contact with the soil, the development would shake less during an earthquake. Arx Pax has obtained four **patents** for the technology, according to Greg Henderson, chief executive officer and co-founder of Arx Pax.

"We are looking at urban in-fill areas that are already subject to flooding," Henderson said. "We are not touching the wetlands at all with this; we are not touching salt ponds. We are being totally respectful of the environment."

The company believes its SAFE Foundation system would make development more **feasible** in areas that now are often shunned because it is difficult to make projects "pencil out" as feasible developments.

(Adapted from *https://www.santacruzsentinel.com / 2018/05/24/ floating-village-eyed-in-san-joses-alviso-area-could-ward-off-floods-quakes-rising-seas /*)

注释：

1.hamlet 小村庄
2.deploy 部署，调度，展开
3.pontoons 浮码头，浮舟
4.self-adjusting 自动调节的
5.excavate 挖掘，开掘
6.interlock 互锁，相互扣住
7.indicative 指示的，预示的
8.influx 流入，汇集
9.patent 专利
10.feasible 可行的，可用的

Word Power

Fill in the blanks with the words given below. Change the form where necessary. Each word can be used only once.

deploy, interlock, excavate ,infuse, tap

(1)We need to ________ young and healthy blood into our company.

(2)He leans back and ________ his fingers, then cracks them extravagantly.

(3)Using a large bulldozer, the men began to ________ the site by operating the machinery's claw continuously into the soil.

(4)It is regrettable that it has become necessary to ________ policemen in schools, but it is needed as an emergency shock treatment.

(5)He owes his election to having ________ deep public disillusion with professional politicians.

Summary

Fill in the blanks with words or phrases from Reading Passage 1.

In Silicon Valley, a place known for (1)________ thinking and risk taking, tech firms have historically played it safe when it comes to their work spaces. They often opt for (2)________ garages and tilt-up buildings over futuristic architecture that mirrors the (3)________ happening inside. But now tech firms are not only looking for utilitarian spaces but environments that (4)________ their workplace culture and (5)________ creativity and better teamwork. This tech construction (6)________ is also part of a pattern that has happened throughout history in areas (7)________ with wealth.

Listening

Scan the code and listen to a microlecture about Silicon Valley. Please choose the best answer to each of the following questions.

(1)What is the secret sauce of Silicon Valley, according to William Miller?

A.It offers cheap land to companies.

B.It attracts graduates from Stanford University.

C.It provides favorable habitat.

D.it gains support from the government.

(2)What is the biggest social problem in Silicon Valley?

A.Sexual harassment. B. Racial discrimination.

C.Gender discrimination. D. Income inequality.

(3)The word silicon in "Silicon Valley" refers to ________ in this area.

A. silicon chip manufacturers B. computer company

C. technology company D. information technology

Speaking

Please briefly introduce "floating village" project in San Jose. How would it work? Refer to the following words and expressions if necessary.

concrete pontoons / a mixed-use village of / floods and earthquakes / excavate / interlock / platform / disconnected / shake less / patent

Writing

1. Example Sentence

First, a site would be excavated. Then, water would fill the site to a shallow depth. Next, a series of platforms consisting of concrete pontoons would be interlocked and laid over the water. Finally, the development would be constructed atop the interlocked floating pontoons.

2. Analysis

(1)这段文字是典型的说明文文体。它解释了"漂浮房屋"的工作流程。

(2)说明"流程"时,重要的是使用表示步骤顺序的词:first、then、next、finally。

(3)流程说明文中不强调动作的发出者,所以一般使用被动语态。

(4)这是描述一个已经发生的工作流程,所以作者在时态上统一使用了过去时。

3. Practice

请根据下面的步骤提示写出制作微电影的步骤。

Write the script. Find a location. Rehearse the lines. Shoot the movie. Edit the movie. Add titles and credits.

第二节　谷歌的新总部

谷歌是世界上最具品牌价值的公司之一，它以搜索引擎起家，主营互联网广告、互联网搜索、云计算等领域。仅仅经历了20年的发展，它已是全球最大的互联网公司。然而为人们所津津乐道的，却不是它怎能如此迅速地积累财富，而是它宽松的员工工作环境、科幻般的可穿戴数字产品、趣味无穷的谷歌涂鸦、横扫围棋界的阿尔法狗。谷歌公司鲜明独特的企业文化，也反映在它的园区建设中，本节中我们将探访谷歌公司的一些基建项目，看看它如何在其中贯彻"以人为本"的公司理念。

Culture Express

自1998年上线以来，谷歌公司对世界产生了不可估量的影响，它不仅改变了我们处理信息的方式，而且改变了我们思考和谈论互联网的方式。由谷歌公司的名字(google)衍生出来的词汇，不仅在人们日常交流中被频繁使用，甚至出现在了新版的权威字典里。

"google"来自一个极大的数字googol，它代表10的100次方，大概是全宇宙中原子数量的1万亿亿倍。所以谷歌公司的取名包含了"穷尽全世界的数据为顾客找到目标"的立意。谷歌创立后不久，这个网站的名称就变成了一个被广泛使用的动词，人们在搜索引擎上"google"着信息，在网上找自己的谷歌分身(googleganger，由google和doppelganger组合而成的新词)，想方设法提供自己公司的谷歌排名(google ranking)，甚至是投放能够影响搜索结果，诱使别人进入错误网页的谷歌炸弹(google bomb)。谷歌公司则将自己的总部大楼命名为Googleplex，它意味着10的googol次方，这已经是大到无法想象的数字了。

Reading Passage 1

导读

总部的设计必然是一家公司形象的招牌，作为全球互联网公司的领头羊，谷歌对自家总部的设计也是费尽了心思。为了让员工既像在家中、在大自然中一样轻松愉悦，又富于工作状态下的创意和效率，Googleplex的设计师曾数易其稿，让我们来看看上一个方案的设计师是如何评价最近采用的新设计的吧。

Eleven years ago, before Google's new proposal for a spectacular, **allegedly** moveable series of **transparent** circus tents designed by Thomas Heatherwick and BIG, Clive Wilkinson Architects designed the first Googleplex in Mountain View, Calif. This Googleplex was 2 million square feet—Pentagon-scale architecture—inspired by a university, where free meals, open floor plans, and cozy **nooks** for meetings **reigned** supreme.

Google plans to keep Wilkinson's core Googleplex buildings **intact**, but people were interested what he—as the architect behind the original Googleplex—thinks about Google's proposed addition. Wilkinson sees the new Google campus as a milestone in reusable, flexible architecture—something that can be literally reshaped to create collaborative environments as Google's teams and projects evolve.

Wilkinson thinks what's impressive about Google's teams is they're dealing with a large employee community. "The challenge is, how do you retain a sense of community without it fragmenting a corporate entity? I think this is very radical proposal." Wilkinson said. It seems extremely community-oriented, extremely people-oriented. The idea of multiple places for enjoying nature and the outdoors being integrated, these moves are extremely positive.

165 years ago, Joseph Paxton's Crystal Palace in London, was probably the most **convulsive** event of the 19th century. It demonstrated the potential of glass and steel in large buildings, ushering in an age of lighter construction, which led to the development of skyscrapers and the iconography (good or bad) of the modern city. It doesn't exist now because it burned down 100 years ago, but it was Earth-shattering. Glass in buildings completely changed going forward.

But it couldn't really last. The glass was fragile, heat buildup was a huge issue. It was very primitive. The internal space they're showing here reminds me very strongly of that moment in architectural history. Probably the only reason it's capable of being done successfully today is that we have incredible industrial materials. This is something we could do today in 2015 that has probably never been possible in history.

The roof has to be **light-sensitive**, and **temperate**, **vis-à-vis** heat build up of the sun, and heat loss is an issue also. Bringing nature in, like trees into a building, hasn't been easy either. That's a challenge this roof will have to adapt to. How do you get the right sunlight within the building so nature thrives and doesn't wither?

It's clear they've got a long way to go on the tech.

(Adapted from *https://www.fastcompany.com/3043076/what-the-googleplexs-original-architect-thinks-of-googles-new-headquarters*)

注释：

1.allegedly 据说
2.transparent 透明的
3.nooks 角落，隐蔽处
4.reign 占主导，盛行
5.intact 完整无缺的
6.convulsive 痉挛性的
7.light-sensitive 感光的
8.temperate 温和的，适度的
9.vis-à-vis 同……相比

Reading Passage 2

导读

谷歌公司在2019年10月宣布它将扩大其在加利福尼亚圣何塞(San Jose)拟建的第二总部的占地面积。在这个总面积约32公顷的建设项目中,有6公顷土地留给了绿地。此外,谷歌还一直试图打破圣何塞市对建筑物的高度限制,以便该公司利用上层空间建造园区,这与传统的硅谷建筑方式有所不同。因此,如果这一项目方案获得通过,圣何塞市区将会变得更绿、更高。

Google has formally applied for plans to build an 80-acre project that consists of up to 7.3 million square feet of office space, higher than the previous 6.5 million originally laid out in August. The company also applied for up to 5,900 units of new housing, more than the 5,000 units previously described.

The expanded ranges allow the company and city greater flexibility as it seeks feedback in the months leading up to a final approval vote next year, company spokesperson Michael Appel told CNBC. Appel added that just because the company increased ranges in certain areas, it wouldn't necessarily develop the maximum space.

The formal proposal comes as Google needs additional space for its rapidly expanding workforce, which is already busting at the **seams** of its existing headquarters and surrounding offices. The company also faces pressure from local **constituents** who fear its growth will further contribute to the already-tight housing market, which is among the country's most expensive.

The San Jose project of Google will include roughly 15 acres of parks and green space, according to the company's proposal. In addition to offices and parks, the company also plans to enable **retail**, cultural spaces and up to 1,100 hotel rooms—most of which will be for "corporate accommodations."

The project will also include a major multi-modal **transit** center, which San Jose mayor Sam Liccardo has dubbed "The Grand Central Station of the West". The proposed campus will also have "flexible" roadways and public bike trails that run throughout the entire development.

Google's also been trying to get the city to expand its building height limits so it can build upward, instead of outward, which would be a departure from the way Silicon Valley structures have traditionally been built.

The company is still soliciting community feedback and will undergo an environmental impact report before taking the proposal for final approval to the city council next year.

(Adapted from *https://www.cnbc.com* / 2019/10/11 / *google-expands-plans-for-second-hq-in-san-jose.html*)

注释:

1.seam 接缝,接合处
2.constituent 选民,要素
3.retail 零售
4.transit 搬运,通过

Word Power

Fill in the blanks with the words given below. Change the form where necessary. Each word can be used only once.

temperate, transparent, reign, intact, transit

(1)A ________ system is a system for moving people or goods from one place to another, for example using buses or trains.

(2)If a person's behaviour is ________, it is calm and reasonable, so that they do not get angry or lose their temper easily.

(3)If a situation, system, or activity is ________, it is easily understood or recognized.

(4)Something that is ________ is complete and has not been damaged or changed.

(5)Someone or something that ________ supreme is the most important or powerful element in a situation or period of time.

Summary

Fill in the blanks with words or phrases from Reading Passage 2.

Google has formally applied for plans to build an 80-acre project that (1)________ up to 7.3 million square feet of office space. The San Jose project of Google will include roughly 15 acres of parks and green space, according to the company's proposal. In addition to offices and parks, the company also plans to enable (2)________, cultural spaces and hotel rooms. The project will also include a major multi-modal (3)________ center with "flexible" roadways and public bike (4) ________ that run throughout the entire development. But, the company is still (5)________ community feedback and will undergo a (an) (6)________ impact report before taking the proposal for final approval to the city council.

Listening

Scan the code and listen to a microlecture about Google. Please choose the best answer to each of the following questions.

(1) Google was founded in 1998 by Larry Page and Sergey Brin while they were Ph. D. students at ________.

A.Stanford University　　B. University of California

C.MIT　　D. Harvard University

(2)Which of the following is not the product of Google?

A.Google glass.　　B. AlphaGo Master.

C.Google map.　　D. Skype.

Speaking

What are the features of the new Google Headquarter in San Jose? You may find the following words and expressions useful.

parks and green space / corporate accommodations / a major multi-modal transit center / flexible road ways

Writing

1. Example Sentence

This Googleplex was 2 million square feet—Pentagon-scale architecture—inspired by a university, where free meals, open floor plans, and cozy nooks for meetings reigned supreme.

2. Analysis

(1)破折号用在解释性的插入语的前面和后面，相当于括号。

(2)Pentagon-scale architecture 指一栋五角大楼规模的建筑物，对前面的面积单位进行解释。

(3)inspired 后面的内容是句子的状语，解释谷歌总部(Googleplex)的灵感来源。

3. Practice

使用破折号对下面句子里的相关内容进行解释。

在美国，居住型房地产业的价值(约为 34 万亿美元)超过美国所有上市公司的市场资本额。

第三节　苹果的新园区

在创始人史蒂夫·乔布斯的领导和推动之下，苹果公司先后推出了 Macintosh、iMac、iPod、iPhone、iPad 等风靡全球的电子产品，深刻地改变了现代通信、娱乐和生活方式。这位“苹果之父”在去世之前，还亲自参与设计了苹果的总部建筑 Apple Park。新总部大楼为环状建筑，中间是大型庭院，用乔布斯自己的话来形容，新大楼像“一艘着陆的宇宙飞船”，媒体则喻之为“巨型玻璃甜甜圈”。

Culture Express

苹果公司的产品相信大家一定不陌生，像 iPhone、iPad、iMac、iWatch 等，这些产品有一个共同的特点，那就是它们的名称都以"i"开头，为什么苹果公司要这样命名自家的产品呢？1998 年苹果创始人乔布斯推出 iMac 电脑时，电脑和因特网还是两个分离的概念。有很多人认为字母 i 在最初的苹果产品名称上代表 internet 一词。而到了现在，苹果公司的这个"i"已经延伸出了更多的含义，例如"individual"（独特的）、"instruct"、（指引）"inform"（告知）、"inspire"（启发）等，象征了苹果在如今这个信息时代中扮演的各种不同角色。

Reading Passage 1

导读

乔布斯生前最后一次出现在公众视野中时，曾很自豪地披露了兴建新的苹果总部的计划。他这样描述新的苹果总部："这将是世界上最好的办公建筑，学习建筑的学生都应该来参观学习。"苹果公司极富未来主义的新总部在建成后，果然得到很多赞扬，赞扬它那炫酷的曲面、世界上最大的碳纤维独立屋顶、整合太阳能面板的弧形玻璃墙、宽大无限制的办公区域……

Apple Park was **derided** as a "retrograde cocoon," the facility was designed with **painstaking** attention to detail to maximize opportunities for creativity and collaboration and to capture founder Steve Jobs' complex vision for the space.

Apple Park covers 2.8 million square feet, **accommodates** 12,000 employees and cost approximately $5 billion to build. The facility, designed by architecture firm Foster + Partners, includes a fitness center, an energy plant and acres of apricot orchards. The ring-shaped building has been compared to a spaceship and the Pentagon.

One of the most distinct aspects of Apple's new headquarters is that it will house 12,000 employees in one structure. Fitting that many people in one building is a logistical hurdle that Apple believes will encourage collaboration between workers and between departments. Jonathan Ive, Apple's chief design officer tells ***Wired*** that the greatest achievement of the campus is that it is "a building where so many people can connect and collaborate and walk and talk." Apple hopes it will foster even greater innovation.

The building will be divided into modular sections, known as pods, that will be used for office work, teamwork and social activities. Everyone from the CEO to summer interns will be placed into these pods, helping employees build connections and discover mentorship opportunities.

Apple's nature-forward approach to the campus's design may sound like good PR, but science supports it. Studies suggest that spending time outside can improve **cognition** and creative thinking. Fittingly, Apple Park includes 6,000 trees and 5.9 million square feet of landscaping. A green courtyard in the middle of the facility will allow employees to walk through nature as they cut across campus.

In a press release, Apple CEO Tim Cook said, "The workspaces and parklands are designed to inspire our team as well as benefit the environment. We've achieved one of the most **energy-efficient** buildings in the world and the campus will run entirely on **renewable** energy."

Cook explained that Apple's late founder Steve Jobs had been inspired by the Californian environment and that the company hopes that this **eco-friendly** setting will help spur the company's next generation of breakthroughs. "Steve was **exhilarated**, and inspired, by the California landscape, by its light and its **expansiveness**," he said, "It was his favorite setting for thought. Apple Park captures his spirit **uncannily** well."

(Adapted from *https://www.cnbc.com / 2017/09/13 / the-science-and-design-behind-apples-innovation-obsessed-new-workspace.html*)

注释:

1.deride 取笑,嘲笑

2.painstaking 不辞劳苦的,煞费苦心的

3.accommodate 容纳

4.*Wired* 一本叫作《连线》的技术杂志,它关注技术对政治、文化、社会和伦理道德带来的冲击,被誉为极客的圣经,隶属国际著名杂志出版商康泰纳什集团旗下

5.cognition 认知

6.energy-efficient 高能效的

7.renewable 可再生的

8.eco-friendly 有益于生态环境的

9.exhilarate 使高兴

10.expansiveness 夸张性

11.uncannily 离奇地

Reading Passage 2

导读

苹果新总部的建筑设计在广受好评的同时,也有建筑师对它的天价建筑成本、"倒退"的设计元素、与周围环境完全不契合的建筑风格提出了质疑和批评。通过阅读下文,你将了解这些批评和质疑的声音并不是空穴来风。

While the project's overall look is impressive from afar (it boasts the largest glass panels in the world), some of its **interiors** left people scratching their heads—or, in this case, bandaging their noggins. Shortly after opening, a handful of Apple employees hurt themselves by walking into the building's signature glass walls. Some of the injuries sustained were serious enough to warrant calls to 911.

The fact that the project does not connect more to the surrounding community—Apple Park contains about 14,200 parking spaces, more room than is dedicated to offices, and was required to add no additional housing for its 12,000 employees—has become one of Cupertino's most glaring errors, a bug that will have a lasting effect for years to come.

Wired, one of the only publications granted access to the campus for an architecture story, later published a **caustic** review of the headquarters, criticizing it for not being more friendly with its small-town surroundings: "Apple's new headquarter is a **retrograde**, literally inward-looking building with **contempt** for the city where it lives and cities in general."

People rightly credit Apple for defining the look and feel of the future; its computers and phones seem like science fiction. But by building a mega-headquarters straight out of the middle of the last century, Apple has **exacerbated** the already serious problems **endemic** to 21st-century suburbs like Cupertino—transportation, housing, and economics. Apple Park is an **anachronism** wrapped in glass, **tucked** into a neighborhood.

(Adapted from *https://sf.curbed.com* / 2019/6/28/19102722/*apple-park-jony-ive-design-architecture-silicon-valley*)

注释：

1.interior 内部
2.caustic 尖刻的
3.retrograde 逆行，倒退
4.contempt 轻视
5.exacerbate 恶化
6.endemic 地方性的，流行的
7.anachronism 不合乎时代的人或事
8.tuck 塞入，藏入

Word Power

Fill in the blanks with the words given below. Change the form where necessary. Each word can be used only once.

endemic, caustic, contempt, exhilarate, exacerbate

(1)If a disease or illness is ________ in a place, it is frequently found among the people who live there.

(2)If you have ________ for someone or something, you have no respect for them or think that they are unimportant.

(3)If you are ________ by something, it makes you feel very happy and excited.

(4)A ________ remark is extremely critical, cruel, or bitter.

(5)If something ________ a problem or bad situation, it makes it worse.

Summary

Fill in the blanks with words or phrases from Reading Passage 2.

While the overall look is (1)________, Apple's new headquarter has become one of Cupertino's most glaring (2)________, a bug that will have a lasting effect for years to come. Shortly after opening, a handful of Apple employees hurt themselves by walking into the building's (3) ________ glass walls. Some of the injuries sustained were (4)________ enough to warrant calls to 911. It also has been criticized for not being more friendly with its (5)________ surroundings. Literally, its inward-looking building with (6)________ for the city separates itself with the city.

Listening

Scan the code and listen to a microlecture about Apple's new headquarter. Please choose the best answer to each of the following questions.

(1)In terms of aesthetics, the new headquarter of Apple is so impressive because its curved shape is like a ________.

A.ring　　B. diamond

C. oval　　D. spade

(2)The new headquarter of Apple is powered by 100% renewable energy, with the installation of ________.

A.rooftop solar system　　B. wind power system

C. ventilation system　　D. glass roof

Speaking

What are the main features of Apple Park? Refer to the following words and expressions if necessary.

encourage collaboration / nature-forward approach / panel of curved glass / renewable energy / eco-friendly setting

Writing

1. Example Sentence

Apple's new headquarter is a retrograde, literally inward-looking building with contempt for the city where it lives and cities in general.

2. Analysis

literally 是一个副词，它在这里的意思是“确实地，真正地，不夸张地”。在口语中，literally 还经常被用作“简直”。

3. Practice

用 literally 翻译下面的句子。

这座剧院是一项浩大的工程，说要涉及数千人真的是一点也不夸张。

第五章　食品生产大国

概　述

民以食为天。美国不仅有强大的经济实力，同时，人口众多的她也是农业生产大国、食品工业大国。本章我们将走进美国最著名的两个农产区——加利福尼亚州的中央谷地和堪萨斯州。我们将了解这些农产区的历史和生产规模。食品的营销策略和人们的饮食习惯与农产区的发展有着密不可分的联系。过量摄入高热量的食物将给人们的身体健康带来极大的危害，而美国的传统饮食多为高热量的碳水化合物。随着肥胖问题日益严重，人们意识到，健康的饮食是永恒的目标。

美国文学也与经济和科技发展息息相关。大量优秀的文学作品都是以特定地区以及当地的农业、工业、政治等为创作背景，人物的行为和情节的推动也离不开特定的历史发展阶段。以农产区为背景的著名文学作品在美国文学中占有相当大的比重，这让我们在欣赏作品的同时，也了解到本章提到的农产区的地域风情及其对美国社会发展的历史意义。

第一节　中央谷地

本节我们将对美国加州的中央谷地进行简要的了解，并着重介绍番茄的生产规模及其对人们饮食的重要性。美国西部的发展具有十分重要的历史意义，整个过程也是一部农民的血泪史和资本主义的发家史，并衍生出无数著名的文学作品。从这些作品中，我们能够更好地了解美国的历史和文化。马克·吐温的代表作之一《卡拉维拉斯县著名的跳蛙》就是以这里为故事发生地。

Culture Express

在人们的日常饮食中，番茄及其加工品是非常重要的存在。番茄也是美国人民餐桌上最常见的蔬菜之一，是汉堡、比萨、三明治、薯条等多种食物的最佳搭档。在美国伊利诺伊州的科林斯维尔还矗立着一座50多米高的番茄酱瓶雕塑，可见人们对番茄酱的热爱。

食品加工厂商对于番茄酱包装的设计从来都不缺少独具匠心的创意。从 10 千克的桶装到瓶装，还有快餐店里方便携带的小袋装，各种包装形式和规格应有尽有，能满足顾客不同的需求。近来一种新型的番茄加工品进一步证明了美国人民对番茄酱的无限热爱，那就是切片番茄酱。切片番茄酱的优点在于 100%纯天然，无任何添加剂，并且能解决传统番茄酱流淌不畅或四处喷洒的缺点。然而美国人民对这种新产品的态度却褒贬不一。

有意思的是，食用番茄酱在法国却受到了限制。“在法国学校的食堂，禁止提供无限量的自助式番茄酱或蛋黄酱。”法国人的理由很简单也很奇怪，他们认为番茄酱太甜，味道过于浓重，会降低孩子们的味觉敏感度，也会造成肥胖，影响孩子们的身体健康。

Reading Passage 1

导读

下文介绍了美国加州中央谷地的地理概况、地名轶闻及其农业发展状况。

General Introduction

California's Central Valley is a large, flat valley that dominates the geographical center of the U.S. state of California. Bounded by the **Sierra Nevada** to the east and the **Coast Ranges** to the west, it is California's single most productive agricultural region and one of the most productive in the world, providing more than half of the fruits, vegetables and nuts grown in the United States. The valley also has many major cities, including the state capital **Sacramento**; as well as Redding, Stockton, Modesto, Fresno and Bakersfield.

Name

The Central Valley is commonly known to residents simply as "the Good Valley." Older names include "the Great Valley," and "Golden Empire." The valley gives its name to **Valley Fever** which is primarily a disease of the lungs that is common in the southwestern United States and northwestern Mexico. It is caused by one kind of **fungus** which grows in soils in areas of low rainfall, high summer temperatures, and moderate winter temperatures. These fungal **spores** become **airborne** when the soil is disturbed by winds, construction, or farming. This illness frequently takes many weeks or months to resolve. Occasionally Valley Fever is life-threatening and even fatal.

Agriculture

Agriculture is the primary industry in most of the Central Valley. More than 230 crops are grown there. Its agricultural productivity relies on irrigation from both **surface water diversions** and **groundwater pumping** from wells. Virtually all non-tropical crops are grown in the Central Valley, which is the primary source for a number of food products throughout the United States, including tomatoes, **almonds**, grapes, cotton, apricots, and **asparagus**.

[Adapted from *https://encyclopedia.thefreedictionary.com / Central + Valley + (California)*]

注释：

1. Sierra Nevada 内华达山脉
2. Coast Ranges 海岸山脉
3. Sacramento 萨克拉门托(加州首府)
4. Valley Fever 溪谷热(一种由土壤中真菌引发的肺部感染疾病，属于地方性疾病，多发于美国得克萨斯州西部、亚利桑那州和墨西哥北部到加利福尼亚圣华金河谷中部及华盛顿州中南部一带的沙漠地区)
5. fungus 真菌，霉菌
6. spore 孢子
7. airborne 空气传播的，飞行中的，空降的
8. surface water diversion 地表水引流
9. groundwater 地下水
10. pump (用泵)抽取
11. almond 杏仁，杏树
12. apricot 杏
13. asparagus 芦笋

Reading Passage 2

导读

19 世纪后期的加州淘金热为美国中西部带来了大量的人口，从而促进了当地的经济。尤其是通过科技创新和兴修水利，美国中西部的农业迅速发展。资本主义在积累财富的同时，也衍生出了人性和政治上的现实问题。下文介绍了美国小说家马克·吐温的成名短篇小说《卡拉维拉斯县著名的跳蛙》。小说的创作背景正是 19 世纪后半期美国西部的淘金热。小说针对当时的社会现实问题进行了批判。

"*The Celebrated Jumping Frog of Calaveras County*" is an 1865 short story by Mark Twain. It was his first great success as a writer and brought him national attention.

The narrator is sent by a friend to interview an old man, Simon Wheeler, who might know the location of an old acquaintance named Leonidas W. Smiley. Finding Simon at an old **mining camp**, the narrator asks him if he knows anything about Leonidas; Simon appears not to, and instead tells a story about Jim Smiley, a man who had visited the camp years earlier.

Jim loves to **gamble** and will offer to bet on anything and everything, from horse races to dogfights to the health of the local parson's wife. He catches a frog, whom he names Dan'l

Webster and trains to jump. When a stranger visits the camp, Jim shows off Dan'l and offers to bet ＄40 that he can out-jump any other frog in **Calaveras** County.

The stranger says that he would take the bet if he had a frog, and Jim goes out to catch one. But during this time, the stranger pours **lead shot** down Dan'l's throat. Once Jim returns, he and the stranger set the frogs down and let them **loose**. The stranger's frog jumps away while Dan'l does not **budge**, and the surprised and disgusted Jim pays the ＄40 **wager**.

After the stranger has departed, Jim notices that Dan'l appears baggier than usual. Picking Dan'l up, Smiley explodes in rage, "Why, blame my cats, if he don't weigh FIVE POUND!!!" He turns the frog upside down, and Dan'l **belches out** two handfuls of the lead shot. Realizing that he has been cheated, Jim chases after the stranger but never catches him.

(Adapted from *https://encyclopedia.thefreedictionary.com / The+Celebrated+Jumping+Frog+of+Calaveras+County*)

注释:

1. mining camp 采矿营地
2. gamble 赌博
3. Calaveras 卡拉维拉斯(美国加州地名)
4. lead shot 铅弹
5. loose 宽松的,不受束缚的
6. budge 挪动
7. wager 赌注
8. blame my cats (如果他没有五磅重)为什么责怪我的猫! 表示"岂有此理"
9. belch out 吐出

Word Power

Match each word in the following sentences with its meaning.

Words	Meanings
(1) A resurgence of this **airborne** disease disproportionately affects the poor.	a. to make water, air, gas, etc. flow in a particular direction by using a pump or something that works like a pump
(2) The city of Tianjin was supposed to be the main beneficiary of the water **diversion**.	b. free to move around; not tied up
(3) The engine is used for **pumping** water out of the mine.	c. in the air or carried in the air
(4) The sheep had got out and were **loose** on the road.	d. a special route arranged to follow when the normal route cannot be used
(5) I **gambled** all my winnings on the last race.	e. to risk money on games

Summary

Fill in the blanks with an appropriate word from Reading Passage 1.

	General Introduction	Name	Agriculture
Central Valley	• It is a large, (1)____ valley. • It is one of the most productive (2)____ region.	the Good Valley; the (3)____ Valley; Golden Empire; "Valley Fever"	• Agriculture is the (4) ____ industry. • More than (5) ____ crops are grown there.

Listening

Scan the code and listen to a microlecture about the Food Machine-Tomato. Please choose the best answer to each of the following questions.

(1) Why did many people go to California in the 18th century?

A. To get foods. B. To get gold.

C. To go sightseeing. D. To provide aids.

(2) What does "eat humble pie" mean?

A. Accept shame, apologize or face humiliation.

B. Eat small pie.

C. Have dinner with somebody.

D. Be invited to a party.

(3) The money here in "Reno Tomatina" is ________.

A. To support the poor people. B. To build infrastructure.

C. To support cancer research. D. To build schools.

Speaking

Central Valley was a desert known as "land of the dead." How did it become the granary it is today? Refer to the following words and expressions if necessary.

California Gold Rush / millions of people / settled down / industrialization / irrigation

Writing

1. Example Sentence

They've been placed here in the middle of Reno, Nevada, **not so that** the good people of this town can eat them, **but so that** they can throw them at each other.

2. Analysis

这句话的意思是:这些放在内华达州雷诺市中心的西红柿不是供人们食用的,而是供人们互相投掷的。

...not so that...，but so that...：做什么不是为了……而是为了……。not...but...后面分别跟了两个目的状语从句，都是由 so that 引导。注意 so that 后面如果跟情态动词则为目的状语从句，如果没有情态动词，则为结果状语从句。

3. Practice

用 not so that...，but so that...翻译下面的句子。

他逃走不是为了躲避惩罚，而是为了追寻真正的凶手。

第二节　独特的灌溉技术

美国加利福尼亚州的中央谷地是美国最大的农业生产区。这里有肥沃的土地、充足的阳光和四季适宜的气候，适合种植各种农作物和水果。美国50%的水果和坚果出自加州的中央谷地，这是一个由太阳能提供动力的巨大的露天食品工厂。在气候与水文上，这里缺乏水资源，但同时水资源又是中央谷地之所以能从荒漠变成农产区的重要原因。那么这个问题是如何解决的呢？本节我们将介绍一种著名的灌溉技术，以及加州农作物种植的主要用水来源。此外，我们还将介绍一部以美国西部发展为历史背景的文学作品——《愤怒的葡萄》。

Culture Express

中心枢轴灌溉

中心枢轴灌溉也称时针式喷灌，指一种特殊的灌溉方法：喷洒设备围绕一个枢轴转动并浇灌庄稼。由此设备浇灌出来的区域就形成了一个圆形，从高空俯瞰，农作物的种植区域也就因此成为一个圆形。中心枢轴灌溉最初是利用水力驱动喷灌桁架，如今大多由电动马达驱动。

1940 年，科罗拉多州斯特拉斯堡的一位名叫弗兰克的农民发明了中央枢轴灌溉系统。这种系统灌溉效率高，并有助于节约水资源，增加灌溉面积。

相比许多其他的表面灌溉和沟灌技术，中心枢轴灌溉也能够减少劳动力成本，而其他的地面灌溉技术则需要更多的劳动力，例如需要挖掘沟渠。中心枢轴灌溉可以减少土壤耕作，降低水的径流量，还能减少地面灌溉所带来的土壤侵蚀。土壤耕作的减少意味着更多的有机材料和农作物残余物得以保存并分解至土壤中，减轻了土壤压实程度。

在美国的半干旱高原，早期定居者最大的困扰就是不断循环的干旱天气不利于农作物种植，尤其是在 20 世纪 30 年代，时常出现具有毁灭性的沙尘暴。二战结束后，中心枢轴灌溉得以应用，带有地下蓄水层的中高平原才被改造成世界最大的农业生产区之一。

Reading Passage 1

导读

半沙漠化状态下的美国西部是如何发展成为全国最大的粮仓的呢？水利的兴修和科技的发展是其中最主要的两个原因。下文介绍了美国加州著名的度假休闲风景区——沙斯塔湖。沙斯塔大坝的修建形成了沙斯塔湖，那么沙斯塔大坝给加州又带来了什么样的影响和作用呢？让我们一起来阅读吧！

Shasta Lake is **impounded** by Shasta Dam, the ninth tallest dam in the United States. Shasta Dam was constructed between 1935 and 1945 across the **Sacramento River**, and Shasta Lake was formed in 1948.

Shasta Dam which is known as the keystone of the Central Valley Project creates Shasta Lake for long-term water storage, flood control, **hydroelectricity** and protection against the intrusion of **saline water**. The largest reservoir in the state, Shasta Lake can hold about 4,500,000 acre feet (5.6×10^9 m^3).

Even before its dedication, Shasta Dam served an important role in World War II providing electricity to California factories, and still plays a vital part in the management of state water resources today. However, it has greatly changed the environment and ecology of the Sacramento River, and flooded **sacred** Native American **tribal** lands. In recent years, there has been debate over whether or not to raise the dam in order to allow for increased water storage and power generation.

Criticism

The Shasta Dam has had a severe negative effect on populations of Pacific salmon in the Sacramento River **watershed** ever since its gates were first closed in 1943. The massive structure completely prevents salmon migration from the lower reaches of the river to the Upper Sacramento, Pit, McCloud and other **tributary** streams. It is estimated that half of the best salmon habitat in the Sacramento basin lies upstream of Shasta Dam. Also, the dam caused temperatures in the river to rise because it released waters from higher **elevations** of Shasta Lake, which are warmed by the sun far more than the surface of the original river pre-dam. Warm waters are harmful to salmon, which prefer colder temperatures, and also impact other fish populations such as **steelhead** and wild California **trout**.

Tours and Recreation

Reclamation holds guided tours of the Shasta Dam year round, each taking two to three hours. There also are a visitor center and auditorium. The tours **comprise** a 428-foot (130 m) elevator ride to the base of the dam, and visits to the dam's inner galleries and the powerhouse among other areas. Shasta Lake has a surface of 30,310 acres

(12,270 ha) at full pool and is surrounded by the Shasta-Trinity National Forest. Many public and private **marinas**, campgrounds, RV parks, resorts and boat launches border the reservoir, one of the most popular recreational lakes in California. **Houseboating**, water-skiing, swimming and fishing are among the numerous activities available at the lake; hiking, picnicking, mountain biking, hunting and camping are popular in the mountainous **vicinity** surrounding it.

(Adapted from *https://encyclopedia.thefreedictionary.com / Shasta+Dam*)

注释:

1. impound 关入,(水坝)拦水
2. Sacramento River 萨克拉门托河
3. hydroelectricity 水力发电
4. saline water 海水,盐水
5. sacred 神圣的
6. tribal 部落的
7. watershed 流域,分水岭
8. tributary 支流
9. elevation 高地,海拔
10. steelhead 北美鳟鱼,虹鳟
11. trout 鳟鱼,鲑鱼
12. comprise 包含
13. marina 游船码头
14. houseboat 乘居住船游览
15. vicinity 邻近,周围地区

Reading Passage 2

导读

下文介绍了一部与美国西部发展历史有关的小说《愤怒的葡萄》。该小说发表于1939年,作者是美国现代小说家约翰·斯坦贝克。这部作品描写的是美国大萧条时期大批农民破产和逃荒的斗争故事。故事的创作背景是当时美国中西部处于半沙漠化状态,沙尘暴破坏了当地的农业,农民们不得不踏上继续西征的道路。通过阅读本篇文章,读者可以更深刻地了解美国中西部的风土人情和历史发展历程。该小说曾获得美国国家图书奖和美国普利策文学奖。

General Introduction

Set during the **Great Depression**, the novel focuses on the Joads, a poor family of tenant farmers driven from their Oklahoma home by drought, economic hardship, agricultural industry changes and **bank foreclosures** forcing tenant farmers out of work.

Due to their nearly hopeless situation, and in part because they are trapped in the **Dust Bowl**, the Joads set out for California. Along with thousands of other "Okies," they seek jobs, land, dignity, and a future.

Plot

The narrative begins just after Tom Joad is paroled from McAlester prison, where he had been imprisoned after being **convicted** of homicide. On his return to his home near Sallisaw, Oklahoma, Tom meets former preacher Jim Casy. When they arrive at Tom's childhood farm home, they find it **deserted**. They were told that the banks have **evicted** all the farmers. They have no option but to seek work in California, described in handbills as fruitful and offering high pay.

Traveling west on **Route 66**, the Joad family find the road crowded with other migrants. The family unit **dwindles**: Granpa dies along the road; Granma dies close to the California state line; and both Noah (the eldest Joad son) and Connie Rivers (the husband of the pregnant Joad daughter, **Rose of Sharon**) split from the family. Led by Ma, the remaining members realize they can only continue, as nothing is left for them in Oklahoma.

Reaching California, they find the state oversupplied with labor, so wages are low, and workers are **exploited** to the point of starvation. The big corporate farmers are in **collusion**, and smaller farmers suffer from collapsing prices.

In response to the exploitation, Casy becomes a labor organizer and tries to recruit for a labor union. The remaining Joads work as **strikebreakers** in a peach orchard, where Casy is involved in a strike that eventually turns violent. When Tom Joad witnesses Casy's fatal beating, he kills the attacker and flees as a **fugitive**. The Joads later leave the orchard for a cotton farm, where Tom is at risk of being arrested for the homicide.

Tom bids his mother farewell and promises to work for the **oppressed**. Rose of Sharon's baby is **stillborn**. Ma Joad remains **steadfast** and forces the family through the **bereavement**. With rain, the Joads' dwelling is flooded, and they move to higher ground. In the final chapter of the book, the family takes shelter from the flood in an old barn. Inside, they find a young boy and his father, who is dying of starvation. Rose of Sharon takes pity on the man and offers him her breast, to save him from starvation.

Critical Reception

The Grapes of Wrath is referred to as a Great American Novel. According to *The New York Times*, it was the best-selling book of 1939 and 430,000 copies had been printed by February 1940. In that month it won the **National Book Award**. Soon it won the **Pulitzer Prize for Fiction**.

The book was noted for Steinbeck's passionate depiction of the **plight** of the poor, and many of his contemporaries attacked his social and political views. Bryan Cordyack writes, "Steinbeck was attacked as a **propagandist** and a socialist from both the left and the right of the political **spectrum**. The most **fervent** of these attacks came from the Associated Farmers of California; they were displeased with the book's depiction of California farmers' attitudes and conduct toward the migrants. They **denounced** the book as a 'pack of lies' and labeled it 'communist propaganda.'"

In 1962, the Nobel Prize committee cited The *Grapes of Wrath* as a "great work" and as one of the committee's main reasons for granting Steinbeck the Nobel Prize for Literature. In 2005 *Time* magazine included the novel in its "TIME 100 Best English-language Novels from 1923 to 2005." In 2009, *The Daily Telegraph* of the United Kingdom included the novel in its "100 novels everyone should read."

(Adapted from *https://encyclopedia.thefreedictionary.com / the+grapes+of+wrath*)

注释:

1. Great Depression (美国)经济大萧条
2. bank foreclosures 银行止赎(取消抵押品赎回权)
3. Dust Bowl 风沙侵蚀区(尤指20世纪30年代的美国中西部或南部)
4. convict 证明有罪
5. desert 遗弃,离弃(某地)
6. evict 驱逐,赶出
7. Route 66 美国66号公路(曾是通往美国西部的主要通道,在20世纪30年代年代的Dust Bowl尤其是如此)
8. dwindle 减少,缩小
9. Rose of Sharon 木槿(莎伦玫瑰,此处为人名)
10. exploit 剥削
11. collusion (尤指国家或组织间之间秘密或非法的)串通,勾结
12. strikebreaker 破坏罢工者
13. fugitive 逃亡者,逃犯
14. oppress 压迫,压抑
15. stillborn 死产的,胎死腹中的
16. steadfast 坚定不移的
17. bereavement 亲友丧亡,丧亲之痛
18. National Book Award (美国)国家图书奖
19. Pulitzer Prize for Fiction 普利策文学奖
20. plight 困境
21. propagandist 宣传者,传播者
22. spectrum 光谱,范围,(政治)派别

23. fervent 强烈的，炽热的

24. denounce 谴责，公然抨击

Word Power

Fill in the blanks with the words given below. Change the word form where necessary.

comprise, steadfast, evict, propagandist, fugitive

(1) They have been ________ by the landlord for not paying the rent.

(2) He was a journalist and ________.

(3) A large number of rules ________ the grammar of a language.

(4) Thank you for your ________ commitment to national security.

(5) The ________ is believed to be headed for the border.

Summary

Fill in the blanks with words or phrases from Reading Passage 1.

Shasta Lake is a reservoirs within the Whiskeytown-Shasta-Trinity National (1) ________ Area, operated by the Shasta-Trinity National Forest. It is (2) ________ by Shasta Dam and Shasta Lake was formed in 1948. Shasta Dam creates Shasta Lake for long-term water storage, flood control, (3) ________ and protection against the intrusion of saline water.

Shasta Dam has greatly changed the environment and ecology of the Sacramento River, and flooded (4) ________ Native American tribal lands. The Shasta Dam has had a severe (5) ________ effect on populations of Pacific salmon in the Sacramento River watershed ever since its gates were first closed in 1943.

Reclamation holds guided tours of the Shasta Dam year round, each taking two to three hours. The tours (6) ________ a 428-foot (130 m) elevator ride to the base of the dam, and visits to the dam's inner galleries and the powerhouse among other areas.

Listening

Scan the code and listen to a microlecture about the Food Machine-Irrigation. Please choose the best answer to each of the following questions.

(1) "Pay dirt" refers to the Central Valley. It means ________.

A. earth or ore that yields a profit to a miner

B. a useful or remunerative discovery or object

C. sudden success

D. a profitable or productive land of agriculture

(2) Where does the water for irrigation come from in Central Valley?

A. Rain. B. Columbia River.

C. Shasta Lake. D. Mississippi River.

(3) What does it need for California's food machine to work on the scale it does?

A. People's interest. B. Great demand.

C. Monumental infrastructure. D. High reward.

Speaking

How did Central Valley solve the problem of lacking water? Refer to the following words and expressions if necessary.

Shasta Dam / impressive water supply / 20 dams and reservoirs / tunnels and canals / center-pivot irrigation / other techniques

Writing

1. Example Sentence

But the Ogallala aquifer was out of reach until after World War II, when they finally had engines powerful enough to pump that underground water, spanning 174,000 square miles to the surface.

2. Analysis

这句话的意思是:但是奥加拉拉蓄水层的水却无法获取,直到二战以后,人们才终于有了动力足够强大的机器把地下水抽到地面上来,用以浇灌45万平方千米(174000平方英里)的土地。

(1) 这句话是一个长难句,包含了多个从句。首先我们必须找到主句中的主语和谓语,然后正确分析各个从句,例如名词从句、定语从句和状语从句。

(2) 这句话的主干是第一句,其中使用了一个常见的结构:not...until,译为"直到……才","out of reach"表示否定。

(3) when引导的是时间状语从句,修饰"after World War II",最后一句话"spanning..."为现在分词作状语成分,用来修饰前面的整句话,表示结果。

3. Practice

翻译下面的句子。

Robert Fulton once wrote, "The mechanic should sit down among levers, screws, wedges, wheels, etc., like a poet among the letters of the alphabet, considering them as an exhibition of his thoughts, in which a new arrangement transmits a new idea."

第三节　堪萨斯

本节我们将对堪萨斯州的概况和历史进行简单的了解。作为美国的另一个重要的农业生产区，堪萨斯州盛产小麦、高粱、大豆、棉花、玉米和盐。堪萨斯州东部是美国中部粮食主产区“谷物带”的一部分。玉米有很多用途：玉米是世界许多地区的主食，是主要的牲畜饲料，玉米淀粉还可以制成塑料、织物、黏合剂和许多其他化工产品；玉米也被用作生产乙醇的原料，以减少汽车使用石油燃料所排放的污染物。由于玉米的价格趋向于跟踪石油的价格，因此玉米也是期货市场中重要的交易品。

经典文学作品《绿野仙踪》即是以堪萨斯州为背景的。

Culture Express

玉米面包知多少

玉米面包是一个统称，指含有玉米面的各种速食面包，通常用酵母粉来发酵。

在欧洲探险家抵达新世界之前，美洲的原住民食用玉米就已经有上千年的历史了。人们喜欢玉米面包的口感和香味，称它为美国南部饮食的“基石”。

美洲原住民将玉米粒浸泡在含有氢氯化钙（一种碱性盐）的热水中，经过冲洗和浮选，使玉米粒脱离玉米麸，其被软化并泡大。这种去胚的玉米粒经研磨而得粗玉米面，其中的烟酸和氨基酸被最大化地释放出来，从而提高了营养价值。这种古老的技术被称为“灰化”。

由于玉米面包价格低廉，可以用多种方式加工，因此玉米面包在美国内战期间广泛流行起来。玉米面包可以烤、煎甚至蒸。尽管蒸的方式很少见，但是蒸出来的玉米面包更软，更有嚼劲，更像是玉米布丁。玉米面包还可以被烤成玉米蛋糕。

除了玉米面包之外，美洲原住民还用玉米做出了很多其他的食品，例如大家熟知的玉米粗粉和酒精饮料（如安第斯吉开酒）。

Reading Passage 1

导读

下文介绍了美国堪萨斯州的农业发展过程以及玉米产业的规模。大部分日常食品中都包含玉米。

Remember Dorothy from *The Wizard of Oz*? Kansas is where Dorothy's from. It's the natural world that Dorothy wanted to get back to after being stuck in that **artificial** land of Oz. But if she saw Kansas today, she wouldn't recognize it. Seen from up, a **dazzling** pattern of circular fields stretches as far as the eye can see. This is one of the greatest land transformations in American history. The food industry is a giant factory that's designed to feed us. The farmland is just the factory floor.

In the last 60 years, American farmers, on average, have tripled their yield, **dwarfing** the productivity of every previous generation. What changed? How did they get to that scale? There are two essential factors—irrigation and commercial fertilizer. America's post-war chemical industry revolutionized farming by **mass-producing** key soil nutrients like **nitrogen**, **phosphorus**, and **potassium**. When fertilizer became available, it was an immediate miracle drug to these crops. People could inject a small amount and **quadruple** the productivity without doing anything else.

Where farmers grew a variety of crops in the last 60 years, now 80% of these fields grow just one, a single species that has come to dominate the farming landscape and the American diet. At 322 million tons a year, they produce more of this one grain than anything else, making it the key ingredient of the food machine, which is corn.

Every time we go to the supermarket, though we might not know it, we're surrounded by corn. The average store has over 45,000 products on its shelves. Roughly a third of them are created using corn. Thanks to modern refining and processing, **cornstarch** can be broken down and **reassembled** as sweeteners, fillers and additives to make anything. In fact, the average American eats about 100 pounds of corn products every single year, and most of them don't even realize it. Check the labels of those products, people will find that corn is in almost everything, even in beef.

(Adapted from *American Reviewed*)

注释:

1. artificial 虚构的,人造的
2. dazzling 眼花缭乱的,耀眼的
3. dwarf 使相形见绌,使显得矮小
4. mass-produce 大规模生产
5. nitrogen 氮
6. phosphorus 磷
7. potassium 钾
8. quadruple 成为四倍
9. cornstarch 玉米淀粉
10. reassemble 重新组合

Reading Passage 2

导读

堪萨斯州在文学作品中最著名的一次亮相是小说《绿野仙踪》(*The Wizard of Oz*)中的主人公多萝西·盖尔(Dorothy Gale)的家。这部小说之所以被称为美国"土生土长"的第一个童话故事,正是因为书中提到了美国的两个地名——堪萨斯和奥马哈。作者鲍姆认为,虽然该书的受众是儿童,但他也想创作一个包含美国元素的故事,例如把美国的农业和工业元素融入故事的背景或情节。正是这部出色的儿童文学作品赋予了堪萨斯州独特的文化魅力。

General Introduction

The Wizard of Oz is an American children's novel written by author L. Frank

Baum and illustrated by W. W. Denslow, originally published by the George M. Hill Company in Chicago on May 17, 1900.

The novel is one of the best-known stories in American literature and has been widely translated. **The Library of Congress** has declared it "America's greatest and best-loved **homegrown** fairytale."

Plot Summary

Dorothy is a young girl who lives with her Aunt Em and Uncle Henry and her little dog Toto on a Kansas farm. One day, Dorothy and Toto are caught up in a **cyclone** that **deposits** her farmhouse into Munchkin Country in the magical Land of Oz. The falling house has killed the Wicked Witch of the East, the evil ruler of the Munchkins. The Good Witch of the North gives Dorothy the magical Silver Shoes and tells Dorothy that the only way she can return home is to go to **the Emerald City** and ask the great and powerful Wizard of Oz to help her.

The Wicked Witch of the West sends a pack of wolves to tear them to pieces, but **the Tin Woodman** kills them with his axe. She sends wild crows to **peck** their eyes out, but **the Scarecrow** kills them by breaking their necks. She sends her Winkie soldiers to attack them, but **the Cowardly Lion** stands firm to repel them. Finally, she uses the power of the Golden Cap to send the winged monkeys to capture Dorothy, Toto, and the Cowardly Lion, **unstuff** the Scarecrow, and **dent** the Tin Woodman. Dorothy is forced to become the Wicked Witch's personal slave. Angered, Dorothy throws a bucket of water at her and is shocked to see the witch melt away. The Winkies ask the Tin Woodman to become their ruler, which he agrees to do after helping Dorothy return to Kansas.

When Dorothy and her friends meet the Wizard of Oz again, Toto **tips over** a screen in a corner of the **throne room** that reveals the Wizard. He sadly explains he is a **humbug**—an ordinary old man who, by a hot air balloon, came to Oz long ago from Omaha. The Wizard provides the Scarecrow with a head full of **bran**, pins, and needles ("a lot of **bran-new** brains"), the Tin Woodman with a silk heart stuffed with sawdust, and the Cowardly Lion a **potion** of "courage." Their faith in the Wizard's power gives these items a focus for their desires. The Wizard appoints the Scarecrow to rule in his stead, which he agrees to do after Dorothy returns to Kansas. Toto chases a kitten in the crowd and Dorothy goes after him, but the **tethers** of the balloon break and the Wizard floats away.

Dorothy is informed that Glinda the Good Witch of the South may be able to help her return home. On the way, the Cowardly Lion kills a giant spider who is **terrorizing** the animals in a forest. The animals ask the Cowardly Lion to become their king, which he agrees to do after helping Dorothy return to Kansas. Glinda reveals that the Silver Shoes Dorothy wears can take her anywhere she wishes to go. Dorothy embraces her friends, all of whom will be returned to their new kingdoms through Glinda's three uses of the Golden Cap: the Scarecrow to the Emerald City, the Tin Woodman to the Winkie Country, and the Lion to the forest; after which the cap shall be given to the King of the Winged Monkeys, freeing them. Dorothy takes Toto in her arms, knocks her heels together three times, and wishes to return home. Instantly, she begins **whirling** through the air and rolling through the grass of the Kansas prairie, up to her Kansas farmhouse. Dorothy runs to her Aunt Em, saying "I'm so glad to be at home again!"

(Adapted from *https://encyclopedia.thefreedictionary.com / The＋Wonderful＋Wizard＋of＋Oz*)

注释：

1. the Library of Congress (美国)国会图书馆
2. homegrown 国产的，自家种植的
3. cyclone 旋风
4. deposit 牢牢地放置在某处
5. the Emerald City 翡翠城
6. the Tin Woodman 铁皮人
7. peck 啄食
8. the Scarecrow 稻草人
9. the Cowardly Lion 胆小的狮子
10. unstuff 拆出填充物(stuff 的反义词)
11. dent 产生凹痕(打扁)
12. tip over 使翻倒
13. throne room 王宫大殿
14. humbug 骗子，谎话
15. bran 麸，糠
16. bran-new (brand-new)全新的
17. potion 一剂，一服
18. tether 系绳，拴绳
19. terrorize 实施恐怖统治，恐吓
20. whirl 旋转，(思绪)恍惚，接连不断

Word Power

Fill in the blanks with the words given below. Change the word form where necessary.

terrorize, artificial, dwarf, whirl, reassemble

(1) Leaves ________ in the wind.

(2) We had to take the table apart and ________ it upstairs.

(3) The old houses were ________ by the huge new tower blocks.

(4) Their point is to ________ people.

(5) These are ________ flowers, so they won't wither.

Summary

Fill in the blanks with words or phrases from Reading Passage 1.

Seen from up, a (1)________ pattern of circular fields stretches as far as the eye can see. This is one of the greatest land (2)________ in American history. The food industry is a giant factory that's designed to feed us. The farmland is just the factory floor.

In the last 60 years, American farmers, on average, have tripled their yield, (3)________ the productivity of every previous generation. There are two essential factors—irrigation and commercial fertilizer.

Now 80% of these fields grow just one, a single species that has come to (4)________ the farming landscape and the American diet. At 322 million tons a year, they produce more of this one grain than anything else, making it the key ingredient of the food machine, which is corn. Every time we go to the supermarket, though we might not know it, we're (5)________ by corn.

Listening

Scan the code and listen to a microlecture about the Food Machine—Corn. Please choose the best answer to each of the following questions.

(1) A chicken nugget contains ________ different ingredients coming from corn.

A. 100　　B. 37　　C. 30　　D. 60

(2) Which of the following species is produced more than anything else?

A. Corn.　　B. Tomato.　　C. Onion.　　D. Wheat.

(3) People feed all these cattle with ________.

A. hey　　B. fodder　　C. grass　　D. corn

Speaking

What's the connection between the modern feedlot business and the corn business? Refer to the following words and expressions if necessary.

CAFO / an extension / transform grain into marketable product / demand of the producer and the consumer / industrial scale / more efficient

Writing

1. Example Sentences

(1) At 322 million tons a year, we produce more of this one grain than anything

else, **making it the key ingredient of our food machine.**

(2) The average store has over 45,000 products on its shelves and roughly a third of them are created **using corn.**

(3) Just look at the label of any processed meal, **including the drink you wash it down with**, and you'll find that corn is in almost everything.

2. Analysis

以上例句中都出现了动词的现在分词作状语。

例 1 中的现在分词作状语,表示结果;例 2 中的现在分词作状语,表示行为方式或手段;例 3 中的现在分词作状语,表示解释说明。

3. Practice

翻译下列句子。

(1) He sat beside the window **reading a book.**

(2) **Following the instruction,** I began to use the washing machine.

(3) He made a choice, **leaving his family all in danger.**

第四节 大都市的美食

由于食品市场的全球化,无论什么季节,无论距离食物有多远,人们都可以随心所欲地选择自己想要的食物。那么,到底是什么推动了人类美食的发展呢?人们又是怎样选择美食的呢?除了生存的基本需求外,人们对于美食的渴望是首要动力。食品市场的营销策略也刺激了人们的消费,商家所获得的高利润进而影响了食品原材料的生产。本节我们将对经典的美国美食进行简单介绍。此外,本节还探讨了肥胖和健康饮食的相关问题。

Culture Express

经典的美国美食

美国许多地区和民族的菜肴都表现了饮食文化,它们共同构成了标准的或经典的美国菜。这些菜肴一般很丰盛、饱腹感很强而且简单。下面我们就一起来了解一下美国人民一日三餐中的经典美食吧!

1. 经典的重口味美式早餐:鸡蛋(煎、炒、水煮蛋或其他多种美味的蛋制品,例如火腿蛋松饼 eggs benedict),培根、香肠或火腿,咸牛肉土豆泥,炸薯饼、烤薄饼或枫糖浆华夫饼。

清淡的美式早餐:冷麦片(玉米片、燕麦片)或热麦片(燕麦粥)、干酪。

早餐通常配有松饼、吐司、橙汁、咖啡或茶。

2. 经典的美式午餐:汉堡包、法兰克福香肠、三明治(培根、生菜和番茄,即所谓 BLT—— bacon, lettuce, tomato)、金枪鱼沙拉、金枪鱼三明治、鸡肉沙拉、鸡蛋沙拉、烤奶酪、火腿、切成薄片的火鸡、意大利香肠、烤牛肉、咸牛肉、通心粉和芝士砂锅。

3. 美式晚餐或鸡尾酒会开胃菜：芥末蛋、鸡尾酒虾。

美国经典的肉类主菜往往以牛肉、猪肉和鸡肉以及海鲜为基础。炖肉通常是用价格低廉的块状牛肉，将其与洋葱和其他蔬菜一起放在水中炖制。肉饼由绞碎的肉与面包屑或其他调味料混合，并在长条烤盘中进行烤制。鸡肉的做法是烤制或用平底锅油炸。肋排（牛肉或猪肉）通常在甜味或醋味等调味料中缓慢煮熟。牛排、猪排和鱼片经油炸或烤制而成。在感恩节和圣诞节，火鸡则是必备食物。

砂锅菜（在美国，casserole 指食物，而不是指烹饪器皿）主要包括金枪鱼罐头或绿豆、面条和各种蔬菜、调味料。砂锅菜成本不高但是营养丰富，易于烹制。

肉馅饼是把炖煮的鸡肉或牛肉放在饼内烘烤而成。其肉馅通常是大量生产的冷冻肉馅，新鲜的肉馅口感自然更佳。

美国常见的配菜是法式炸土豆、土豆泥、烤豆子、凉拌卷心菜、通心粉沙拉、带有多种调味料的绿色沙拉以及诸如胡萝卜、西兰花或青豆等蔬菜。烤玉米棒也是典型的美国食品。

4. 苹果派是经典的美国甜点。在美国文化中，苹果派具有深厚的内涵。我们可以从苹果派的味道中闻出妈妈甚或奶奶、姨妈的溺爱以及家的温暖。正如那句谚语所说“as American as an apple pie”，我们可以翻译为“地道的美国味”“经典美国式的”，由此可见苹果派在美国文化中的地位。其他水果派，例如樱桃、桃等，也很受欢迎。正餐之后，一个并不花哨的巧克力蛋糕或冰激凌也会使这顿饭变得非常圆满。

午餐或晚餐的饮料：苏打水（可乐或柑橘类苏打水）、果汁（苹果汁或橙子汁）和啤酒。葡萄酒也为美国人所广泛接受，但还算不上最受欢迎的酒水。

当今美国的食品种类繁多并且日趋国际化，因此上述这些经典的美国菜肴也许将不再主宰人们的餐桌。来自世界各地的异国美食和食材以及美国各地区的特色美食都在美国的饮食文化中有着一席之地，而其中墨西哥和美国西南部风味的影响力最强。

Reading Passage 1

导读

美国人非常热爱甜点。在纽约有几百家大大小小的甜品店，各种风格和口味应有尽有。其中的黑白曲奇饼干是纽约市最著名的甜点之一。美国前总统奥巴马在大选前为了获得加州犹太人的支持而参加亲民活动时，就曾有一段与黑白曲奇饼干有关的故事。

A black-and-white cookie, or half-and-half cookie, is a soft, sponge-cake-like **shortbread** which is iced on one half with vanilla **fondant**, and on the other half by chocolate fondant. Notably, this style of cookie is often seen as a particularly “New York” snack. Few New York desserts are as **iconic** as black-and-white cookies. Almost every bakery, **bagel** store, and corner **deli** has them.

The exact origin of the black-and-white cookie is unknown. The half-moon common in **Upstate** New York and New England is sometimes confused with the black-and-white cookie but is made with a different recipe. Nonetheless, while the two names are often used **interchangeably** , there are considerable differences between the two; most notably in the textures of the base and the **icing**, with black-and-whites having a drier, cookie-like base and fondant **frosting**. And with the cookie also being bigger than most half-moons.

On October 19, 2008, Barack Obama **dubbed** them Unity Cookies at a deli in Hollywood, Florida.

In a nod to large Jewish population in South Florida and ever eager to **court** the influential Jewish community, Barack Obama made a surprise stop Tuesday at Hollywood's Deli Den, ordering a **plethora** of traditional food including whitefish, some bagels and the **requisite** dessert—with the assistance of Reps. Robert Wexler and Debbie Wasserman Schultz.

Wexler—Obama's biggest champion in the Jewish community—insisted Obama didn't need his help ordering, though he did appear a bit shaky when he asked for "whitefish."

"Whitefish salad?" Wasserman Schultz clarified. "Of course," Obama said, "Like we need a whole fish."

He also told Wasserman Schultz he'd get a couple of **oatmeal raisin cookies**, "a great Jewish tradition," he joked.

"Yes," Wasserman Schultz said, laughing, "Growing up we had so many of them." Wexler suggested a few black- and white- cookies **for the road**.

"One black-and-white-cookie." Obama said.

Wasserman Schultz **piped up**, "make it two."

"Now that's a tradition," Obama replied, "It's a unity cookie."

(Adapted from Sasha Johnson, 21 October, 2008, "Obama: McCain is 'running out of time' and 'making stuff up'")

注释:

1. shortbread 黄油甜酥饼干
2. fondant 方旦软糖料(用于装饰蛋糕)
3. iconic 标志性的,偶像的
4. bagel 百吉饼
5. deli 熟食店
6. upstate 州的北部
7. interchangeably 可交换地
8. icing 糖衣,酥皮
9. frosting 霜状白糖
10. dub 起别名,授予称号

11. in a nod to 向……致敬，表示感谢
12. court 设法获得，献殷勤，招致
13. plethora 过多，过剩
14. requisite 必不可少的
15. oatmeal raisin cookies 提子燕麦曲奇饼干
16. for the road 为路上准备
17. pipe up 脱口而出，开始说或唱

Reading Passage 2

导读

众所周知，美国人爱吃高热量的美食，由此导致了严重的肥胖问题。肥胖已经被正式归为一种损害健康的疾病。通过下面的阅读，我们来进一步了解肥胖的成因、危害以及如何预防肥胖。

Obesity is a medical condition in which excess body fat has accumulated to the extent that it may have a negative effect on health. Obesity increases the likelihood of various diseases and conditions, particularly **cardiovascular** diseases, type 2 diabetes, **obstructive sleep apnea** , certain types of cancer, **osteoarthritis** and depression.

Causes

Obesity is most commonly caused by a combination of excessive food intake, lack of physical activity, and **genetic susceptibility.** A few cases are caused primarily by genes, **endocrine disorders**, medications, or mental disorder.

A 2016 review supported excess food as the primary factor. Agricultural policy and techniques in the United States and Europe have led to lower food prices. In the United States, **subsidization** of corn, soy, wheat, and rice through the U.S. farm bill has made the main sources of processed food cheap compared to fruits and vegetables.

As societies become increasingly reliant on **energy-dense**, big-portions, and fast-food meals, the association between fast-food consumption and obesity becomes more concerning.

Effects on Health

The World Health Organization (WHO) predicts that overweight and obesity may soon replace more traditional public health concerns such as **undernutrition** and **infectious** diseases as the most significant cause of poor health.

Obesity is a leading preventable cause of death worldwide, with increasing rates in adults and children. In 2015, 600 million adults (12%) and 100 million children were obese. Authorities view it as one of the most serious public health problems of the 21st century. In 2013, the American Medical Association **classified** obesity **as** a disease.

Management

The main treatment for obesity consists of dieting and physical exercise. Diet quality can be improved by reducing the consumption of energy-dense foods, such as those high in fat and sugars, and by increasing the intake of **dietary fiber**. Diet programs may produce weight loss over the short term, but maintaining this weight loss is frequently difficult and often requires making exercise and a lower food energy diet a **permanent** part of a person's lifestyle.

(Adapted from *https://encyclopedia.thefreedictionary.com / Obesity*)

注释:

1. cardiovascular 心血管的
2. obstructive sleep apnea 阻塞性睡眠窒息症
3. osteoarthritis 骨关节炎
4. genetic susceptibility 遗传易感性
5. endocrine disorders 内分泌紊乱
6. subsidization 补贴
7. energy-dense 高能量的
8. undernutrition 营养不良
9. infectious 传染性的
10. classify...as... 把……分类为……
11. dietary fiber 膳食纤维
12. permanent 永久的,不变的

Word Power

Fill in the blanks with the words given below. Change the word form where necessary.

iconic, requisite, undernutrition, infectious, permanent

(1) ________ is a main cause in one-third of all deaths in children under five.

(2) Those patients are still ________.

(3) The condition can be ________ or last for a few days.

(4) You need the ________ experience for the job.

(5) There are many ________ brands around in our lives.

Summary

Fill in the blanks with words or phrases from reading passage 2.

Obesity is a medical condition in which (1) ________ body fat has accumulated to the (2)________ that it may have a negative effect on health. Obesity is most commonly caused by a combination of excessive food intake, lack of (3)________ activity, and genetic susceptibility. A 2016 review supported excess food as the (4)________ factor.

The World Health Organization (WHO) predicts that overweight and obesity may soon (5)________ more traditional public health concerns such as undernutrition and infectious diseases as the most significant cause of poor health. The main treatment for obesity (6)________ of dieting and physical exercise.

Listening

Scan the code and listen to a microlecture about the Food Machine—Crave Ability. Please choose the best answer to each of the following questions.

(1) 30 years ago, why did people go to restaurants?

A. For recreation.　　B. For delicious foods.

C. For parties.　　D. For celebration.

(2) What does "hit big" mean?

A. Strike hard.

B. Come against something / somebody with force.

C. Score points by hitting a ball.

D. Achieve great success or become very popular.

(3) Which of the following helps people decide what to eat with all this choice?

A. Crave-ability.　　B. Advertisements.

C. Friends' recommendation.　　D. Celebration.

Speaking

What are the reasons for American people's obesity? Refer to the following words and expressions if necessary.

survival tactic / high-calorie foods / not aware of healthy diet / lack of physical exercises / expensive fruits and vegetables / working people / busy

Writing

1. Example Sentence

(1) It's not surprising that crave-ability usually means adding calories.

(2) Over the last half-century, the food machine made it cheap and easy for us to put away an average of 600 additional calories per person per day.

2. Analysis

(1) "it"可以作为形式主语和形式宾语。当不定式、动名词、从句等用作主语时，为了避免头重脚轻，通常在句首使用"it"作为形式主语，在句尾使用真正的主语。当不定式、动名词、从句等用作宾语，且其后跟宾语补语时，形式宾语"it"应该用在宾语补语之前，而真正的宾语应该移到句末。

(2) 例1中的"it"是形式主语，真正的主语是句末的"that"从句。例2中的"it"是形式宾语，真正的宾语是句末的不定式结构。

3. Practice

用it作形式主语或形式宾语的形式来翻译下列句子。

(1)要想按时完成任务是不可能的。

(2)我觉得大家一起去爬山是很有意思的一件事。

(3)据报道，几天后气温会有所升高。

第六章　行走中的国度

概　述

人们的生活离不开吃、住、行。本章介绍了美国人各种不同的出行方式以及一些相关建筑。交通出行是人们生活中重要的一部分,如何让交通建筑既实用又美观,是自古以来人们一直在探索研究的课题。本章中,首先我们将走进纽约,了解那里与众不同的地形和环境,并对纽约的地标性地铁建筑进行介绍;然后我们去往芝加哥,对那里的火车站、铁路桥等相关地标建筑进行介绍;机场航站楼及其周边的建筑历来也是体现建筑艺术的载体。我们还将进一步了解汽车文化对美国人生活的影响,以及多层停车场的设计理念。

第一节　寸步难行的纽约

纽约拥有美国最复杂、最古老的交通基础设施。纽约州内多变的地形和拥挤的城市带来了很多难以克服的交通问题。该州的人口扩张遵循了早期的水路路线,首先是哈德逊河和莫霍克河,然后是伊利运河。19 世纪,铁路沿河修建;20 世纪又沿着同样的线路修建了高速公路。本节我们将对纽约的交通建筑,特别是 2016 年新建成的纽约世贸中心交通枢纽站进行介绍。

Culture Express

纽约的交通建筑

纽约是美国最大、最繁华的城市。由于纽约的地形多样,其交通运输状况十分复杂。

纽约市内有很多河流港湾,因此众多的桥梁和隧道是纽约交通的一大特色。对于四面环水的曼哈顿岛来说更是如此。

布鲁克林大桥是纽约市最早的大桥,落成于 1883 年,是当时世界上最长的悬索桥。后来政府在曼哈顿区周围的水域上架起了更多的桥梁,例如威廉斯堡大桥和曼哈顿大桥;

竣工于1909年的皇后区大桥是一座悬臂桥，连接曼哈顿区和皇后区；20世纪30年代，三区大桥落成。该桥前端分岔为三路，分别连接皇后区、布朗克斯区及曼哈顿区三区，因此得名“三区大桥”。在哈德逊河上，乔治·华盛顿大桥也随后完成。韦拉札诺海峡悬索大桥横跨纽约湾南部的韦拉札诺海峡，连接纽约史泰登岛与布鲁克林。

纽约的隧道有穿过哈德逊河底的林肯隧道、荷兰隧道。1940年竣工的皇后区-航港局客运总站是全美最繁忙的公交总站，也是州际公共汽车进出纽约市的主要门户。

2016年3月启用的纽约世贸中心交通枢纽站是纽约的新地标。这个换乘中心集地铁站和购物中心为一体。整座建筑从外观上看像一只张开翅膀的和平鸽。这是纽约最大的地铁换乘枢纽，有九条地铁线，共27个入口，每天的乘客人数达30万人次，还有超过6000平方米的零售和商业办公空间。

Reading Passage 1

导读

2016年3月，刚刚落成的纽约世贸中心交通枢纽站正式向公众开放。这个被称为“Oculus”的枢纽站是在911恐怖袭击近15年后，耗资40亿美元重新建立的地铁站。它也被誉为纽约的新地标。下文简要介绍了这座地铁站的外形、由来和强大的运输功能。

World Trade Center is a terminal station in Lower Manhattan for **PATH** rail service. It was originally opened on July 19, 1909, as Hudson Terminal, but was torn down, rebuilt as World Trade Center, and re-opened on July 6, 1971. Following the September 11, 2001 attacks, a temporary station opened in 2003. This station serves as the **terminus** for the **Newark**-World Trade Center and **Hoboken**-World Trade Center routes. The main station house, the **Oculus**, opened on March 4, 2016, and the terminal was renamed the World Trade Center Transportation Hub, or World Trade Center for short.

The World Trade Center Transportation Hub is the **Port Authority of New York and New Jersey**'s formal name for the new PATH station and the associated transit and retail complex. It was designed by Spanish architect Santiago Calatrava and composed of a train station with a large and open **mezzanine** under the National September 11 Memorial plaza. This mezzanine is connected to an aboveground **head house** structure called the Oculus—located between 2 World Trade Center and 3 World Trade Center—as well as to public **concourses** under the various towers in the World Trade Center complex.

In addition, the station was designed to connect the PATH to the New York City Subway system, and to **facilitate** a below ground east-west passageway that connects to the various modes of transportation in Lower Manhattan, from the **Fulton Center** to the **Battery Park City Ferry Terminal**. Furthermore, to replace the lost retail space from the original mall at the World Trade Center, significant portions of the Hub are devoted to the new 365,000 square feet (33,910 m^2) Westfield World Trade Center mall.

Calatrava said that the Oculus **resembles** a bird being **released** from a child's hand. The roof was originally designed to mechanically open to increase light and **ventilation** to the enclosed space. Herbert Muschamp, architecture critic of *The New York Times*, compared the design to the **Bethesda Terrace and Fountain** in Central Park. However, Calatrava's original **soaring spike** design was **scaled back** because of security issues. The design was further modified in 2008 to **eliminate** the opening and closing roof mechanism because of budget and space **constraints**.

(Adapted from *https://encyclopedia.thefreedictionary.com / World + Trade + Center + (PATH + station)*)

注释:

1. PATH (Port Authority Trans-Hudson)连接纽约曼哈顿和新泽西北部的地铁系统
2. terminus 终点站,终点
3. Newark 纽瓦克市(美国新泽西州港市)
4. Hoboken 霍博肯(美国新泽西州城市)
5. Oculus 眼睛(纽约世贸中心交通枢纽建筑的别名)
6. Port Authority of New York and New Jersey 纽约和新泽西港务局
7. mezzanine 夹层
8. head house 候车室,井口建筑物
9. concourse 大厅,广场
10. facilitate 使更容易便利,促进,帮助
11. Fulton Center 纽约富尔顿中心
12. Battery Park City Ferry Terminal 炮台公园城市渡轮码头
13. resemble 像,类似
14. release 释放,发布
15. ventilation 通风
16. Bethesda Terrace and Fountain 纽约中央公园的贝塞斯达露台和喷泉
17. soaring 不断上升的,高耸的
18. spike 猛增,急升,尖状物
19. scale back 相应缩减,按比例缩减
20. eliminate 消除,淘汰
21. constraint 约束,限制

Reading Passage 2

导读

纽约世贸中心交通枢纽站还未建成时,各界媒体和建筑师就对其发表了褒贬不一的评论。本文节选自卡巴科·本杰明(著名编辑,主持编辑一档关于纽约城市交通的新闻博客 *Second Ave. Sagas*)所写的一篇评论《为什么大型交通工程不能既美观又实用?》,从中

我们可以思索关于建筑的永恒话题:美观和实用孰轻孰重？二者能否兼顾？

Why Can't Transportation **Mega-Projects** Be both Beautiful and Practical?

In New York City's ＄4 billion PATH Hub, form overtakes function.

From a practical perspective, where Grand Central **seamlessly** integrates commuters with its purpose as a rail **depot**, the Port Authority's new hub fails its customers, the PATH-riding public. One platform is already completed, and its design flaws are obvious. Staircases are too narrow to **accommodate** the morning crowds who come streaming out of the trains from Hoboken, Jersey City, and beyond, while the narrow platforms quickly fill with **irate** commuters. Anyone trying to catch a train back to the **Garden State** risks a **stampede**. The marble, bright and **sterile**, picks up any spill, and a drop of water creates dangerously slippery conditions until a Port Authority janitor **scurries** out of some unseen door, mop in hand. Passenger flow and comfort, two of the most important elements of terminal design, seem to be an afterthought. The PATH Hub is shaping up to be an example of design divorced from purpose.

On a national level, the Calatrava PATH Hub is symbolic of the battle between form and function, between architects and planners, between grand visions and out of control costs, between **utilitarian pragmatists** and **starchitects** looking to leave their mark. The sacrificing of passenger needs for design flourishes happens everywhere.

In his writings and lectures on "Why Architecture Matters", the architectural critic Paul Goldberger writes: "When architecture is art, it does not escape the obligation to be practical, and its practical shortcomings should not be forgiven." Politicians choose architects who create buildings with visual designs that leave a mark in the public memory. For an occasional visitor to Lower Manhattan, Calatrava's building is a sight to see, but for an occasional PATH rider, Caltrava's platforms and staircases are a reminder that transit users in the eyes of celebrity **crafters** are afterthoughts. The riders don't post photos to **Instagram** and **swoon over** a **stegosaurus** -like structure rising out of the ashes of the Twin Towers; they **grumble about** narrow staircases and **shoddy** construction.

Transit **advocates** are often **accused of** being too willing to sacrifice beauty for function. Would I rather have a **drab** box with more Hudson River crossings than a station headhouse that **invokes** memories and a feeling of appreciation for transit design and architectural beauty? No. But I would rather spend ＄4 billion to improve regional mobility than **assuage** the **whims** of another Calatrava. Of course, there must be a middle ground; there always is. Form and function was an achievable balance over 100 years ago, as the lasting **grandeur** of Grand Central proves. Why can't we do the same today?

(Adapted from Benjamin Kabak ,October 7, 2014, "Why Can't Transportation Mega-Projects Be both Beautiful and Practical?")

注释：

1. Mega-Project 大型项目或工程
2. seamlessly 无瑕疵地，无缝地
3. depot 火车站或汽车站
4. accommodate 容纳
5. irate 发怒的
6. Garden State 花园州（美国新泽西州的别名）
7. stampede 人群的蜂拥，惊跑
8. sterile 无菌的
9. scurry 碎步疾跑
10. utilitarian 实用的，功利的
11. pragmatist 实用主义者
12. starchitect 明星建筑师
13. crafter 工匠
14. Instagram 照片墙（一款图片分享应用）
15. swoon over 痴迷，神魂颠倒，失去知觉
16. stegosaurus 剑龙
17. grumble about 抱怨，发牢骚
18. shoddy 粗制滥造的，劣质的
19. advocate 拥护者
20. accuse of 控告，谴责
21. drab 单调的
22. invoke 唤起，引起
23. assuage 平息，减轻
24. whim 突发的念头，虚妄
25. grandeur 壮丽，宏伟，庄严

Word Power

Fill in the blanks with the words given below. Change the word form where necessary.

release, soaring, constraint, assuage, accommodate

(1) Her father gave her a present to ________ her grief.

(2) All prisoners have been ________ from custody.

(3) The university can ________ more than 20,000 students.

(4) Due to financial ________ we decided to change the original plan.

(5) Our government is struggling with the ________ price of food.

Summary

Fill in the blanks with words or phrases from Reading Passage 1and Passage 2.

World Trade Center is a (1)________ station in Lower Manhattan for PATH rail service. The World Trade Center Transportation Hub is the associated transit and retail (2)________. It (3)________ of a train station with a large and open mezzanine. The Oculus (4)________ a bird being released from a child's hand.

From a practical perspective, where Grand Central seamlessly (5)________ commuters with its purpose as a rail depot, the Port Authority's new hub fails its customers, the PATH-riding public. Passenger flow and comfort, two of the most important elements of terminal design, seem to be an (6)________. The PATH Hub is shaping up to be an example of design divorced from purpose.

Transit advocates are often accused of being too willing to (7)________ beauty for function. Form and function was an (8)________ balance over 100 years ago, as the lasting grandeur of Grand Central proves.

Listening

Scan the code and listen to a microlecture about the Nation on the Move—Transportation Challenge in NY. Please choose the best answer to each of the following questions.

(1) Which station is mentioned in the video clip?

A. Cincinnati Union Station.　　B. Chicago Union Station.

C. Los Angeles Union Station.　　D. Grand Central Terminal.

(2) How many different transportation modes mentioned in the two video clips?

A. 2.　　B. 3.　　C. 4.　　D. 5.

(3) Which of the following is true about a transport hub?

A. It is a place where passengers and cargo are exchanged between vehicles or between transport modes.

B. It is the central part of a car wheel.

C. It is a focal point around which events revolve.

D. It is a device for connecting computers in a network.

Speaking

What do you know about New York City's strong transportation system and the problem of traffic congestion? What's the beneficial impact of the subway on people's lives and the city as a whole? Refer to the following words and expressions if necessary.

various modes of transportation in NY / efficient / convenient / challenge / gridlock / subway

Writing

1. Example Sentence

(1) The transportation network **moves** millions even while straining under their weight.

(2) A flight **comes** and **goes** every 24 seconds.

(3) By 7:00 a.m., thousands of yellow cabs are **picking up** their first fares of the day at the airports and **heading for** Manhattan.

(4) One fleet alone **carries** 65,000 commuters a day.

(5) They all **converge** at America's busiest commuter hub.

(6) Trains **stream** into another bustling train station, Grand Central Terminal.

2. Analysis

在主语为非人的事或物的句子中通常会使用拟人的修辞手法来具体说明主语的功能或作用。以上例句中的主语皆为物,即各种各样的交通工具,谓语动词皆为主动式,用拟人的修辞手法表现出这些交通工具的作用,强调其对人们出行的重要意义。

3. Practice

用上述方法翻译下列句子。

(1) 大家在这次会议上各抒己见。

(2) 调查结果显示,肥胖与饮食之间有着直接的关系。

(3) 这个难题是用计算机算出来的。

第二节　交通发达的芝加哥

铁路系统连接了美国的东海岸和西海岸,使美国逐步走上了现代化道路。自19世纪起,芝加哥就成为美国中部地区铁路运输的中心,多个铁路公司将线路修筑到市区并形成了绵密放射状铁路网。本节我们将了解芝加哥的铁路交通,另外对芝加哥联合车站、贝弗利/摩根铁路区等与铁路交通相关的地标区域或建筑进行简单介绍。

Culture Express

芝加哥的铁路交通

芝加哥是美国第三大城市,是一个重要的交通枢纽,同时该市也是美国北部主要的货运铁路枢纽。它是全球物流的重要组成部分,是仅次于香港和新加坡的全球第三大综合联运港。

伊利诺伊州区域交通管理局(RTA)负责协调三个运输系统:芝加哥交通管理局(CTA)、梅特拉(Metra)和佩斯(Pace)。

芝加哥交通管理局负责管理芝加哥市区和郊区的公共交通,包括一个广阔的公共汽车网络，以及一个被称为“L”（意为“高架”）的快速高架路交通和地铁系统，其也连接中途机场和奥黑尔机场。这些线路通过颜色来区分，包括红线、蓝线、绿线、橙线、棕线、紫线、粉线和黄线。红线和蓝线是穿过市区的地铁，提供 24 小时服务，全年无休，另一个提供 24 小时服务的城市是纽约。美国第二大区域客运铁路网梅特拉在芝加哥市区和郊区运营 11 条通勤铁路。佩斯在芝加哥周边的 200 多个郊区提供公交和辅助交通服务，并延伸到市区。

美国铁路公司的长途服务起源于联合车站。芝加哥是美国最大的客运铁路服务中心之一。列车的终点站包括旧金山、华盛顿特区、纽约市、印第安纳波利斯、新奥尔良、波特兰、西雅图、密尔沃基、昆西、圣路易斯、卡本代尔、波士顿、大急流城、休伦港、庞蒂亚克、洛杉矶和圣安东尼奥等。20 世纪初，芝加哥纽约电气化公司试图建造芝加哥和纽约之间的直通铁路，但最终该项目没有完成。

七条一级铁路中除了堪萨斯城南方铁路，其他六条均在芝加哥会合。2002 年，芝加哥曾经发生过一次严重的货运火车拥堵事件：火车需要两天的时间才能从芝加哥地区经过，而从美国西海岸到芝加哥也只需要两天的时间。全国大约 1/3 的货运列车都经过这个城市，使它成为全国主要的交通瓶颈。2003 年宣布的《芝加哥地区环境与运输效率方案》（*Chicago Region Environmental and Transportation Efficiency*，*CREATE*）投入了大约 15 亿美元用来改善铁路基础设施，减少了约 1/3 的货运拥堵。

Reading Passage 1

导读

下文介绍了芝加哥地标建筑之一——芝加哥联合车站。

Chicago Union Station

Chicago Union Station is a major railroad station that opened in 1925 in Chicago, Illinois. It is the only remaining intercity rail terminal in Chicago, as well as being the city's primary terminal for commuter trains. The station stands on the west side of the Chicago River between West Adams Street and West Jackson Boulevard, just outside the Chicago Loop. Including approach and **storage tracks**, it is about nine and a half city blocks in size. Its **facilities** are mostly underground, buried beneath streets and **skyscrapers**.

Chicago Union Station is the third-busiest rail terminal in the United States, after Grand Central Terminal and Penn Station in New York City. It is Amtrak's overall fourth-busiest station. It handles approximately 120,000 passengers on an average weekday and is one of Chicago's most iconic structures, **reflecting** the city's strong architectural **heritage** and historic achievements. Its combination of Bedford **limestone Beaux-Arts facades**, massive **Corinthian** columns, sparkling marble floors, and magnificent Great Hall, all **highlighted** by brass lamps, create an environment that captures the imagination of passengers and visitors who enter its **premises**. In addition to standing out architecturally, Union Station has features that reflect its commitment to

sustainability. In 2011, its lighting system was replaced with more energy-efficient light bulbs and **motion sensors**, reducing the station's **carbon footprint** by 4 million tons annually. Unlike other major American intercity / commuter rail hubs, such as Grand Central Terminal and Penn Station in New York, 30th Street Station in Philadelphia, South Station in Boston, and Union Station in Los Angeles, Union Station does not have any direct connection to local rapid transit service. However, there are several rapid transit stations within walking distance of Union Station, and numerous bus lines that stop directly at Union Station.

Chicago Union Station was **designated** as one of America's "Great Places" in 2012 by the American Planning Association (APA) for **promoting** social activity and community **cohesiveness.** These places are unique in their cultural and historical significance, sense of community, and vision. Other **criteria** include "architectural features, **accessibility**, functionality, and community involvement." These spaces are safe and inviting, well-maintained, and attractive, both visually and in functionality. In addition, local culture and history are reflected within the space.

(Adapted from *https://encyclopedia.thefreedictionary.com / Chicago+Union+Station*)

注释：

1. storage track 存车线
2. facility 设施，设备
3. skyscraper 摩天大楼
4. reflect 反映，倒映
5. heritage 遗产，传承
6. limestone 石灰岩
7. Beaux-Arts 艺术，美术
8. facade 建筑物正面，外观
9. Corinthian 科林斯柱式
10. highlight 加亮，视觉上突出，强调
11. premise (经营或办公)场所，房屋或土地
12. sustainability 持续性
13. motion sensor 动作传感器
14. carbon footprint 碳排放量
15. designate 指定，定名为……
16. promote 促进，提升
17. cohesiveness 凝聚力
18. criteria 标准，条件
19. accessibility 可及性，无障碍环境

Reading Passage 2

导读

下文介绍了芝加哥的另外两个与交通有关的地标建筑(群)——贝弗利/摩根铁路区和芝加哥伊利诺伊州西部铁路桥。

The Beverly / Morgan Railroad District

The Beverly / Morgan Railroad District is a historic district in the Beverly, Morgan Park, and Washington Heights community areas of Chicago, Illinois, United States. It was designated a Chicago Landmark on April 15, 1995.

The district **consists of** the six train stations at 91st, 95th, 99th, 107th, 111th and 115th Streets along the Rock Island District commuter line of Metra. The stations were built between 1889 and 1945 by various **architects.**

The six structures in this "**thematic**-style" district **represent** rare, surviving examples of late-19th and early-20th century commuter railroad stations in Chicago. These type of stations helped promote the development of the city's **outlying** areas, including — in this case — the suburban communities of Beverly, Morgan Park, and Washington Heights, which have since been **annexed** by the city. The architecture of the stations, which were designed for the Chicago, Rock Island & Pacific Railroad, reflect the **Colonial Revival, Queen Anne,** and **Richardsonian Romanesque** styles of the surrounding **residences.**

The stations, and the railroad tracks themselves, also are unique for their grade-level location, unlike other facilities which have been raised on **viaducts** and **embankments** .

(Adapted from City of chicago Department of Planning and Development, 2003, "Beverly / Morgan Railroad District")

注释:

1. consists of 包含,由……组成
2. architect 建筑师
3. thematic 主题的;主题式的
4. represent 代表,表现
5. outlying 偏远的
6. annex 并吞,获得,附加
7. Colonial Revival 殖民复兴
8. Queen Anne 安妮女皇
9. Richardsonian Romanesque 理查森罗马式
10. residence 住宅,居民楼

11. viaduct 高架铁路,高架桥
12. embankment (公路或铁路)路堤

Chicago & Illinois Western Railway Bridge

The Chicago & Illinois Western Railway Bridge was built in 1914 by Theodor Rall. It was designated a Chicago Landmark on December 12, 2007.

The Chicago & Illinois Western Railway Bridge is a **rare-surviving** example of a **patented** bridge design by Theodor Rall. Although this bridge type was invented by Rall, the patent was held by the contractor, Strobel Steel Construction Company of Chicago. The Rall type was one of the designs most frequently used by the railroads in the early twentieth century and is significant for combining the **bascule** bridge technologies of both rolling and **trunnion** motion. The bridge is a single track, **single-leaf** bascule span which runs on an east-west **axis** over a slip in the **Chicago Sanitary and Ship Canal**. This **low-profile** bridge is supported by three **unevenly-spaced piers** made from reinforced concrete. Visible **struts** are located on the sides of the bridge along with a trunnion, which when engaged by an electric motor, pulls the leaf up and rolls it backwards along the **horizontal** track **girders**. Today, the bridge's mechanism has been disabled and it remains in fixed position.

(Adapted from *http://webapps*1. *chicago. gov / landmarksweb / web / landmarkdetails.htm*? *lanId*＝13103)

注释:

1. rare-surviving 幸存的,尚存的
2. patented 专利的
3. bascule 竖旋桥,活动桥
4. trunnion 耳轴
5. single-leaf 单片钢板
6. axis 轴,轴线
7. Chicago Sanitary and Ship Canal 芝加哥环境船舶运河(芝加哥排水运河)
8. low-profile 低调的
9. unevenly-spaced 间隔不均匀的
10. pier 支墩
11. strut 支柱
12. horizontal 水平的,地平线的
13. girder 大梁,主梁

Word Power

Fill in the blanks with the words given below. Change the word form where necessary.

heritage, designate, cohesiveness, consist, outlying

(1) We need to improve our national ________.

(2) Her diet ________ largely of vegetables.

(3) People in the ________ villages and towns had difficulty going out.

(4) This building has been ________ a non-smoking area.

(5) Every country has its customs and ________.

Summary

Fill in the blanks with words or phrases from the Reading Passage 1.

Chicago Union Station is a (1) ________ railroad station, the only (2) ________ intercity rail terminal in Chicago, as well as being the city's primary terminal for (3)________ trains. It (4) ________ approximately 120,000 passengers on an average weekday and is one of Chicago's most iconic structures, (5) ________ the city's strong architectural heritage and (6) ________ achievements. In 2011, its lighting system was (7) ________ with more energy-efficient light bulbs and motion sensors, reducing the station's carbon (8) ________ by 4 million tons annually.

Listening

Scan the code and listen to a microlecture about the Nation on the Move-Railroads. Please choose the best answer to each of the following questions.

(1) Where did all national rail lines end?

A. Chicago. B. New York.

C. Los Angles. D. Washington.

(2) For nearly 100 years, what is the fastest and most popular way to travel?

A. Bus. B.Railway.

C. Plane. D. Car.

(3) Which of the following first connected the country from coast to coast and made modern America possible?

A. The freight. B. The airplanes.

C. The railroads system. D. The subway.

Speaking

What is a hump yard? What is it used to do? Refer to the following words and expressions if necessary.

a man-made hill / at freight train stations / railway yard / separate railway cars / classify the cars

Writing

1. Example Sentence

(1) The network we depend on to ship our goods depend on Jack, his remote control, and a surprisingly simple process known as humping.

(2) Everything that moves through America moves through these yards.

2. Analysis

(1) 两个句子都是复合句,主语之后都有一个后置定语从句,分别是"we depend on to ship our goods"和"…that moves through America"。

(2) 两个句子的主句中,谓语分别是"depend on Jack, his remote control, and a surprisingly simple process known as humping"和"moves through these yards"。

(3) 从句和主句的谓语部分相同,使句义层层递进,能够起到强调和对比的作用。

3. Practice

合并下列句子。

(1) The commuter plane connected the bigger city with the smaller communities.

(2) The commuter plane connected the remote areas with the rest of the world.

第三节　飞遍世界

乘坐飞机出行无疑是比乘坐火车更快、更适于长途旅行的一种交通方式。但是航班的导航和指挥是最为复杂和烦琐的。而且,机场航站楼既需实用,能带给乘客们舒适和方便,同时也要美观,能让人欣赏到建筑的美感,故而也逐渐成为建筑艺术的载体。本节我们将简单介绍与空中交通有关的建筑物——机场航站楼,并重点介绍美国著名的约翰·肯尼迪国际机场和丹佛国际机场。

Culture Express

机场航站楼

机场航站楼是旅客上下飞机进行中转的机场建筑。在航站楼内,乘客购买机票,托运行李,并通过安检。有些大机场只有一个航站楼,通过天桥、通道或地下隧道与多个候机大厅相连(例如丹佛国际机场、世界上最繁忙的亚特兰大国际机场)。还有些大机场有多个航站楼,每个航站楼有一个或多个候机大厅(如纽约的肯尼迪国际机场)。

弗罗默旅行指南提到,大多数机场航站楼都是朴素风格的,"20 世纪 60 年代和 70 年代的混凝土建筑在 20 世纪 90 年代和 21 世纪初被玻璃建筑取代。最好的航站楼做了大胆尝试,融合了'光'和'空气'的概念"。很多机场被认为是建筑杰作,如纽约肯尼迪机场的五号航站楼。还有一些机场是为了反映特定地区的文化而设计的,例如新墨西哥州的阿尔伯克基国际太阳港,其航站楼就是以普韦布洛复兴为风格设计的。

由于客运航班的迅速崛起，20 世纪三四十年代美国建立了许多航站楼，它们都反映了当时流行的装饰艺术风格。其中保存至今的一个例子是休斯敦机场航站楼。早期的机场航站楼直接面对停机坪开放，乘客可以步行或乘公共汽车到达飞机脚下。这种设计在小型机场中仍然很常见，甚至许多大型机场都有“巴士登机口”来容纳主航站楼以外的飞机。

卫星楼是与其他机场建筑分离的建筑，也称子航站楼。飞机可以停放在卫星楼的四周。洛杉矶国际机场利用地下人行隧道将卫星楼与主航站楼连接起来。坦帕国际机场是第一个使用自动载人通道将主航站楼与卫星楼连接起来的机场，这也是如今所有机场的标准设置。

有些机场是半圆形航站楼，飞机停在一边，汽车停在另一边。这种设计的结果是乘客需要长距离步行，但大大缩短了登机手续办理处和登机口之间的距离。按照这一模式设计的机场包括达拉斯/沃斯堡国际机场、堪萨斯城机场等。

Reading Passage 1

导读

本文介绍了纽约的约翰·肯尼迪国际机场。其中 5 号航站楼被沙里宁设计成大鹏展翅的形状，外部和内部都采用大量柔和的曲面，室内的装饰细节也都是统一的风格。这座建筑体现了典型的象征主义风格。

John F. Kennedy International Airport is the primary international airport serving New York City. It is the busiest international air passenger gateway into North America, the fifth busiest airport in the United States and the busiest airport in the New York City airport system, handling just under 59 million passengers in 2016. Over ninety airlines operate out of the airport, with non-stop or direct flights to destinations in all six **inhabited** continents.

JFK features six passenger terminals and four runways. It serves as a hub for American Airlines and Delta Air Lines and is the primary operating base for JetBlue Airways. Opened as New York International Airport in 1948, it was commonly known as Idlewild Airport before being renamed in 1963 in memory of John F. Kennedy, the 35th President of the United States, following his **assassination.**

Terminal 5 opened in 2008 for JetBlue Airways, the manager and primary (then only) **tenant** of the building and serves as the base of their large JFK hub. It sits behind the **preserved** Eero Saarinen-designed terminal originally known as the TWA Flight Center, which is now connected to the new structure and is considered part of T5. The Saarinen building was reopened in 2018 as a hotel. The terminal was re-designed by Gensler and constructed by Turner Construction, and it is known for its many gift shops and **gourmet** restaurants, including a steak house and a sushi restaurant.

Thoroughly modern and thoroughly New York, JetBlue's **award-winning** T5 at JFK delivers a state-of-the-art airport experience as inspiring and unique as the city we call home. T5 makes flying fun again with convenient check-in **kiosks** and self-tagging, unique dining and retail options, free Wi-Fi and **abundant** charging stations throughout—even an outdoor rooftop deck. Plus, enjoy seamless in-terminal connections with our partners Aer Lingus, Hawaiian Airlines and TAP Air Portugal, and easy access to other terminals via the **AirTrain.** T5 offers a world of options to recharge (literally and figuratively) or relax—before, after and between flights.

The T5 Rooftop & Wooftop Lounge is located across from Gate 28. Passengers can get some air before they're up in the air. Open daily from 6a.m.-11p.m., people will find places to **plug in**, and enjoy inspiring views and a dog walk. TWA Hotel is connected to T5 via Eero Saarinen's iconic flight tubes, and JFK's only on-airport hotel is now open, with the landmark Saarinen building as its centerpiece.

(Adapted from *https://www.jetblue.com / at-the-airport / terminal-5-at-jfk*)

注释:

1. inhabited 有人居住的
2. assassination 暗杀，行刺
3. tenant 房客，住户
4. preserved 保存的，腌制的
5. gourmet 菜肴精美的；美食家
6. award-winning 备受赞誉的，应获奖的
7. kiosk 自助服务终端，小摊，凉亭
8. abundant 丰富的，充裕的
9. AirTrain 机场内捷运，机场轻轨
10. plug in 充电

Reading Passage 2

导读

位于美国科罗拉多州丹佛市的丹佛国际机场素来被称为“神秘的机场”。其神秘之处在于:多层地下建筑不为人所知，机场大厅诡异的壁画和艺术陈列品、蓝色野马雕塑等。下文摘自《丹佛邮报》的一篇关于蓝色野马的评论文章。人们对这座雕塑爱恨交织，称其为“Bluecifer”(Blue ＋ Lucifer，蓝色 ＋ 路西法)，希望政府能够将其移走。

“Mustang,” a 32-foot sculpture of a wild horse, is seen at Denver International Airport. Now that the controversial public work of art has been in place for five years, it is possible for citizens to petition to have it removed.

We come before you today to **fend off** any notion of **rounding up** a **posse** and going after the **ferocious** animal looming on a small piece of range east of this ol' cowtown.

With its bulging muscles, **lurid** veins and **eerie** red eyes, the great blue beast has been the **bane** of many a man, woman and child since it came to town on Feb. 11, 2008.

Known to some in these parts as "Blucifer", "Devil Horse", or "The Blue Stallion of Death", it could soon be open season on the creature properly known as "Mustang", the sculpture that stands guard at Denver International Airport.

As reported last week by Westword, **petitions** to remove public art in Denver are accepted after five years—a policy intended to avoid **knee-jerk** decisions on placement, fit and **aesthetic.**

Though a half-serious effort four years ago drew considerable interest, to our knowledge no one is proposing the piece be sent out to pasture. And we hope no one does.

For the last five years, the **anatomically** correct creature has prompted **untold** commentary and criticism.

"Mustang" is the work of noted Hispanic artist Luis Jimenez. It was the subject of **controversy** even before landing in Denver some 16 years after it was **commissioned.** Some people believe the sculpture is cursed—pointing out that Jimenez was killed after a portion of it fell off and crushed him (it was completed by family members).

Yet "Mustang" has found admirers among art critics, parents looking to entertain children and many others.

In 2011, it was honored as one of the "most **bizarre** " pieces of public art by Yahoo. com. But it is more than that—it also **evokes** feelings of the region's historical and cultural heritage.

The sculpture is—in the true sense of the word—remarkable.

And that's the point of public art, Colleen Fanning, a consultant in Denver who worked on the project, told *The Denver Post*'s Colleen O'Connor in 2011. Most of us, she said, "want to choose things that evoke thought and maybe, hopefully, make someone stop and wonder what that is all about."

"Mustang" is a sort of bizarre Mr. Ed in that it's a horse that gets people unexpectedly talking—about art.

That is an amazing accomplishment and one that warrants letting the piece **stay put** on the plains east of town for the **foreseeable** future.

(Adapted from "Keep remarkable 'Mustang' sculpture at DIA", *The Denver Post*. February 6, 2013.)

注释:

1. fend off 打跑,避开,挡住
2. round up 聚拢,总结
3. posse 一群,一队(志同道合者);武装队
4. ferocious 凶猛的,凶恶可怕的
5. lurid 血红的,可怕的,耸人听闻的

6. eerie 怪异的，可怕的
7. bane 痛苦之源，祸害
8. petition 请愿，恳求
9. knee-jerk 下意识的，不经思考的；膝反射的
10. aesthetic 美感，美学
11. anatomically 生理结构上地
12. untold 数不尽的；未说过的
13. controversy 争论，争议
14. commission 委任，委托
15. bizarre 奇异的
16. evoke 引起，唤起
17. stay put 留在原地不动
18. foreseeable 可预知的，能预测的

Word Power

Match the word with its appropriate meaning in English. Fill in the blanks with the letters in front of the words.

a. assassination, b. preserved, c. gourmet, d. bane, e. aesthetic

(1) ________ nicer or more unusual or sophisticated foods, often more expensive
(2) ________ something causes misery or death
(3) ________ murder of a public figure by surprise attack
(4) ________ concerning or characterized by an appreciation of beauty or good taste
(5) ________ kept intact or in a particular condition

Summary

Fill in the blanks with words or phrases from the Reading Passage 1.

John F. Kennedy International Airport is the primary international airport serving New York City. Over ninety airlines operate out of the airport, with non-stop or (1)________ flights to destinations in all six (2)________ continents. It serves as a (3)________ for American Airlines and Delta Air Lines and is the primary operating base for JetBlue Airways.

Terminal 5 opened in 2008 for JetBlue Airways, the manager and primary (then only) tenant of the building and serves as the base of their large JFK hub. Thoroughly modern and thoroughly New York, JetBlue's (4)________ winning T5 at JFK delivers a state-of-the-art airport experience as (5)________ and unique as the city we call home. T5 offers a world of options to recharge (literally and figuratively) or relax—before, after and between flights. TWA Hotel is connected to T5 via Eero Saarinen's iconic flight tubes, JFK's only on-airport hotel is now open, with the landmark Saarinen building as its (6)________.

Listening

Scan the code and listen to a microlecture about the Nation on the Move—Air Transportation and Air Beacon. Please choose the best answer to each of the following questions.

(1) Which is the fastest and most popular way to travel nowadays?

A. Railroads. B. Airplanes.

C. Cars. D. Subway.

(2) Which is the only way for flying navigation in the area off the grid?

A. GPS. B. Radar.

C. Air beacon. D. Bonfire.

(3) What is Montana called?

A. Big Sky County. B. Land of Opportunity.

C. Sunshine State. D. Golden State.

Speaking

Air travel is so common today that the airways are filled with all kinds of travelers. Do you know who they are and why they need to fly? Refer to the following words and expressions if necessary.

road warriors / business trip / dead bodies / for burial / prisoners / distant court hearings / penitentiaries

Writing

1. Example Sentence

(1) Many deceased retirees are flown home for burial.

(2) The air beacon on the top of the continental divide is the only way for flying navigation.

2. Analysis

在一些通常需要动词、形容词或从句才能表达含义的句子中，可以把它们转化为名词。名词化可以使句子更紧凑、简洁且更正式。如上面例句中的 burial、navigation。

3. Practice

翻译下列句子。

(1) 我看到他来了。

(2) 在第五大道发生了一起事故。

(3) 警察对这起案件进行了调查。

第四节　自驾出行

20 世纪初汽车被发明出来，自此其对人们越来越重要。世界各地都有汽车的影子，尤其是在比较发达的国家，汽车已经成为最受欢迎的交通方式。汽车的普及在就业模式、社会交往、基础设施和商品物流等方面都带来了翻天覆地的变化。本节我们将讨论汽车对人们生活的影响，并简单介绍与汽车相关的建筑——多层停车场。

Culture Express

汽车对社会和文化的影响

汽车给人们的日常生活带来了什么样的影响？这一直是一个有争议的话题。一方面，汽车的大量生产意味着一场交通革命，这极大地方便了人们的出行。另一方面，汽车普及所带来的负面影响也是广泛的：汽车使用的是不可再生能源；交通事故导致的意外死亡率急剧上升；人们住得越来越远；驾车导致身体锻炼的减少和日益严重的肥胖问题；造成了严重的空气和噪声污染；城市逐渐向郊区蔓延，由此导致了市中心的衰败。

英国建筑师马丁 · 波利（Martin Pawley）在他的著作《私人未来》（*The Private Future*，1973 年）中称汽车是“私有化的象征，意味着离开群体”。他认为，汽车是一个私人世界，是一个允许人进行天马行空的想象和逃避外界的地方。波利预言，汽车的规模和技术含量将继续扩大成增长。

随着时间的推移，汽车已经不再是单纯的交通工具或身份象征了，很多人把驾驶当作了一种兴趣爱好，他们欣赏汽车的制造工艺和性能，还组织了很多各种各样的驾驶比赛。这些喜爱汽车和驾驶的人被称为“汽车爱好者”。

这种爱好的一个主要方面是收集汽车，尤其是经典的车型，其被认为具有审美、娱乐和历史价值。这样的需求产生了投资潜力，使一些汽车能够具有极高的价值，从而成为一种金融工具。

汽车爱好的第二个主要方面是汽车改装，许多汽车爱好者改装他们的汽车以实现性能改进或视觉增强。这种操作还衍生出许多亚文化，例如快车手（Hot Rodders）和纯粹主义者（Purists）。前者喜欢改装或者定制车辆，主要是基于外观或复制 1948 年之前的美国汽车设计，也包括其他各地一些二战期间甚至更早的汽车设计。此外，来自世界各地爱好者经常聚集在一起参加各种赛车运动（包括专业的和业余的）来展示他们的汽车。

许多汽车俱乐部的成立也促进了社会交往，俱乐部的成员都以拥有、驾驶和展示汽车为荣。当今世界上许多著名的社交活动都围绕这个爱好展开，其中一个著名的例子就是美国加州卵石滩的优雅古典车展。

Reading Passage 1

导读

下文简要介绍了多层停车场的外观、功能和不足之处。

A multi-storey car park (also called a parking garage, parking structure, parking **ramp**, **parkade**, parking building, parking deck or indoor parking) is a building designed for car parking and where there are a number of floors or levels on which parking takes place. It is essentially an indoor, **stacked** parking lot.

Many car parks are independent buildings dedicated **exclusively** to that use. The design loads for car parks are often less than the office building they serve (50 psf versus 80 psf), leading to long floor spans of 55-60 feet that permit cars to park in rows without supporting columns in between. The most common structural systems in the United States for these structures are either **prestressed** concrete double-tee floor systems or post-tensioned **cast-in-place** concrete floor systems.

In recent times, car parks built to serve residential and some business properties have been built as part of a larger building, often underground as part of the basement, such as at the Atlantic Station redevelopment in Atlanta. This saves land for other uses (as opposed to a parking lot), is cheaper and more practical in most cases than a separate structure, and is hidden from view. It protects customers and their cars from weather such as rain, snow, or hot summer sunshine that raises a vehicle's interior temperature to extremely high levels.

Car parks which serve shopping centers can be built **adjacent to** the center for easier access at each floor between shops and parking. One example is Mall of America in Bloomington, Minnesota, USA, which has two large car parks **attached to** the building, at the eastern and western ends.

These garages often have low ceiling **clearances**, which restrict access by full-size vans and other large vehicles. On 15 December 2013, a man was killed during a robbery in the garage at The Mall at Short Hills in Millburn, New Jersey. The ambulance responding to the shooting was delayed because it was too large to enter the garage.

These structures are not usually known for their architectural value. As Architectural Record has noted, "In the **Pantheon** of Building Types, the parking garage **lurks** somewhere in the **vicinity** of prisons and **toll plazas.**" *New York Times* has labeled parking structures as "the grim afterthought of American design."

A handful of parking garages have received considerable praise for their design, including 1111 Lincoln Road, in the South Beach section of Miami Beach, Florida, designed by the internationally known Swiss architectural firm of Herzog & de Meuron; Santa Monica Place Public Parking Structures at Frank Gehry's Santa Monica Place Mall, by the architectural firm Brooks + Scarpa.

(Adapted from *https://encyclopedia.thefreedictionary.com / Multi-storey+car+park*)

注释：

1. ramp 坡道
2. parkade (parking arcade) 停车场
3. stacked 放有大量……的，成堆的
4. exclusively 专有地，排外地
5. prestressed 预应力的
6. cast-in-place 现场浇筑
7. adjacent to 与……邻近的
8. attached to 附属于……的
9. clearance 空隙，间隙；清除；准许
10. pantheon 万神殿；名流群
11. lurk 潜伏，躲藏
12. vicinity 邻近，附近
13. toll plaza 收费站

Reading Passage 2

导读

在美国佛罗里达州的迈阿密海滩，林肯大道 1111 号是一座集地上多层停车场、住宅中心和购物中心为一体的奇特建筑。这座极富艺术美感和实用价值的建筑凸显了美国的汽车文化，并改变了地下停车场单调阴暗的色彩，赋予了停车场极高的建筑美感。本文节选自网站“建筑记录”(Architectural Record)中对林肯大道 1111 号的一篇评论。

A robust house of cards, 1111 Lincoln Road is a composition of cast-in-place concrete **slabs** that function as floor plates, columns, and ramps **winding** through the compressions and expansions in heights of the six parking levels, which range from 8 to 34 feet. The building is anchored by ground-floor retail and topped by a restaurant and Wennett's **penthouse.** A **canopy** above the retail spaces continues across the existing building to the new one, marrying the two structures that are otherwise linked only by bridges at each level. To carry life up off the street, the team **wedged** a **boutique** between the garage's decks. And the soaring seventh-floor parking level does **double-duty** as an event space, hosting fashion shows, parties, and concerts.

While the building may appear **whimsical**, its sculptural expression is the product of structural logic, say the architects. Their decision to vary the parking slabs both horizontally and vertically resulted in triangulated columns that lean out to **buttress** the **cantilevers** and split to accommodate ramps and long spans. In a nod to the building type's humble **pedigree**, the team used class B concrete, so **pockmarks** and imperfections **abound.** But in the interest of differentiating the garage from its **brethren**, they employed an open stair and indirect lighting. And to keep lines clean, they used frameless elevators, limited exposed piping and lighting, and embedded the sprinkler system, lending the space the restrained **ruggedness** of a well-groomed five o'clock shadow.

While in some ways **otherworldly**, the building is very much of Miami. Inspired by Lapidus's Tropical Modern canopies, fountains, and **pavilions** on the **promenade** below, the architects also nod to the local **vernacular** with the use of concrete and **overhangs**. Dispensing with exterior walls eliminates the need for air-conditioning and limits electrical lighting requirements. It also lends the building a gravity-defying **flamboyance** and affords expansive views and an awe-inspiring feeling of connection to the city and the elements.

The team has made a contribution to Miami Beach by providing a valuable **amenity** and creating a landmark and a vibrant public space that transcends shopping. In doing so, they have also pulled off quite the **coup** by transporting an apartment above the fray on a fantastic **pedestal**. But most of all, they are helping break the mold for the lowly parking garage, lifting it up out of its gloomy **limbo** into the light and air.

(Adapted from *https://www.architecturalrecord.com / articles / 8232-lincoln-road*)

注释:

1. slab 平板,厚片
2. winding 蜿蜒曲折的
3. penthouse 阁楼,顶层公寓
4. canopy 天篷,遮篷
5. wedge 用楔子固定
6. boutique 精品店
7. double-duty 两种用途
8. whimsical 异想天开的,古怪的
9. buttress 扶壁,支撑力量
10. cantilever 悬臂
11. pedigree 血统,家谱
12. pockmark 麻面,凹坑
13. abound 大量存在,富于
14. brethren 同胞,兄弟
15. ruggedness 强度,坚固性
16. otherworldly 超凡脱俗地
17. pavilion 楼阁,亭子
18. promenade 散步长廊
19. vernacular 本国的,地方的
20. overhang 突出部分,伸出物
21. flamboyance 华丽,艳丽

22. amenity 舒适,便利
23. coup 妙计
24. pedestal 基座,基架
25. limbo 监狱,地狱边境

Word Power

Match the word with its appropriate meaning in English. Fill in the blanks with the letters in front of the words.

a. dedicated, b. adjacent, c. considerable, d. whimsical, e. humble, f. dispense, g. transcend

(1) ________ large or relatively large in number or amount or extent or degree
(2) ________ determined by chance or impulse rather than by necessity or reason
(3) ________ of low birth or station
(4) ________ devoted to a cause or ideal or purpose
(5) ________ administer or bestow, as in small portions
(6) ________ nearest in space or position

Summary

Fill in the blanks with words or phrases from the Reading Passage 1.

A multi-story car park is a building (1) ________ for car parking and where there are a number of floors or levels on which parking takes place. It is essentially an indoor, (2) ________ parking lot. Many car parks are independent buildings dedicated (3) ________ to that use.

In recent times, car parks built to serve (4) ________ and some business properties have been built as part of a larger building, often underground as part of the basement. This saves land for other uses (as opposed to a parking lot), is cheaper and more practical in most cases than a (5) ________ structure, and is hidden from view. Car parks which serve shopping centers can be built (6) ________ to the center for easier access at each floor between shops and parking.

These structures are not usually known for their (7) ________ value. However, a handful of parking garages have received (8) ________ praise for their design,

Listening

Scan the code and listen to a microlecture about the Nation on the Move—Driving in Dallas and Las Vegas, Driving in Los Angeles. Please choose the best answer to each of the following questions.

(1) Which is the better way of dealing with traffic pressure in Los Angles?

A. More roads. B. Fewer cars.

C. High price of oil. D. Mass transit.

(2) Which of the following is not the reason for traffic jam?

A. Cheap oil. B. More cars.

C. More neighborhoods. D. More highways.

(3)Which of the following blocked construction of new roads in 1940s?

A. Lack of technology. B. Lack of money.

C. Neighborhoods. D. Time pressure.

Speaking

How can people cope with traffic jam and congestion? Refer to the following words or expressions if necessary.

building more new roads / widen the roads / increase highway patrol / using technical device / monitor or traffic lights

Writing

1. Example Sentence

(1) These freeways were designed to cut through neighborhoods.

(2) You're looking at an old streetcar route that was paved over years ago and now it's being reclaimed for a new light rail line.

2. Analysis

通常情况下,主动式比被动式的使用范围更广。但有些句子更倾向于使用被动式。例如,当主语未知或不重要时,当受动者被强调或更重要时,或在一些描述科技或实验步骤等方面的文章中施动者没有必要出现,句子用被动式来表达会更准确、更恰当。如上例,主语分别为公路和轨道,谓语是设计和铺设、改造,施动者未知,强调的是动作的过程和结果,所以皆为被动句。

3. Practice

翻译下列句子。

(1) 那座旧房子拆了。

(2) 她觉得有人正在跟踪她。

(3) 这些大巴车是用来运送游客的。

第七章　用电大国

概　述

能源使人类的生活进入了现代化。能源产生电，人们在黑夜中有了电灯，工厂的机器能够转动；能源产生热能，人们在冬季有了温暖；能源可作为燃料，人类有了汽车、火车、飞机等各种交通工具。

美国是地球上人均能源消费量最高的国家。本章我们将看到美国巨大的能源机器如何为所有人提供能量；我们还将发现能源从何而来；人们如何利用它，人们又是如何浪费它的，如何把它送到全国各个家庭和工作场所。能源危机已经出现，能源的未来是什么？保持能源的持续供应对人类来说是一项艰巨的任务。人们对可持续能源的探索研究正处于最艰难的时刻，目前我们需要千方百计地节约能源以缓解能源危机。本章我们还将了解与能源相关的各种建筑，这些建筑不仅美观实用，还能最大限度地节省能源，体现了可持续发展的设计理念。

第一节　照明与建筑

本节介绍了照明对建筑的作用。照明是为了达到实用或美学效果。照明包括使用人工光源（如灯具和其他照明装置）以及自然光源。采光（使用窗户、天窗等）在白天被用作建筑物照明的主要方式，可以代替人工光源来节省能源，而人工光源是建筑能源消耗的一个主要组成部分。室内照明通常使用灯具来完成，这也是室内设计的关键部分。照明是建筑或景观项目的一个必不可少的组成部分。照明得当可以提高工作效率，改善区域外观，甚至对人产生积极的心理影响。

Culture Express

照明设计应用于建筑环境被称为“建筑照明设计”，包括使用自然光和人工光源。建筑照明涉及美学因素以及实际需要的光量、建筑物的居住者、能源效率和成本。建筑照明设计主要考虑建筑或空间照明的三个基本方面：建筑的美学作用、功效学以及能源效率问题。照明设计师将详细研究这三个方面的细节。在设计过程中通常还要考虑以下因素：需要照明的人类活动的种类、所需的光量、影响景观和整体环境的光色、光线在室内空间或室外空间的分布以及照明系统本身对受光者的影响。设计者要意识到，照明是否成功的最终标准是人类的反应——“是否清晰、直观、无不适”。照明设计师必须了解光产生和分布的原理、人类感知光的生理和心理过程、人眼的结构以及视杆细胞和视锥细胞对光的反应。

Reading Passage 1

导读

下文详细介绍了建筑照明设计的概念。

Extensive **luminaire** photometric designing calls for consideration of the amount of functional light present, the energy expended, as well as the aesthetic impact supplied by the lighting system. Some buildings, like surgical centers and sports facilities, are primarily concerned with providing the appropriate amount of light for the associated task. Some buildings, like warehouses and office buildings, are primarily concerned with saving money through the energy efficiency of the lighting system. Other buildings, like **casinos** and theatres, are primarily concerned with enhancing the appearance and emotional impact of architecture through lighting systems. Therefore, it is important that the sciences of light production and luminaire photometrics are balanced with the artistic application of light as a medium in our built environment. These electrical lighting systems should also consider the impacts of, and ideally be **integrated** with, daylighting systems. Factors involved in lighting design are essentially the same as those discussed above in energy **conservation.**

Architectural lighting design focuses on three fundamental aspects of the illumination of buildings or spaces. The first is the aesthetic appeal of a building, an aspect particularly important in the illumination of retail environments. Secondly, the **ergonomic** aspect: the measure of how much of a function the lighting plays. Thirdly is the energy efficiency issue to ensure that light is not wasted by over-illumination, either by illuminating vacant spaces unnecessarily or by providing more light than needed for the aesthetics or the task.

Each of these three aspects is looked at in considerable detail when the lighting designer is at work. In aesthetic appeal, the lighting designer attempts to raise the general attractiveness of the design, measure whether it should be subtly **blended into** the background or whether it should stand out, and assess what kind of emotions the lighting should evoke. The functional aspects of the project can **encompass** the need for the project to be visible (by night mostly, but also by day), the impact of daylight on the project and safety issues (glare, color confusion etc.).

(Adapted from *https://encyclopedia.thefreedictionary.com / Architectural + lighting + design*)

注释：

1. luminaire 光源，照明装置
2. casino 赌场，娱乐场
3. integrate 使完整，使结合
4. conservation 保护，保存
5. ergonomic 人类环境改造学的，人体工学的
6. blend into 融入，融合
7. encompass 包含；包围，环绕

Reading Passage 2

导读

下文介绍了照明设计的典范建筑之一——西格拉姆大厦。西格拉姆大厦位于纽约市曼哈顿中城第 52 街和第 53 街之间的公园大道 375 号。整座大厦包括石面大厅、独特的玻璃以及青铜色外观，全部由美国德裔建筑师路德维希·密斯·凡·德·罗(Ludwig Mies van der Rohe)设计。

The Seagram Building stands 515 feet (157 m) tall with 38 stories, and was completed in 1958. It stands as one of the most notable examples of the **functionalist** aesthetic and a prominent instance of corporate modernism.

This structure, and the International style in which it was built had enormous influences on American architecture. One of the style's characteristic **traits** was to express or **articulate** the structure of buildings externally. It was a style that argued that the functional utility of the building's structural elements when made visible, could **supplant** a formal decorative articulation; and more honestly converse with the public than any system of applied **ornamentation.**

The plaza created a procession to the entry of the building, providing the **threshold** that linked the city with the skyscraper. This threshold continues into the building as a horizontal plane in the plaza that cuts into the lobby. The lobby also has a white ceiling that stretches out over the entry doors further eroding the defined line between interior and exterior.

The office spaces above the lobby have flexible floor plans lit with **luminous ceiling** panels. These floors also get maximum natural lighting with the exterior being glass **panes** of gray **topaz** that provide floor-to-ceiling windows for the office spaces. The gray topaz glass was used for sun and heat protection, and although there are Venetian blinds for window coverings they could only be fixed in a limited number of positions so as to provide visual consistency from the outside.

The detailing of the exterior surface was carefully determined by the desired exterior expression Mies wanted to achieve. The metal bronze skin that is seen in the facade is nonstructural but is used to express the idea of the structural frame that is underneath.

Additional **vertical** elements were also welded to the window panels not only to **stiffen** the skin for installation and wind loading, but to aesthetically further enhance the vertical articulation of the building.

The Seagram Building, with its use of modern materials and setback from the city grid, became a **prototype** for future office buildings designed by Mies as well as a model for many buildings erected in its surroundings. This building, fifty years after its completion, is still admired by many visitors everyday and sets an example of an International style skyscraper amidst the New York skyline.

(Adapted from *https://encyclopedia.thefreedictionary.com / Seagram + Building*, *https://www.archdaily.com* / 59412 / *ad-classics-seagram-building-mies-van-der-rohe*)

注释:

1. functionalist 实用主义者,功能主义者
2. trait 特性,特点
3. articulate 明确表达,使相互连贯
4. supplant 取代,排挤掉
5. ornamentation 装饰物
6. threshold 入口,门槛
7. luminous ceiling 流明天花板,发光顶棚
8. pane 窗格
9. topaz 黄玉,托帕石
10. vertical 垂直的
11. stiffen 变硬
12. prototype 原型;标准,模范

Word Power

Match the word with its appropriate meaning in English. Fill in the blanks with the letters in front of the words.

a. luminaire b. integrate c. conservation d. vacant e. trait f. articulate g. decorative h. vertical

(1) ________ an occurrence of improvement by virtue of preventing loss or injury or other change

(2) ________ express or state clearly

(3) ________ empty; not being used

(4) ________ a complete electric light unit

(5) ________ serving an aesthetic rather than a useful purpose

(6) ________ a distinguishing quality

(7) ________ make into a whole or make part of a whole

(8) ________ at right angles to the plane of the horizon or a base line

Summary

Fill in the blanks with words or phrases from the Reading Passage 1.

Extensive (1)________ photometric designing calls for consideration of the amount of (2)________ light present, the energy expended, as well as the (3)________ impact supplied by the lighting system. Therefore, it is important that the sciences of light production and luminaire photometrics are balanced with the artistic application of light as a medium in our built environment. These electrical lighting systems should also consider the impacts of, and ideally be (4) ________ with, daylighting systems. Factors involved in lighting design are essentially the same as those discussed above in energy (5) ________.

In aesthetic (6) ________, the lighting designer attempts to raise the general attractiveness of the design, measure whether it should be subtly (7)________ into the background or whether it should stand out, and assess what kind of emotions the lighting should evoke. The functional aspects of the project can (8) ________ the need for the project to be visible (by night mostly, but also by day), the impact of daylight on the project and safety issues (glare, color confusion etc.).

Listening

Scan the code and listen to a microlecture about the Electric Nation—New Energy Awareness and Nuclear Energy. Please choose the best answer to each of the following questions.

(1) Which of the following is renewable source?

A. Nuclear power. B. Methane gas.

C. Coal. D. Natural Gas.

(2) When did the first commercial reactor came online?

A. In 1962. B. In 1957.

C. In 1948. D. In 1969.

(3) Who created America's first central power plant?

A. Einstein. B. Washington.

C. Franklin. D. Edison.

Speaking

How important is energy to people's lives? Without energy what would happen? Refer to the following words and expressions if necessary.

keep the lights on / keep the homes heated / vehicles / modern lives / no electricity or gasoline / life in darkness and cold

Writing

1. Example Sentence

(1) **With** their powerful engines, these cars will burn through nearly 10,000 gallons of gasoline.

(2) **With** the project finished, he began to look for a new challenge.

2. Analysis

(1) 介词 with＋名词,表示"带着……"或"怀有……",通常放在句首作状语,与主句之间的关系为因果关系。

(2) 类似的结构是介词 with＋名词＋补语,表示"随着"或"由于"。

3. Practice

翻译下列句子。

(1) 怀着对工作的热情和细心,他努力成了一名出色的医生。

(2) 钱花光了,我必须去找份工作。

(3) 孩子们都长大了,那对夫妻开始环球旅行。

第二节　电,从哪里来

如果为国家电网供电的能源或用作汽车燃料的能源严重不足,就将产生能源危机。近年来,工业发展和人口增长导致全球能源需求激增。人类步入 21 世纪以来,这种新的需求,连同中东局势紧张、美元贬值、石油储备减少、石油峰值论以及油价投机等共同引发了新世纪的能源危机。

当前,人类能源结构正在逐步由不可再生能源向可再生能源转变。本节我们将了解能源危机产生的原因和政府的应对措施,并简单了解与水力发电和太阳能发电相关的建筑。

Culture Express

能源危机的原因以及带给人类的思索

能源危机的产生原因是多方面的。其中最主要的就是工业发展和市场发展的需求。政府采取的一系列措施,例如增税、能源公司国有化和能源部门监管等,使能源供求偏离经济平衡。当市场出现垄断时，市场调节就有可能失效。工会组织的罢工和政府的禁运等劳工行动也可能引发危机。由于过度消耗、基础设施老化、炼油厂和运输港口设施停滞等限制了燃料供应，或者用于取暖的能耗增加，在寒冷的冬季就可能会出现能源紧张的情况。这些都是能源危机的成因。

能源危机对人类社会的影响是方方面面的。由供应震荡引发的能源危机对宏观经济的影响很大，将影响其他各行各业的所有资源。当能源市场瘫痪时，能源短缺必然出现。对消费者来说，用于汽车和其他交通工具的燃料价格将上涨。电力短缺直接体现在供暖、烹饪以及水资源供应上。因此，持续的能源危机可能演变为人道主义危机。大到核电站，小到电热毯，能源短缺的现象将影响公众的态度。

如果能源短缺的现象持续不断，政府将进入危机管理阶段。政府可进行能源审核，以监察能源的使用情况。为了保护能源，政府或将实行各种宵禁措施以减少电量消耗。例如，为了应对中亚能源危机、节约电力，塔吉克斯坦当局曾下令酒吧和咖啡馆在烛光下营业。在严重的能源危机中，社会可能需要实行能源配给和燃料配给，许多设施为节省取暖用油而关闭；人们可能出现恐慌性购买；工厂削减生产量，解雇工人；通货膨胀加剧。

人们正在努力寻求新技术来提高能源利用效率。其他应对措施包括开发非常规石油资源，如合成燃料、商业化的可再生能源以及使用替代技术。另外，能源供应还可以依靠小型发电机组及水力、太阳能和其他绿色能源。建筑施工技术，例如保温隔热，使用反光屋顶、热效率高的窗户等，都可以降低能源消耗。

Reading Passage 1

导读

胡佛水坝是美国最著名的水力发电站。胡佛水坝位于美国亚利桑那州和内华达州交界处的科罗拉多河布莱克峡谷。它建于 1931～1936 年的大萧条时期，并于 1935 年 9 月 30 日由富兰克林·罗斯福总统主持落成。胡佛水坝蓄积了美国最大的水库——米德湖。大坝的发电机为内华达州、亚利桑那州和加利福尼亚州的公共和私人设施提供电力。胡佛水坝还是一个重要的旅游景点，每年有近 100 万人参观。本文主要介绍了胡佛水坝的设计和建筑特点。

Denver artist Allen Tupper True was hired to handle the design and decoration of the walls and floors of the new dam. True's design scheme incorporated **motifs** of the Navajo and Pueblo tribes of the region. True researched **authentic** decorative motifs from Indian sand paintings, textiles, baskets and **ceramics.** The images and colors are based on Native American visions of rain, lightning, water, clouds, and local animals—lizards, **serpents**, birds—and on the Southwestern landscape of stepped **mesas.** In these works, which are integrated into the walkways and interior halls of the dam, True also reflected on the machinery of the operation, making the symbolic patterns appear both ancient and modern.

True also devised an **innovative** color-coding for the pipes and machinery, which was **implemented** throughout all BOR projects. True's work on the Hoover Dam was humorously referred to in a poem published in *The New Yorker*, part of which read, "lose the spark, and justify the dream; but also worthy of remark will be the color scheme."

The Norwegian-born, naturalized American sculptor Oskar J.W. Hansen designed many of the sculptures on and around the dam. His works include the monument of dedication plaza, a **plaque** to memorialize the workers killed and the **bas-reliefs** on the elevator towers. In his words, Hansen wanted his work to express "the **immutable** calm of intellectual resolution, and the enormous power of trained physical strength, equally enthroned in **placid** triumph of scientific accomplishment", because "the building of Hoover Dam belongs to the sagas of the daring." Hansen's dedication plaza, on the Nevada abutment, contains a sculpture of two winged figures **flanking** a flagpole.

Surrounding the base of the monument is a **terrazzo** floor embedded with a "star map." The map depicts the Northern Hemisphere sky at the moment of President Roosevelt's dedication of the dam. This is intended to help future astronomers, if necessary, calculate the exact date of dedication. The 30 feet (9.1 m) high bronze figures, dubbed "Winged Figures of the Republic", were each formed in a continuous pour. To put such large bronzes into place without marring the highly polished bronze surface, they were placed on ice and guided into position as the ice melted. Hansen's bas-relief on the Nevada elevator tower depicts the benefits of the dam: flood control, navigation, irrigation, water storage, and power. The bas-relief on the Arizona elevator depicts, in his words, "the **visages** of those Indian tribes who have inhabited mountains and plains from ages distant."

(Adapted from *https://encyclopedia.thefreedictionary.com / Hoover+Dam*)

注释:

1. motif 图案,纹样
2. authentic 真正的,逼真的
3. ceramics 陶瓷工艺,陶瓷制品
4. serpent 巨蛇,巨蟒
5. mesa 台地,方山
6. innovative 革新的,新颖的
7. implement 实施,执行
8. plaque 牌匾,饰板
9. bas-relief 浮雕
10. immutable 不可变的
11. placid 平静的,温和的
12. flank 在侧面
13. terrazzo 水磨石
14. visage 容貌,外表

Reading Passage 2

导读

下文介绍了一种新型建筑模式——被动式太阳能建筑。

In **passive solar building** design, windows, walls, and floors are made to collect, store, and distribute solar energy in the form of heat in the winter and reject solar heat in the summer. This is called passive solar design or climatic design because, unlike active solar heating systems, it doesn't involve the use of mechanical and electrical devices.

The key to designing a passive solar building is to best take advantage of the local climate. Elements to be considered include window placement and **glazing** type, **thermal insulation**, thermal mass, and **shading**. Passive solar design techniques can be applied most easily to new buildings, but existing buildings can be "**retrofitted.**"

Passive solar technologies use sunlight without active mechanical systems (as contrasted to active solar). Such technologies **convert** sunlight **into** usable heat (in water, air, and thermal mass), cause air-movement for ventilating, or future use, with little use of other energy sources. A common example is a **solarium** on the equator-side of a building. Passive cooling is the use of the same design principles to reduce summer cooling requirements.

Some passive systems use a small amount of **conventional** energy to control **dampers**, **shutters**, night insulation, and other devices that enhance solar energy collection, storage, and use, and reduce undesirable heat transfer.

Passive solar technologies include direct and indirect solar gain for space heating, solar water heating systems based on the **thermosiphon**, use of thermal mass and phase-change materials for slowing indoor air temperature swings, solar cookers, the solar chimney for enhancing natural ventilation, and earth sheltering.

More widely, passive solar technologies include the solar furnace and solar forge, but these typically require some external energy for **aligning** their concentrating mirrors or receivers, and historically have not proven to be practical or cost effective for widespread use. "Low-grade" energy needs, such as space and water heating, have proven, over time, to be better applications for passive use of solar energy.

(Adapted from *https://encyclopedia.thefreedictionary.com / passive + solar + building + design*)

注释：

1. passive solar building 被动式太阳能建筑
2. glazing 玻璃装配，上釉
3. thermal insulation 热绝缘，隔热

4. shading 遮光网(篷、漆)
5. retrofit 改进,设计更新
6. convert...into... 把……转化成……
7. solarium 日光浴室
8. conventional 传统的,惯例的
9. damper 风门,气闸;阻尼器;减震器
10.shutter 百叶窗,遮板
11.thermosiphon 温差环流系统;热虹吸管
12.align 排列

Word Power

Match the word with its appropriate meaning in English. Fill in the blanks with the letters in front of the words.

a. authentic b. implement c. flank d. visage e. insulation f. retrofit g. convert h. align

(1) ________ a material that reduces or prevents the transmission of heat or sound or electricity

(2) ________ be located at the sides of something or somebody

(3) ________ change the nature, purpose, or function of something

(4) ________ the human face or the appearance conveyed by a person's face

(5) ________ place in a line or arrange so as to be parallel or straight

(6) ________ conforming to fact and therefore worthy of belief

(7) ________ fit in or on an existing structure, such as an older house

(8) ________ apply in a manner consistent with its purpose or design

Summary

Fill in the blanks with words or phrases from the Reading Passage 2.

In passive solar building design, windows, walls, and floors are made to collect, store, and (1) ________ solar energy in the form of heat in the winter and (2) ________ solar heat in the summer. This is called passive solar design or climatic design because, unlike (3) ________ solar heating systems, it doesn't (4) ________ the use of mechanical and electrical devices. The key to designing a passive solar building is to best take advantage of the local climate.

Passive solar technologies use sunlight without active (5) ________ systems (as contrasted to active solar). Such technologies (6) ________ sunlight into usable heat (in water, air, and thermal mass), cause air-movement for ventilating, or future use, with little use of other energy (7) ________.

Passive solar technologies include direct and indirect solar gain for space heating, solar water heating systems based on the thermosiphon, use of thermal mass and phase-change materials for slowing indoor air temperature swings, solar cookers, the solar chimney for enhancing natural (8) ________, and earth sheltering.

Listening

Scan the code and listen to a microlecture about the Power Grid and the Coal Energy. Please choose the best answer to each of the following questions.

(1) Which of the following is not one of the possible reasons for lines damaged?

A.A lightning strike.　　B. Being old.

C.Blackout.　　D. Corroding.

(2)Which of the following was not one of the consequences of New York blackout mentioned in the video clip?

A. People had to walk.

B. There were no phone service, no computers, no cellphones.

C. 80% of the people were left without power.

D. People had no food to eat.

(3) Most power plants are still burning the same ancient fuel which is ________.

A. natural gas　　B. coal

C. nuclear　　D. oil

Speaking

What do you think of fossil fuels? While providing people with energy, what disadvantages has it brought to human beings and the environment as well? Refer to the following words and expressions if necessary.

abundant / reliable and cheap / run out sooner or later / pollution / security risks

Writing

1. Example Sentence

You might think that would have killed coal mining, but not here in Wyoming.

2. Analysis

这句话的意思是:你可能认为那已经导致了煤矿的关闭,但在怀俄明州不是这样。句子使用了虚拟语气,来表达与事实相反的情况,表示其不太可能发生或不能确定。注意谓语部分的时态为 would+have+done,表示应该已经发生了什么,而实际上却没有发生。

3. Practice

翻译下列句子。

(1) If the dam **collapsed**, many acres of good farmland **would** disappear.

(2) If this **had** not been allowed to happen, the dam **would not have** collapsed.

(3) Without music, the world would be a dull place.

第三节　可持续性建筑设计

为了节约能源,建筑物的设计越来越倾向于降低能源消耗,并且最大限度地使用可再生能源。由此衍生出了多种多样的建筑设计理念,例如可持续性建筑、绿色建筑、自然建筑以及零能耗建筑等。可持续性建筑指的是建筑及其内部的设施具有环保责任性并能高效地利用资源,这体现在绿色建筑的整个生命周期中,包括从规划到设计、施工、运营、维护、改造和拆除。整个过程需要承包商、建筑师、工程师和客户在所有项目阶段密切合作。这些不断创新的建筑设计更注重建筑物的经济性、实用性、耐用性和舒适性,拓展并补充了传统。

Culture Express

节约能源

节能是指减少某种能源的消耗。节能不同于高效利用能源;少开车是节能,如何利用等量的能源行驶更远的里程则是高效利用能源。二者都属于节能技术。

尽管节能减少了对某种能源的使用,可能给人们的生活带来少许不便,但它可以改善环境质量,节省经济成本。节能在可持续能源体系中处于重要位置,降低能源的消耗有利于防止未来的资源枯竭。

在建筑方面,节能的主要方法之一是进行能源审计。能源审计是对建筑物、工序或某个系统的能源使用情况进行检查和分析,以减少能源输入,从而避免输出的负面影响。能源审计通常是由训练有素的专业人员完成,并经过国家计划项目讨论。此外,智能手机中的应用程序也能使房主独立完成相对复杂的能源审计。建筑技术和智能仪表可以让企业和住户以图形方式看到能源使用对工作场所或家庭的影响。先进的实时能源审计能够帮助人们采取正确的措施来节约能源。

Reading Passage 1

导读

下文介绍了可持续性建筑的设计理念及其某些方面的不可行性。可持续性建筑通过对材料、能源、发展空间和整个生态系统的有效利用和适度使用,将建筑对环境的负面影响最小化。可持续性建筑在设计中有意识地考虑到环境的能源使用和生态保护等问题。但由于政策、法规等原因,可持续性建筑的实现还面临多方面的障碍。

The design of sustainable architecture is focused on making a building energy-efficient, so as to reduce its energy consumption, water consumption, operating costs, and environmental impact. Such efficiencies include the maximal use of natural lighting,

low-e glass, solar electric systems, energy-efficient lighting systems, energy-efficient ventilation systems including the use of the **chimney effect**, and newer sustainable materials and techniques that minimize heat loss in buildings.

The idea of sustainability, or ecological design, is to ensure that our actions and decisions today do not inhibit the opportunities of future generations.

Energy efficiency over the entire life cycle of a building is the most important goal of sustainable architecture. Architects use many different passive and active techniques to reduce the energy needs of buildings and increase their ability to capture or generate their own energy.

There is no doubt Green Technology has made its **headway** into the architectural community, and the implementation of given technologies have changed the ways we see and perceive modern day architecture. While green architecture has been proven to show great improvements of ways of living both environmentally and technologically the question remains—is all this sustainable? Many building codes have been **demeaned** to international standards. "LEED" (Leadership in Energy & Environmental Design) has been criticized for exercising flexible codes for building to follow. Contractors do this to save as much money as they possibly can. With companies cutting paths to make shortcuts with sustainable architecture when building their structures it fuels to the irony that the "sustainable" architecture isn't sustainable at all. Sustainability comes in reference to longevity and effectiveness.

Ethics and Politics also play into sustainable architecture and its ability to grow in urban environment. Conflicting viewpoints between engineering techniques and environmental impacts still are popular issues that **resonate** in the architectural community. With every revolutionary technology or innovation, there comes criticisms of **legitimacy** and effectiveness when and how it is being utilized. Many of the criticisms of sustainable architecture do not reflect every aspect of it, but rather a broader **spectrum** across the international community.

(Adapted from *https://encyclopedia.thefreedictionary.com / Sustainable + architecture*)

注释：

1. low-e glass 低辐射玻璃，建筑节能玻璃
2. chimney effect 烟囱效应，抽吸效应
3. headway 前进，进步
4. demean 降低，贬抑
5. resonate 共鸣
6. legitimacy 合法，正统
7. spectrum 范围，光谱，频谱

Reading Passage 2

导读

下文介绍了自然建筑的设计特点。

A similar concept to green building is natural building, which is usually on a smaller scale and tends to focus on the use of natural materials that are available locally. A natural building involves a range of building systems and materials that place major emphasis on sustainability. Ways of achieving sustainability through natural building focus on durability and the use of minimally processed, plentiful or renewable resources, as well as those that, while recycled or **salvaged**, produce healthy living environments and maintain indoor air quality. Natural building tends to rely on human labor, more than technology. As Michael G. Smith observes, it depends on "local ecology, geology and climate; on the character of the particular building site, and on the needs and personalities of the builders and users."

The basis of natural building is the need to lessen the environmental impact of buildings and other supporting systems, without sacrificing comfort or health. To be more sustainable, natural building uses primarily abundantly available, renewable, reused or recycled materials. The use of rapidly renewable materials is increasingly a focus. In addition to relying on natural building materials, the emphasis on the architectural design is **heightened**. The **orientation** of a building, the utilization of local climate and site conditions, the emphasis on natural ventilation through design, fundamentally lessen operational costs and positively impact the environmental. Building **compactly** and minimizing the ecological footprint is common, as are on-site handling of energy acquisition, on-site water capture, alternate sewage treatment and water reuse.

The materials common to many types of natural building are clay and sand. When mixed with water and, usually, straw or another fiber, the mixture may form cob or **adobe** (clay blocks). Other materials commonly used in natural building are: earth (as **rammed** earth or earth bag), wood (**cordwood** or **timber frame**/**post-and-beam**), straw, **rice-hulls**, bamboo and stone. A wide variety of reused or recycled **non-toxic** materials are common in natural building, including urbanite (salvaged chunks of used concrete), vehicle windscreens and other recycled glass.

(Adapted from *https://encyclopedia.thefreedictionary.com/Natural+building*)

注释：

1. salvage 回收；抢救
2. heighten 增高；加强
3. orientation 定向；方向

4. compactly 紧密地，简洁地
5. adobe（建筑用）黏土，土砖
6. ram 夯实，捣实
7. cordwood（建筑用）堆积材
8. timber frame 木构架
9. post-and-beam 柱梁
10. rice-hull 稻壳
11. non-toxic 无毒的

Word Power

Match the word with its appropriate meaning in English. Fill in the blanks with the letters in front of the words.

a. sustainable b. consumption c. acquisition d. compact
e. orientation f. salvage g. legitimacy h. inhibit

(1) ________ the act of assuming or acquiring possession of something
(2) ________ the act of determining one's position
(3) ________ involving the use of natural products and energy in a way that does not harm the environment
(4) ________ lawfulness by virtue of being authorized or in accordance with law
(5) ________ the utilization of economic goods to satisfy needs or in manufacturing
(6) ________ closely and firmly united or packed together
(7) ________ limit the range or extent of
(8) ________ collect discarded or refused material

Summary

Fill in the blanks with words or phrases from the Reading Passage 2.

A natural building involves a (1) ________ of building systems and materials that place major emphasis on (2) ________. Natural building tends to rely on human labor, more than technology. The basis of natural building is the need to (3) ________ the environmental impact of buildings and other supporting systems, without (4) ________ comfort or health. To be more sustainable, natural building uses primarily abundantly available, renewable, reused or recycled materials. In addition to relying on natural building materials, the emphasis on the architectural design is heightened. The (5) ________ of a building, the utilization of local climate and site conditions, the emphasis on natural ventilation through design, fundamentally lessen operational costs and positively impact the environmental.

Listening

Scan the code and listen to a microlecture about the Electric Nation—Wind and Solar Energy, Methane Gas. Please choose the best answer to each of the following questions.

(1) Which of the following technology is taking off so fast that by mid-century it could surpass coal as the number-one power source on the grid?

A. Solar. B. Nuclear.

C. Wind. D. Oil.

(2) Which of the following is not mentioned by pastor Earl Trent in his speech about solar energy?

A. Renewable energy. B. Lowered cost.

C. Energy efficiency. D. Energy conservation.

(3) Which of the following is not a drawback of making electricity by using methane gas?

A. It doesn't come cheap.

B. It doesn't need to dig, drill or pipe in.

C. It can't provide enough energy for the whole country.

D. It needs millions of cows to make sufficient electricity.

Speaking

Do you know anything about renewable resources for energy, such as wind, solar and methane gas? What are the advantages and drawbacks of them? Refer to the following words and expressions if necessary.

renewable / clean / not enough / volatile / technical or mechanical problems

Writing

1. Example Sentences

(1) I've come to the Columbia River gorge myself to get a closer look at what's driving this phenomenal growth of wind power.

(2) It represents a small but growing trend that's changing **how** we get our power.

2. Analysis

例1的意思是:我独自来到哥伦比亚河谷,近距离观察到底是什么使风能发展得如此迅速。例2的意思是:它代表了一种虽小但不断发展的趋势,它改变了我们获得能源的方式。两句话中都出现了宾语从句,其分别由“what”和“how”引导,是名词性从句,充当“look at”和“change”的宾语。

3. Practice

翻译下列句子。

(1)老师不知道他们什么时候才能交上作业。

(2)妈妈问我饿不饿。

(3)彼得问我那个女孩住在哪里。

第八章　改变美国的建筑

概　述

在本章中，我们将带你穿越美国，发现建筑物建造之初其背后或令人震惊或怪诞或伤感的故事。这是一次探索之旅、时间之旅，也是建筑师的想象力之旅。这些建筑物改变了现代美国人的生活、工作和娱乐方式。为什么很多美国的公共建筑都拥有希腊罗马神庙的外观？风靡全球的室内购物商场缘何起源于美国的郊区？是谁开创了这些设计先河？答案将在本章中一一被揭晓。本章所介绍的建筑物有：美国公共建筑物的代表——弗吉尼亚州议会大厦和波士顿三一教堂，摩天大楼的鼻祖——温莱特大厦以及室内购物中心的起源——南谷购物中心。

第一节　弗吉尼亚州议会大厦

法国作家雨果曾说："建筑是石头的史书。"建筑总能唤起我们对诸多历史和故事的好奇。美国的建筑风格，正如美国这个国家，是各种风格的混合。不像欧洲的建筑风格那样一步步逐渐发展演变而来，美国在同一时期接纳了许多种成熟的建筑风格，它们相互之间又有融合和影响。弗吉尼亚州议会大厦就是如此。而且，作为承前启后的重要建筑，在它之后的很多公共建筑都受其影响。

Culture Express

由托马斯·杰弗逊等人设计的弗吉尼亚州议会大厦开放于1785年。为了纪念美国独立战争的胜利，杰弗逊和法国建筑师按照法国南部一座罗马神庙的样子在弗吉尼亚州的里士满建造了弗吉尼亚州议会大厦。

托马斯·杰弗逊虽然出身贵族，但他一生都是平民治国理念的追随者和实践者。"人人生而平等"是著名的《独立宣言》的开篇，它用简单有力的语言向古往今来的权贵和不平等发出了呐喊。作为其建筑成名作，弗吉尼亚州议会大厦完全摒弃了殖民地时期的建筑风格，是杰弗逊从建筑角度向英国发出的独立宣言，宣告美国将不再依附于大英帝国。

Reading Passage 1

导读

美国50个州拥有各自的议会大厦，其内涵与独特性使其都称得上是每个州的门面。下文介绍了弗吉尼亚州议会大厦作为公共建筑物的主要特色和设计师的灵感来源等相关信息。

The Virginia State Capitol is the seat of state government of the Commonwealth of Virginia, located in Richmond, the third capital city of the U.S. state of Virginia. It houses the oldest elected **legislative** body in North America.

As the designer of the Virginia State Capitol, Thomas Jefferson, the founding father of the United States, was passionate about America's independence from Britain. He didn't like the king of England and was no fan of the **Georgian architecture** which bore the name of the English king. So this building was more like his **Dear John Letter** to the Great Britain.

When the state of Virginia needed a new government building, Thomas Jefferson—a **self-taught** architect and former governor of that state—**took his inspiration from** a classical Roman temple in southern France, **Maison Carrée** dating back to 16 B.C. When he was invited to design the building, he served as America's minister to France at that time. He fell in love with Maison Carrée the first time he saw it and was thoroughly **entranced** by this monumental ancient structure, writing about his first face-to-face encounter with the temple, "Here I am, gazing whole hours at the Maison Carrée, like a lover at his mistress."

Given its Classical Revival style of architecture along with the fact that its color is white, the Virginia State Capitol was seen in many films. The Capitol was the **double** for the exterior shots of the White House featured in the movie *The Contender* (2000) starring Gary Oldman, Jeff Bridges, Christian Slater.

In the 2012 film ***Lincoln***, the Virginia State Capitol was used as a **stand-in** for the United States Capitol in Washington D.C. during the Civil War era and the exteriors of the White House. Filming took place in Richmond, Fredericksburg, and Petersburg, Virginia. In reference to Petersburg, according to location manager Colleen Gibbons, "one thing that attracted the filmmakers to the city was the 180-degree vista of historic structures," which is "very rare."

(Adapted from *http://www.virginiaplaces.org/vacities/26capitals.html*)

注释：

1.legislative 立法的

2.Georgian architecture 乔治风格建筑（代指殖民地时期英式风格建筑）

3.Dear John Letter 分手信

4.self-taught 自学成才的

5.take inspiration from 从……中获得灵感

6.Maison Carrée 方形神殿(位于法国南部尼姆的一座古代建筑,是保存状态最为良好的古罗马时期神殿建筑之一)

7.entranced 着迷的,狂喜的

8.double、stand-in 替身

9.*Lincoln*《林肯》,上映于2012年的电影,讲述了美国第16任总统经历南北战争,维护美国统一的故事。影片主要的取景地是弗吉尼亚州的里士满,该片选取了多个当地场景和地点,其中就包括弗吉尼亚州议会大厦

Reading Passage 2

导读

弗吉尼亚州是一个“盛产”总统的州,美国建国以来有八位总统诞生于此。所以在弗吉尼亚州,有很多的总统故居。除了杰弗逊亲自设计建造的自家庄园蒙蒂塞洛(Monticello)之外,美国开国总统乔治·华盛顿(George Washington)的庄园——弗农山庄(Mount Vernon)也位于弗吉尼亚州。本文介绍了弗农山庄的相关信息。

The building began as a one and one-half stories house built in 1734 by George Washington's father, Augustine Washington. When George Washington's ancestors acquired the estate, it was known as Little Hunting Creek Plantation, after the nearby Little Hunting Creek. However, when Washington's older half-brother, Lawrence Washington, inherited it, he changed its name to Mount Vernon in honor of Vice Admiral Edward Vernon who was a very famous **admiral** and had been Lawrence's **commanding officer** in the British Royal Navy.

George Washington had been in very good relation with his half-brother. But sadly, Lawrence died pretty young and George Washington inherited the property and retained the name.

George Washington began running Mount Vernon in 1754, and over the next 45 years he slowly enlarged the dwelling to create the 21-room **residence** we see today. Washington oversaw each renovation, advising on design, construction, and decoration, despite being away much of the time. Conscious that the world was watching, Washington selected architectural features that expressed his growing status as a Virginia gentleman and ultimately as the leader of a new nation.

On December 12, 1799, Washington spent several hours riding over the plantation, in snow, hail and freezing rain. He ate his supper later that evening without changing from his wet clothes. The following day, he awoke with a severe **sore throat** and became increasingly hoarse as the day progressed. All the available medical treatments failed to improve his condition, and he died at Mount Vernon on December 14, 1799, aged 67.

On December 18, 1799, a funeral was held at Mount Vernon, where his body was interred. Congress passed a joint resolution to construct a marble monument in the United States Capitol for his body, an initiative supported by Martha. Southerners who wanted his body to remain at Mount Vernon defeated the measure.

(Adapted from *https://www.tripsee.travel/destinations/United + States/Oregon/Mount+Vernon*)

注释:

1.admiral 海军将领

2.commanding officer 指挥官

3.residence 住宅,住处

4.sore throat 咽喉痛

Word Power

Match the word with its appropriate meaning in English.

a.vista, b.self-taught, c.neoclassical, d.passionate, e.monumental

(1)________ having or showing strong feelings of enthusiasm for something or belief in something

(2)________ acquire knowledge or skills on one's own

(3)________ very important and having a great influence, especially as the result of years of work

(4)________ art and architecture that is based on the style of ancient Greece or Rome, or music, literature, etc. that uses traditional ideas or styles

(5)________ a beautiful view, for example, of the countryside, a city, etc

Summary

Fill in the blanks with words or phrases from Reading Passage 1.

Designer	Designed by the founding father ________.
Function	Served as (2)________ of the state of Virginia.
Inspiration	Took inspiration from a classical Roman temple in southern France,(3) ________.
Influence	The declaration of (4) ________ from British architecture.
Films	As stand-in mainly for (5)________ and (6) ________ in films like *The Contender* and *Lincoln*.

Listening

Scan the code and listen to a microlecture about Virginia State Capitol. Please choose the best answer to each of the following questions.

(1) Virginia State Capitol is located in ________.

A. Richmond B. Washington

C. New York D. Williamsburg

(2) Which of the following man is one of the America's Founding Fathers?

A. Thomas Jefferson. B. Abraham Lincoln.

C. Franklin Roosevelt. D. Theodore Roosevelt.

(3) Which of the following is not the distinctive features of the Virginia State Capitol?

A. Symmetry. B. Column.

C. White color. D. Round dome.

Speaking

In the previous sections, the distinctive features of the Virginia State Capitol have been introduced. Please summarize the architecture styles by yourself. Can you think of some public architectures in America which share similar designs? Please refer to the following words and expressions if necessary.

Greek and Roman architecture / column / temple / public building

Writing

1. Example Sentence

This was always intended **that there would be these magnificent front steps.**

2. Analysis

(1)指示代词 this 代指后面的从句"that there would be these magnificent front steps"。

(2)本句也可改写为："These magnificent front steps were always included in his design."。

(3)当句子的主语相对较长时，为了避免头重脚轻通常用一个代词来代替，而将真正的主语放在后面。常见的句式有 This is... that... / It is... that... 等。

3. Practice

翻译下面的句子。

一直以来我的梦想是毕业后当一名外交官。

第二节　波士顿三一教堂

公共建筑三一教堂位于马萨诸塞州的波士顿。波士顿(Boston)创建于1630年,是美国马萨诸塞州的首府和最大城市,也是美国东北部新英格兰地区的最大城市。波士顿三一教堂位于波士顿公共图书馆美威大楼的前方,初建于1733年,是一座典雅的哥特复兴式教堂,被毁于1872年的大火;现在的教堂重建于1877年,是第一座理查德森罗马式(Richardsonian Romanesque)风格的建筑。

Culture Express

纵观波士顿的历史,自由和教育一直是其发展的基石。

16～17世纪,很多欧洲的新教徒无法忍受欧洲大陆的宗教迫害,远渡重洋来到美洲大陆,为的就是追求宗教自由与和平。1630年,欧洲大陆第一批清教徒来到了现在的波士顿并将之称为"高山上的城市"(a city on the hill),希望未来的世界会崇拜这座城市。此外,作为美国最古老、最有文化价值的城市之一,波士顿同时也是美国东北部高等教育和医疗保健的中心,是全美人均受教育程度最高的城市,拥有哈佛大学、麻省理工学院等众多知名高等学府。清教徒到达波士顿仅五年后便建立了波士顿拉丁学校,这也是美国最古老的公立学校。它是美国最好的高中之一,有四位美国总统、四位马萨诸塞州的州长毕业于该校。由此可见,教育在为这座美国最古老的城市不断注入新的活力。

Reading Passage 1

导读

波士顿三一教堂位于波士顿市中心科普利广场(Copley Square)中央。科普利广场地处波士顿最繁华地带,周边矗立着许多重要建筑。其中位于东侧的三一教堂最为亮眼,玫瑰色的朱砂外墙和橘黄色的罗马式屋顶相得益彰。

Boston is one of the oldest municipalities in the United States with its long history. The first settlers arrived here are puritans from the European continent who had come here to seek religious freedom. In Boston's Back Bay at Copley Square sits the architecturally **stunning** Trinity Church. The Back Bay neighborhood was once underwater before being filled in with land. The church actually rests on over 4,000 **wooden piles** that were put underneath fill and clay to keep the church's foundation strong.

Built from 1872 to 1877, Trinity Church is part of the Episcopal Diocese of Massachusetts **parish**. After the parish's church on Summer Street had been burned down in the Great Boston Fire of 1872, construction on the new church began—one in the shape of a modified Greek cross—under the direction of Rector Phillips Brooks, a well-known preacher at the time.

Designed by Henry Hobson Richardson in a **Richardsonian Romanesque** style, Trinity Church is considered the birthplace of this architectural style, and its signature features include a **clay roof, arches, rough stones, and towers.** The style has since been used in many other buildings in the United States.

Inside Trinity Church, there are brightly colored **murals** that cover over 20,000 square feet. While the windows were clear glass at first, they are now beautiful **stained-glass murals.** The church is considered one of the "Ten Most Significant Buildings in the United States" and is the only church in the nation with that honor.

(Adapted from *https://theculturetrip.com / north-america / usa / massachusetts / articles / a-brief-history-of-trinity-church-boston /*)

注释:

1.stunning 眩晕的,极好的
2.wooden piles 木桩
3.parish 教区
4.Richardsonian Romanesque 理查德森罗马式
5.clay roof 黏土屋顶
6.arch 穹顶
7.rough stone 粗糙的石材
8.tower 塔楼
9.mural 壁画
10.stained-glass mural 装饰玻璃壁画

Reading Passage 2

导读

波士顿所在的马萨诸塞州作为欧洲移民最早的定居地之一,一直被视为自由、民主的典范。这一点在建筑上深有体现,在科普利广场中央,古典建筑三一教堂和有着现代玻璃幕墙的汉考克大厦和谐共存。然而,那些曾饱受宗教迫害之苦的人们所理解的宗教自由,似乎只是他们自己所属教派的自由,而不是普遍的宗教自由。虽然他们痛恨其他教派的宗教迫害,但一旦自己获得了自由,在镇压"异端"时便一点也不手软了。在马萨诸塞的一个小镇塞勒姆,就发生了北美殖民地历史上著名塞勒姆的女巫案。

In January 1692, 9-year-old Elizabeth Parris and 11-year-old Abigail Williams (the daughter and niece of Samuel Parris, minister of Salem Village) began having **fits**, including violent contortions and uncontrollable outbursts of screaming. After a local doctor diagnosed **bewitchment**, other young girls in the community began to exhibit similar symptoms. In late February, arrest warrants were issued for a slave, Tituba, along with two other women—the homeless beggar Sarah Good and the poor, elderly Sarah Osborn—whom the girls accused of bewitching them.

The three accused witches were brought before the **magistrates** Jonathan Corwin and John Hathorne and questioned, even as their accusers appeared in the courtroom in a grand display of **spasms**, **contortions**, screaming and **writhing**. Though Good and Osborn denied their guilt, Tituba confessed. Likely seeking to save herself from certain conviction by acting as an **informer**, she claimed there were other witches acting alongside her in service of the devil against the Puritans. As hysteria spread through the community and beyond into the rest of Massachusetts, a number of others were accused, with some being regarded as upstanding members of church and community and even the four-year-old daughter of Sarah Good.

Like Tituba, several accused "witches" confessed and named still others, and the trials soon began to overwhelm the local justice system. In May 1692, the newly appointed governor of Massachusetts ordered the establishment of a special court on witchcraft cases.

Presided over by judges, the court handed down its first conviction. On June 2, one accused witch was hanged on what would become known as **Gallows Hill** in Salem Town. Five more people were hanged that July; five in August and eight more in September. In addition, seven other accused witches died in jail, while an accused man was pressed to death by stones after he refused to enter a plea at his **arraignment**.

In January 1697, the Massachusetts General Court declared a day of fasting for the tragedy of the Salem witch trials; the court later deemed the trials unlawful, and the leading justice Samuel Sewall publicly apologized for his role in the process. The damage to the community lingered, however, even after Massachusetts Colony passed legislation restoring the good names of the condemned and providing financial restitution to their heirs in 1711.

(Adapted from *https://www.coursehero.com/file/ponclkp/In-January-*1692-9-*year-old-Elizabeth-Betty-Parris-and-*11-*year-old-Abigail/*)

注释：

1.fits 癫痫发作
2.bewitchment 魔力，妖术，蛊惑
3.magistrate 地方法官，文职官员
4.spasm 痉挛，抽搐
5.contortion 扭弯，扭歪
6.writhing 翻滚，打滚，因剧痛扭动/蠕动
7.informer 告密者，通知者
8.Gallows Hill 绞架山(塞勒姆女巫案中女巫被绞死的山)
9.arraignment 传讯，提讯

Word Power

Match the words or phrases in the following sentence taken from the above passages with their meanings.

____ (1) The parish's church had burned down in 1872.

____ (2) After the Great Boston Fire of 1872, construction on the new church began - one in the shape of a modified Greek cross

____ (3) Designed in a Richardsonian Romanesque style, Trinity Church is considered the birthplace of this architectural style.

____ (4) Like Tituba, several accused "witches" confessed and named still others...

____ (5) In late February, arrest warrants were issued for a slave and two other women.

a. change something slightly, usually in order to improve it

b. be completely destroyed by fire

c. the place where somebody was born or something began

d. a warrant authorizing officials to bring that person to court

e. to admit, especially formally or to the police, that you have done sth wrong or illegal

Summary

Fill in the blanks with words or phrases from Reading Passage 1.

Boston is one of the (1)________ municipalities in the United States with its long history. The first settlers arrived here are (2)________ from the European continent who had come here to seek religious freedom. In the center of Boston lie two architectures with totally different styles. Boston Trinity Church is the embodiment of classic feature with (3) ________, (4) ________, (5) ________, and (6) ________ while the John Hancock Tower is a sleek 60-story tower with a glass curtain wall.

Listening

Scan the code and listen to a microlecture about the Boston Trinity Church. Please choose the best answer to each of the following questions.

(1) Which of the following is the distinctive feature of Boston Trinity Church?

A. Rough stone. B. Clay roof.

C. White color. D. Arches.

(2) Boston Trinity Church is designed by ________.

A. Henry Hobson Richardson B. Thomas Jefferson

C. Frank Lloyd Wright D. Louis H. Sullivan

(3) The use of stone and heavy walls in Boston Trinity Church is to deliver message and give the sense of ________.

A. confidence　　B. balance

C. solidity　　D. symmetry

Speaking

Although it is one of the oldest cities in American history, Boston is still vibrant and full of energy. Please share your opinions with your classmates about the reasons why Boston possesses such vigor and vitality. Refer to the following words if necessary.

freedom / tolerant / education

Writing

1. Example Sentence

This little sketch is really the embryo of this church. It's like the conception of a baby in a womb.

2. Analysis

(1) 这句话使用了修辞手法——暗喻(metaphor)。

A metaphor is a figure of speech that describes an object or action in a way that isn't literally true, but helps explain an idea or make a comparison.

(2) 把设计师的建筑手稿(sketch)比作胚胎(embryo)。

(3) 把整个设计过程比作胎儿的孕育过程 (conception of a baby in a womb),使其形象生动又富有生命活力。

3. Practice

Metaphors can make your words come to life (or in the case of the exam, to death). Often, you can use a metaphor to make your subject more relatable to the reader or to make a complex thought easier to understand. They can also be a tremendous help when you want to enhance your writing with imagery. As a common figure of speech, metaphors turn up everywhere from novels and films to presidential speeches and even popular songs. When they're especially good, they're hard to miss.

For example, in William Shakespeare's work, metaphor is constantly used to achieve its literary effects. "All the world's a stage, and all the men and women merely players. They have their exits and their entrances."

How would you describe love using the rhetorical device metaphor?

第三节　温莱特大厦

说起摩天大楼,这可是一件让中国人自豪的事情。因为现在世界上超过一半的摩天大楼都在中国。而且中国各大城市都在争相发展,大楼的建造速度也越来越快,这不仅仅是技术和经济发展的象征,更是综合实力的象征。摩天大楼,这种现代文明的典型代表,最早出现在19世纪的美国。

Culture Express

一百多年前,在水泥还没有被发明出来的时候,世界上主要的建筑材料是石头和木材。由于材料的原因,房屋的高度受到了限制。那时,房屋一般仅两三层,很少突破这个瓶颈。到了今天,上百米的高楼变得非常普遍,技艺熟练的工人配合大型的机械,在几个月的时间里,就能完成一座宏伟的建筑,而这在以前是无法想象的事情。世界上第一座摩天大楼位于美国中部工业城市芝加哥,关于它的来历,还有一个故事。

Reading Passage 1

导读

在19世纪前,芝加哥的建筑大多是木质结构,不仅低矮而且无法抵挡火灾的侵袭,一旦失火,就可能让一条街受到影响。木质建筑的寿命越久,木质就越干燥,越容易引发火灾,为城市留下了安全隐患。然而正是人们闻之恐慌的火灾促成了世界上第一座摩天大楼的诞生。

It won't surprise anybody to learn that the very first skyscraper went up in the United States, but it will surprise some to learn that it went up in Chicago. While it didn't take Manhattan long to claim the steel-framed high-rise as its own, the skyscraper boom began in the capital of the American Midwest in 1885 as **William Le Baron Jenney's Home Insurance Building** rose to its then-impressive height of 10 stores (and, after an 1890 addition, 12) by means of metal, rather than just masonry.

Legend has it that Jenney, an engineer by training and an École Centrale Paris classmate of Gustave Eiffel (designer of the **eponymous** tower), first suspected that an iron skeleton could hold up a building when he saw his wife place a heavy book atop a small birdcage, which easily supported its weight. This opened a new chapter in the history of towers, helped by the Great Chicago Fire (in which more than three square miles of the mostly wooden central city burned to the ground in 1871), and by Chicago's surging 1880s economy.

For obvious reasons, when the New York Home Insurance Company wanted a new Chicago headquarters in the city's cleared-out downtown, they wanted it **fireproofed**—but they also wanted it tall, accommodating "a maximum number of small offices above the bank floor." Jenney's metal-framed design won their open contest, not only thanks to the relative **fire-resistance** of its materials, but to the additional protection offered by its outer iron columns, covered in stone.

Unlike its predecessors—the generations of large buildings supported by nothing but their own masonry walls—the Home Insurance Building wouldn't have to get thicker, darker, stuffier and heavier to get taller. It weighed only a third as much in iron and steel as it would have in stone.

After construction got underway, the Home Insurance Company and the City of Chicago temporarily halted the project in order to investigate further whether the building could really stand up on its own. Soon after, Jenney got the idea to switch from an iron frame to an exotic new material, steel, using a supply offered to him by the Steel Company of Pittsburgh. This aroused yet more skepticism. A 1962 Life magazine **retrospective** on the origins of skyscraper recalls how "an aroused critic terrified his fellows at a protest meeting by **impersonating** the **writhing** of a steel beam exposed to a sudden change of temperature."

But in the event, not only did the Home Insurance Building stand up, it came to stand for an entire architectural movement, loosely termed **the Chicago School**, which gave built form to the proud, square-shouldered, technologically forward American ambition that drove the country forward in the late 19th and early 20th century.

(Adapted from *https://www.100resilientcities.org / the-worlds-first-skyscraper-chicagos-home-insurance-building /*)

注释：

1.steel-framed 钢架

2.high-rise 高楼

3.William Le Baron Jenney 威廉·勒巴隆·詹尼，美国建筑师与工程师，被称为"摩天楼之父"

4.Home Insurance Building 位于芝加哥的家庭保险大厦，也是世界上第一座摩天大楼

5.eponymous 同名的

6.fireproofed 防火的

7.fire-resistance 耐火性

8.retrospective 回顾的，怀旧的，可追溯的

9.impersonate 扮演；模仿；拟人，人格化

10.writhe 扭动，翻滚

11.the Chicago School 芝加哥学派(美国19世纪晚期由建筑师和工程师组成的一个学派)

Reading Passage 2

导读

火灾是建筑师探索新型建筑的导火索，但摩天大楼的建造离不开新型材料的使用。英国工程师亨利·贝塞麦(Henry Bessemer)将生铁转变成钢的技术使今天的摩天大楼成为可能。

Construction of skyscrapers was made possible thanks to Englishman Henry Bessemer, who invented the first process to mass-produce steel inexpensively. An American, William Kelly, had held a patent for "a system of air blowing the carbon out of **pig iron**," but bankruptcy forced Kelly to sell his patent to Bessemer, who had been working on a similar process for making steel. In 1855, Bessemer patented his own "**decarbonization process**, utilizing a blast of air." This breakthrough in the production of steel opened the door for builders to start making taller and taller structures. Modern steel today is still made using technology based on Bessemer's process.

While "the Bessemer process" kept Bessemer's name well-known long after his death, **lesser-known** today is the man who actually employed that process to create the first skyscraper: George A. Fuller. Throughout the 19th century, construction techniques had called for outside walls to carry the load of a building's weight. Fuller, however, had a different idea.

He realized that buildings could bear more weight—and therefore soar higher—if he used Bessemer **steel beams** to give buildings a **load-bearing skeleton** on the inside of the building. In 1889, Fuller erected the Tacoma Building, a successor to the Home Insurance Building that became the first structure ever built where the outside walls did not carry the weight of the building. Using Bessemer steel beams, Fuller developed a technique for creating steel cages that would be used in subsequent skyscrapers.

Taller buildings were also made possible through the invention of the electric elevator in 1883, which reduced the amount of time it took to travel between floors. Also **impactful** was the invention of electric lighting, which made it easier to illuminate larger spaces.

(Adapted from *https://www.thoughtco.com / how-skyscrapers-became-possible-1991649*)

注释：

1. pig iron 生铁
2. decarbonization process 脱碳工艺
3. lesser-known 鲜为人知的
4. steel beam 钢梁
5. load-bearing skeleton 承重构架
6. impactful 有效的，有力的

Reading Passage 3

导读

钢筋水泥建筑的安全可靠使现代人不再对高耸入云的摩天大楼产生恐惧。但是在好莱坞电影 *Skyscraper* 中，那令人眩晕的高度仍然让我们感到心惊肉跳。

Skyscraper is a 2018 American action film written and directed by Rawson Marshall

Thurber, and starring **Dwayne Johnson.** Will Sawyer (starred by Dwayne Johnson), a U.S. Marine war veteran and now an FBI **Hostage Rescue Team** (HRT) leader, loses his left leg below the knee when he and HRT colleague Ben Gillespie encounter a hostage taker with a suicide bomb.

Ten years later, Sawyer is a private security consultant who, on a recommendation from Gillespie, is hired to review security for the world's tallest skyscraper, Hong Kong's 3,500-foot, 225-floor tower, "The Pearl", for owner Zhao Long Ji. Sawyer is joined by his wife, Sarah, and twin children, Georgia and Henry, staying with him on the not-yet-opened residential floors.

While on assignment in China, he finds the tallest, safest building in the world suddenly **ablaze**, and has been **framed** for it. A **wanted man** on the run, Will must find those responsible people, **clear his name** and somehow rescue his family who is trapped inside the building... above the fire line.

Skyscraper grossed \$68.4 million in the United States and Canada, and \$236.4 million in other territories, for a total worldwide gross of \$304.9 million, against a production budget of \$125 million.

[Adapted from *https://the－jh－movie－collection－official.fandom.com/Skyscraper_(2018_film)*]

注释：

1.Dwayne Johnson 道恩·强森，美国男演员、制片人、职业摔跤手，主要作品有《速度与激情》《末日崩塌》《摩天营救》等

2.Hostage Rescue Team 人质救援小组

3.ablaze 着火的，闪耀的

4.framed 被陷害的

5.wanted man 通缉犯

6.clear his name 洗清罪名

Word Power

Fill in the blanks with the words or phrases given below. Change the form where necessary. Each word can be used only once.

suspect, atop, surge, accommodate, get, underway

(1)If something ________, it increases suddenly and greatly, after being steady or developing only slowly.

(2)You use ________ when you are stating something that you believe is probably true, in order to make it sound less strong or direct.

(3)If a building or space can ________ someone or something, it has enough room for them.

(4)If something is ________ something else, it is on top of it.

(5)If you ________ with something or if something does ________, you begin doing it or it begins.

Summary

Fill in the blanks with words or phrases from Reading Passage 1.

The very first skyscraper went up in (1) ________, the capital of the American Midwest. It is William Le Baron Jenney's Home Insurance Building, which rose to its then-impressive height of 10 stores by means of (2) ________, rather than just masonry. Jenney first suspected that an (3) ________ could hold up a building when he saw his wife place a heavy book atop a small birdcage, which easily supported its weight. This opened a new chapter in the history of towers, helped by (4) ________ (in which more than three square miles of the mostly wooden central city burned to the ground in 1871), and by Chicago's surging 1880s (5)________.

Listening

Scan the code and listen to a microlecture about New York City. Please choose the best answer to each of the following questions.

(1)Wainwright Building is located in ________.

A.New York B. Washington D.C

C.Chicago D. St. Louis

(2)The early skyscrapers were usually made with ________.

A.masonry B. stone

C. wood D. iron and steel

(3)The very first modern skyscraper, Seagram Building, is located in ________.

A.New York B. Washington D.C

C. Chicago D. St. Louis

Speaking

City life and country life are two entirely different ways of living—each with their own advantages and disadvantages. Please share your ideas with your classmates about these two different ways of living. Refer to the following words and expressions if necessary.

convenience / mail order / public transportation / jobs / career promotion / accommodation / living environment

Writing

1. Example Sentence

It won't surprise anybody to learn that the very first skyscraper went up in the United States, but it will surprise some to learn that it went up in Chicago.

2. Analysis

(1)本句为 but 连接的并列句,前后为转折关系。

(2)but 连接的并列句一般是强调后一句。

(3)这两句是平行结构。"It won't surprise anybody to learn that..., but it will surprise some to learn that...."

平行结构在英语句子中的应用很广泛,值得多留意。

3. Practice

试译培根的《论学问》中的平行结构。

Some books are to be tasted, others to be swallowed, and some few to be chewed and digested.

第四节　南谷购物中心

购物中心起源于18～19世纪欧洲的城市拱廊建筑和商业长廊。其飞速的发展演变,一方面得益于经济的发展和社会的进步,另一方面则是购物中心在传播过程中与各地具体情况相结合的结果。

Culture Express

20世纪50年代,现代意义上的大型区域购物中心——南谷购物中心(Southdale Center),在美国明尼苏达州的郊区伊代纳(Edina)建成。20世纪50年代末期至60年代是购物中心蓬勃发展的时期,大量模仿南谷购物中心的大型室内购物中心相继建成。人们心目中的购物天堂大多是以此为蓝本建成的。

Reading Passage 1

导读

南谷购物中心的重要革新体现在通过人工控制来营造舒适宜人的购物环境和花园气氛,提供开放的公共空间以满足人们社会活动的需要,提供大面积的免费停车场,并将汽车限制在购物中心周围,在内部建立绝对的排除汽车干扰的步行区。

Southdale Center

Southdale Center is a shopping mall located in Edina, Minnesota, a suburb of the Twin Cities. It opened in 1956 and is both the first and the oldest **fully enclosed, climate-**

controlled shopping mall in the United States. When the Southdale Center in Edina, Minnesota opened its doors in 1956, its design was revolutionary.

Southdale Center was developed by the **Dayton Company** and designed by Victor Gruen, an Austrian immigrant and socialist. Gruen was a European-style socialist; he found individual stores in downtown venues to be inefficient, and the suburban lifestyle of 1950s America too "car-centric" and wanted to design a building that would be a **communal** gathering place, where people would shop, drink coffee, and socialize, as he remembered from his native Vienna.

Southdale was the first modern indoor mall in the US, and eventually became a national symbol of car-centric, **consumerist**, postwar suburbia. The shopping mall featured a large central atrium with **escalators** that led to two upper floors. A pair of department stores anchored each end of the climate-controlled complex, which was surrounded by thousands of parking spaces. Over the next half-century, thousands of American malls copied Southdale's layout (which has since gone through several renovations).

The center was constructed to successfully bring the community together by "gathering art, culture and entertainment under one roof with retail." The Dayton's store was modeled after Dayton's **flagship store** in Minneapolis, Minnesota. In November 1956, organic architect Frank Lloyd Wright visited the mall as part of a tour of new buildings in Minnesota; he critiqued Southdale's overall design, stating "[the] garden court has all the evils of the village street and none of its charm", further criticizing several other buildings in nearby Minneapolis. He unfavorably added that Gruen "should have left downtown, downtown."

Despite the outside criticism, Southdale Center was copied by thousands of its followers.

(Adapted from *https://www.travelchannel.com/interests/shopping/articles/top-10-us-shopping-malls*)

注释:

1.fully enclosed 全封闭式的
2.climate-controlled 恒温控制的
3.Dayton Company 美国的代顿公司
4.communal 公共的,社区的
5.consumerist 主张消费主义的人,用户至上者
6.escalator 自动扶梯
7.flagship store 旗舰店

Reading Passage 2

导读

逛昆西市场，品舌尖上的美国。与隐藏在高楼大厦中的购物商场不同，market（市场）对很多城市居民具有独特的吸引力。昆西市场是波士顿著名的购物场所，市场的中央建筑内有许多美食摊位，相邻的两栋大楼内则是时装、装饰品、珠宝与礼品店，加之整个广场上有很多具有历史价值的建筑物，所以这里是波士顿的著名景点，游览、购物两不误的好去处。

Quincy Market is a historic market complex near Faneuil Hall in downtown of Boston, Massachusetts. It was constructed in 1824-26 and named in honor of Mayor Josiah Quincy, who organized its construction without any tax or debt. The market is a designated National Historic Landmark and a designated Boston Landmark in 1996, significant as one of the largest market complexes built in the United States in the first half of the 19th century.

While Quincy Market may be historical, it should not be the first or fifth or even seventieth spot on anyone's "must go" Boston food list. All that said, there are some decent options inside this glorified mall food court.

1.The Monster at the Dog House

Hot dogs are never a bad idea, and the Dog House offers a long list of tasty variations. It also **hawks** Italian sausages and **Polish kielbasa**, but go for a "the Monster"—it's made with a **Fenway Frank**, and you can feel like you're at a Sox game even if it's late November.

2.French Fries at Fisherman's Net

You can't speak for the fried clams or the **chowder** at Fisherman's Net, but the French fries are extraordinary. They're crispy and golden and salty, and they're the perfect snack for the tourist who's hungry but also wants to wait to really eat until figuring out a better dining location than Quincy Market.

3.Clam Chowder Bread Bowl at Boston Chowda Co.

Ignore the **kitschy** phonetic spelling and try the clam chowder because Boston Chowda Co. actually does a very good version, one that would be included on a list of the best clam chowders in Boston. For the more adventurous (and insatiate) eater: Try the clam chowder-filled bread bowl. It's decadent and kind of dumb, but the hollowed out round loaf functions as one giant oyster cracker. Perhaps avoid eating the entire bowl if you plan to continue on to the next stop of this food crawl.

4.M&M Cookie at Carol Ann Bake Shop

M&M cookies aren't exactly lunch food, but just think of this as the snack that bridges the gap between the horror of having to eat at Quincy Market and the elation that comes with finding a proper meal. The baked goods at Carol Ann Bake Shop are made fresh on site daily. Even Rachael Ray cosigns this spot.

(Adapted from *https://boston.eater.com / 2017/11/22/16685330 / best-food-quincy-market*)

注释:

1.hawk 叫卖
2.Polish kielbasa 波兰熏肠
3.Fenway Frank 一种畅销的热狗
4.chowder 海鲜杂烩浓汤
5.kitschy 矫揉造作的

Word Power

Fill in the blanks with the words or phrases given below. Change the form where necessary. Each word or phrase can be used only once.

revolutionary, venue, resort to, accessibility, diminish

(1) ________ is a place where people meet for an organized event, for example a concert, sporting event or conference.

(2) If you ________ something, you try to make use of something, especially something bad, as a means of achieving something, often because there is no other possible solution.

(3) If something is ________, it involves a great or complete change.

(4) If something is ________, it can be reached, entered, used, seen, etc.

(5) If something ________, it becomes or makes something. become smaller, weaker, etc.

Summary

Fill in the blanks with words or phrases from Reading Passage 1.

Southdale Center is a shopping mall located in Edina, Minnesota, a suburb of the Twin Cities. It is the first and the oldest (1) ________, (2) ________ shopping mall in the United States. When the Southdale Center in Edina, Minnesota opened its doors in 1956, its design was (3) ________. Southdale Center was developed by the (4) ________ and designed by Victor Gruen, an Austrian immigrant and socialist. Gruen was a

European-style socialist; he found individual stores in downtown venues to be (5) ________, and the suburban lifestyle of 1950s America too "car-centric" and wanted to design a building that would be a communal gathering place, where people would shop, drink coffee, and socialize, as he remembered from his native Vienna.

Listening

Scan the code and listen to a microlecture about Seattle. Please choose the best answer to each of the following questions.

(1) Victor Gruen's original inspiration of the shopping mall was from his hometown in ________.

A. Vienna, Austria　　B. Paris, France

C. London, the UK　　D. Sydney, Australia

(2) Which of the following word refers to the place outside downtown, the way of life, and the attitudes of the people who live there?

A. Suburb.　　B. Suburbia.

C. Urban.　　D. Downtown.

(3) Which of the following is not the feature of Southdale Center?

A. Sprawling stores.　　B. Fully-enclosed.

C. Climate-controlled.　　D. Plain exterior.

Speaking

In a digital world, is there still room for good old-fashioned shops? Or are we moving towards a hybrid model? Will E-Commerce replace Bricks and Mortar Retailers? Please share your ideas with your classmates. Refer to the following words and expressions if necessary.

Online retailer / brick-and-mortar stores / advantage

Writing

1. Example Sentence

(1) A recent Global Advisor survey of more than 25,000 people across 25 countries shows that half of respondents (51%) say it's easier to buy goods and services online than it was a year ago.

(2) The latest data from the U.S. Department of Commerce shows retail sales rose above forecasts by 0.4% in August, 2019 from the previous month, driven by auto sales and online shopping.

2. Analysis

(1)在文章写作中有很多方式可以表达作者的观点态度，其中最常用的为引用、举例子、列数据等。

(2)以上两句话都使用了具体的数据来表达作者的观点。

(3)使用数据可以使观点更加客观真实,但是一定要注意:数据的来源要真实可靠。

3. Practice

分析下面句子中作者使用数据所要表达的观点。

"Just 0.00545 percent of the 550,000 boys playing high school basketball each year in the United States become a first-round draft pick—1 in 18,333." stated Jeff Rabjohns, a writer for *The Indianapolis Star*, in an article titled "Prep players face long odds of making it to NBA."

第九章　改变美国的街道

概　述

在本章中，我们将带你穿越美国，从著名街道角度解读美国文化的演变，透过建筑设计师的眼光观察美国历史的发展。百老汇缘何被称为“宽街”？华尔街的铜牛是谁设计的？一条街道又为何加速了美国独立运动的胜利？答案都将在本章中一一被揭晓。本章所包含的街道有：美国戏剧和音乐剧的发源地——百老汇大街、金融中心华尔街、美国第一条邮政道路——波士顿邮路以及位于纽约布鲁克林区的东公园路和促进美国西进运动的国家之路。

第一节　百老汇大街

百老汇大街（Broadway）为纽约市重要的南北向道路，南起巴特里公园（Battery Park），由南向北纵贯曼哈顿岛。由于此路两旁分布着为数众多的剧院，是美国戏剧和音乐剧的重要发祥地，“百老汇”也因此成为音乐剧的代名词。

百老汇大街的中心地带位于第 42 街“时报广场”（Times Square）附近，周围云集了几十家剧院，中段是美国商业性戏剧娱乐中心，因而“百老汇”已成为美国戏剧活动的同义词。而今，它也是美国现代歌舞艺术、美国娱乐业的代名词。

Culture Express

百老汇大街两旁分布着几十家剧院，在百老汇大街 44 街至 53 街的剧院被称为内百老汇，百老汇大街 41 街和 56 街上的剧院则被称为外百老汇。内百老汇上演的是经典的、热门的、商业化的剧目，在外百老汇演出的是一些实验性的、还没有名气的、低成本的剧目，但这种区分越来越淡化。

“百老汇”实际上有三层含义：第一层含义是地理概念，指纽约市时报广场附近 12 个街区以内的 36 家剧院；第二层含义是在百老汇地区进行的演出；第三层含义是整个百老汇产业，这个产业也包括在纽约市以外的地区，以演出百老汇剧目为主的那些剧院。总的来说，百老汇是西方戏剧行业的一个巅峰代表，在戏剧和剧场行业中代表着最高级别的艺术成就和商业成就。

Reading Passage 1

导读

纽约之所以能成为世界艺术中心、娱乐的先锋，“百老汇功不可没”。百老汇很像电影圈的好莱坞，具有极强的商业色彩和娱乐性。除了是音乐剧的代名词外，百老汇还被称为“英雄峡谷”(Canyon of Heroes)和“白色大道”(the Great White Way)，这些别称又是如何得来的呢？

Broadway is a road in the U.S. state of New York which is the oldest north-south main thoroughfare in New York City. Broadway runs the length of Manhattan Island, roughly parallel to the North River, from Bowling Green at the south to Inwood at the northern tip of the island. Broadway in Manhattan is known widely as the heart of the American commercial theatrical industry, and is a **boulevard** full of famous theatres where visitors from all over the world gather to watch the top musicals of the season and other great plays. Thus it is often used as a metonym for it, as well as in the names of alternative theatrical ventures such as **Off-Broadway** and **Off-Off Broadway**. There are three types of shows: On-Broadway, Off-Broadway and Off-Off Broadway. The On-Broadway offers the most famous musicals and theatres worldwide, Off-Broadway are less well-known and so on. The avenue is also famous as it cuts Manhattan obliquely into lower Manhattan, Midtown Manhattan, upper west side, etc.

Canyon of Heroes is occasionally used to refer to the section of **lower Broadway** in the Financial District that is the location of the city's **ticker-tape parades**. The traditional route of the parade is northward from Bowling Green to City Hall Park. Most of the route is lined with tall office buildings along both sides, affording a view of the parade for thousands of office workers who create the snowstorm-like jettison of **shredded paper** products that characterize the parade.

While typical sports championship parades have been showered with some 50 tons of **confetti** and shredded paper, the V-J Day parade on August 14-15, 1945—marking the end of World War II—was covered with 5,438 tons of paper, based on estimates provided by the **New York City Department of Sanitation**.

"The Great White Way" is a nickname for a section of Broadway in **Midtown Manhattan**, specifically the portion that **encompasses** the Theater District, between 42nd and 53rd Streets, and encompassing Times Square.

In 1880, a stretch of Broadway between Union Square and Madison Square was **illuminated** by Brush arc lamps, making it among the first electrically lighted streets in the United States. By the 1890s, the portion from 23rd Street to 34th Street was so brightly illuminated by electrical advertising signs that people began calling it "The Great White Way." When the theater district moved uptown, the name was transferred to the Times Square area.

(Adapted from *https://www.flickr.com/photos/kenlund/*46803176814/*in/photostream/*)

注释:

1.boulevard 林荫大道
2.Off-Broadway 外百老汇
3.Off-Off-Broadway 外外百老汇
4.Canyon of Heroes 英雄峡谷
5.lower Broadway 下百老汇
6.ticker-tape parade 纸袋游行
7.shredded paper 碎纸
8.confetti 五彩纸屑
9.New York City Department of Sanitation 纽约市卫生局
10.Midtown Manhattan 曼哈顿中城
11.encompass 包含,包围
12.illuminate 照明

Reading Passage 2

导读

百老汇大街早在1811年纽约市进行城市规划之前就已存在,其中心地带是在第42街时报广场附近,周围云集了几十家剧院。其中有一座被人们称为"派拉蒙剧院"(the Paramount Building)。

As one of New York's most famous avenues, Broadway is known as the heart of the American theatre industry since it is the only oblique street that crosses the city center.

Broadway's most important attraction is Times Square, which cuts 7th Avenue. Times Square's surroundings provide the most important leisure and cultural offerings, with nearly 40 theatres, one of which is called The Paramount Theatre.

The Paramount Theatre was a noted 3,664 seat movie palace located at 43rd Street and Broadway in the Times Square district of New York City. Opened in 1926, it was a premiere showcase theatre and New York headquarters of **Paramount Pictures.** Adolph Zukor, founder of Paramount predecessor Famous Players Film Company, maintained an office in the building until his death in 1976. The Paramount Theatre eventually became a popular live performance **venue.** The theater was closed in 1964 and its space converted to office and **retail** use. The tower which housed it, known as the *Paramount Building* located at 1501 Broadway, is in commercial use as an office building and is still home to Paramount Pictures offices, and remains a Times Square landmark.

Over the years, many of the top stars performed there, including **Frank Sinatra** and dozens of the era's **luminaries.** After years of showing movies and shows, the Paramount Theatre was closed on February 21, 1966 with the James Bond movie "Thunderball." The **auditorium** was destroyed and converted into office space, and the entrance and lobby areas were **gutted** to make way for office and retail space.

(Adapted from *https://www.researchgate.net/publication/*319518386 _ *Paramount* _ *Building*)

注释:

1. Paramount Pictures 派拉蒙电影公司
2. venue 地点,场所
3. retail 零售
4. Frank Sinatra 法兰克·辛纳屈,美国歌手、演员、主持人
5. luminary 杰出人物
6. auditorium 礼堂
7. gut 毁坏……的内部

Word Power

Match the words given below with their meanings.

thoroughfare, metonym, parade, musical, district, convert

(1)________ a public road or street used by traffic, especially a main road in a city or town

(2)________ a play or a film / movie in which part or all of the story is told using songs and often dancing

(3)________ a word, an expression used as a substitute for something else

(4) ________ an area of a country or town, especially one that has particular features

(5) ________ a public procession, especially one for celebrating a special day or event

(6) ________ to change or make something change from one form, purpose, system, etc. to another

Summary

Fill in the blanks with words or phrases from Reading Passage 1.

Broadway is a major route in the U.S. state of (1) ________ which is the oldest north-south main thoroughfare. Broadway in Manhattan is known widely as the heart of the American commercial (2)________ industry and has been a metonym of it. Broadway runs the length of (3)________ Island, roughly parallel to the North River. It also has two nicknames, respectively (4)________ and (5)________. Canyon of Heroes is occasionally used to refer to the section of lower Broadway in the Financial District that is the location of the city's (6)________. "The Great White Way" is a nickname for a section of Broadway in Midtown Manhattan because in 1880, a stretch of Broadway between Union Square and Madison Square was (7)________ by Brush arc lamps, making it among the first electrically lighted streets in the United States.

Listening

Scan the code and listen to a microlecture about Broadway. Please choose the best answer to each of the following questions.

(1)Which of the following is not the synonym of "major route"?

A.Main stem. B. Arterial road.

C. Thoroughfare. D. Main vein.

(2)The name "Brede weg", meaning broadway in English comes from ________.

A.Dutch B. French

C. Italian D. Latin

(3)Broadway is the center of America's ________ industry.

A.economic B. financial

C.theatrical D. car

Speaking

Broadway is famous for its theatrical industry. Some of the Avenue's most successful musicals are presented and applauded. Will you please search for some information and introduce one of the musicals to your classmates? Refer to the following words and expressions if necessary.

The Lion King / Wicked / Les Misérables / The Phantom of the Opera / Chicago / Aladdin

Writing

1. Example Sentence

Broadway is a road which is the oldest north-south main thoroughfare in New York City.

2. Analysis

(1)本句使用了最常见的从句之一——定语从句。

(2)定语从句往往通过从句引导词(如本句中的 which)与主句或其他从句连接。

(3)英语表达中较长的定语经常使用定语从句的形式放在名词的后面，如“road which is...”，汉语则倾向于将定语放在名词前面，如“百老汇是一条纵贯纽约市南北方向的主干道”。

3. Practice

翻译下面的句子，通过句中的逻辑词 but 和 and 厘清句子的逻辑关系。

On the whole such a conclusion can be drawn with a certain degree of confidence **but** only if the child can be assumed to have had the same attitude towards the test as the other with whom he is compared, **and** only if he was not punished by lack of relevant information which they possessed.

第二节　华尔街

华尔街(Wall Street)比任何事物都更能代表金融和经济力量。对美国人而言，华尔街等同于精英主义、强权政治，是美国人资本主义市场经济的骄傲。在美国人的心目中，华尔街是一个依靠贸易、资本主义和创新，而非依靠殖民主义和掠夺成长起来的国家和经济系统的象征。

Culture Express

华尔街，纽约市曼哈顿区南部从百老汇路延伸到东河的一条大街。全长仅为 500 多米，宽仅为 11 米，街道狭窄而短。从百老汇到东河仅有 7 个街段，却以“美国的金融中心”闻名于世。美国摩根财阀、洛克菲勒石油大王和杜邦财团等开设的银行、保险、航运、铁路等公司集中于此。除此之外，它还是主要证券交易所的总部，如纽约证券交易所、纳斯达克、美国证券交易所、纽约期货交易所等。

Reading Passage 1

导读

“华尔街”一词现已超越这条街道本身，成为附近区域的代称，亦可指对整个美国经济具有影响力的金融市场和金融机构。

Anchored by Wall Street, New York City has been called both the most economically powerful city and the leading financial center of the world, and the city is home to the world's two largest stock exchanges by total **market capitalization**, the **New York Stock Exchange** and **NASDAQ.** Several other major exchanges have or had **headquarters** in the Wall Street area, including the **New York Mercantile Exchange, the New York Board of Trade**, and the former American Stock Exchange.

There are varying accounts about how the street got its name Wall Street.

The name of the street originates from an actual wall that was built in the 17th century by the Dutch, who were living in what was then called **New Amsterdam.** The

12-foot (4m) wall was built to protect the Dutch against attacks from pirates and various Native American tribes, and to keep other potential dangers out of the establishment.

The area near the wall became known as Wall Street. Because of its prime location running the width of Manhattan between the East River and the Hudson River, the road developed into one of the busiest trading areas in the entire city. Later, in 1699, the wall was dismantled by the British colonial government, but the name of the street stuck.

The financial industry got its official start on Wall Street on May 17, 1792. On that day, New York's first official stock exchange was established by the signing of *The Buttonwood Agreement*. The agreement, so-called because it was signed under a buttonwood tree that early traders and speculators had previously gathered around to trade informally, gave birth to what is now the modern-day New York Stock Exchange.

(Adapted from *https://www.livescience.com / 32563-why-is-it-called-wall-street.html*)

注释：

1.anchor 抛锚，使固定
2.market capitalization 市值
3.New York Stock Exchange 纽约证券交易所
4.NASDAQ 纳斯达克
5.New York Mercantile Exchange 纽约商业交易所
6.New York Board of Trade 纽约期货交易所
7.New Amsterdam 新阿姆斯特丹（纽约市 1625～1664 年的旧称，当时为荷兰殖民地）
8.*The Buttonwood Agreement*《梧桐树协议》

Reading Passage 2

导读

华尔街的铜牛雕像一直是美国资本主义最为重要的象征之一，也是外来游客必到的景点之一。这座铜牛塑像是由意大利艺术家阿图罗·迪·莫迪卡设计的。迪·莫迪卡是在 1987 年纽约股市崩盘之后，有了创作的灵感。为了筹资，他卖掉了家乡西西里祖传农场的一部分，总共筹得资金 36 万美元。1989 年的一个午夜，他在纽约证券交易所外将这座后来举世闻名的铜牛雕像竖立起来，宣称它是“美国人力量与勇气”的象征。

Charging Bull, sometimes referred to as the *Wall Street Bull* or the *Bowling Green Bull*, is a bronze sculpture that stands on Broadway just north of Bowling Green in the Financial District of Manhattan, New York City. The 7,100-pound (3,200 kg) bronze sculpture, standing 11 feet (3.4 m) tall and measuring 16 feet (4.9 m) long, depicts a bull, the symbol of aggressive financial optimism and prosperity. *Charging Bull* is a popular tourist destination that draws thousands of people a day, symbolizing Wall Street and the Financial District.

The sculpture was created by **Sicilian** artist Maestro Arturo Di Modica **in the wake of** the 1987 Black Monday **stock market crash.** On December 14, 1989, Di Modica arrived on Wall Street with *Charging Bull* on the back of a truck and illegally dropped the sculpture outside of the New York Stock Exchange. After being removed by the New York City Police Department later that day, *Charging Bull* was installed at Bowling Green a week later. Despite initially having only a temporary permit to be located at Bowling Green, *Charging Bull* became a popular tourist attraction. In 2017, another bronze sculpture titled *Fearless Girl* was installed across from *Charging Bull*, though it was later relocated.

The bull has called its current spot in Bowling Green home for nearly three decades. The 7,100-pound statue was initially placed outside the New York Stock Exchange in the middle of the night in 1989. Executives at the exchange didn't like it, however, and Di Modica worked with the city to find a new placement for the bull. The sculpture has become synonymous with Wall Street, and has endured its fair share of controversy. It was the site of protests from the **Occupy Wall Street movement**, and more recently protesters staged a **"die-in"** by pouring fake blood and climbing on the statue to protest climate change.

NBC New York reported in 2019 that the mayor's office confirmed that there are plans to move the statue to a **pedestrian plaza** near the Stock Exchange. The NYSE declined to comment on the location.

(Adapted from *https://blog.shops-net.com* / 446394 / *charging-ball.html*)

注释：

1.Charging Bull 华尔街铜牛
2.Sicilian 西西里人
3.in the wake of 随……而来，紧紧跟随
4.stock market crash 股市崩盘
5.Occupy Wall Street movement 占领华尔街运动
6. die-in 死亡示威
7. pedestrian plaza 步行广场

Word Power

Fill in the blanks with the words given below. Change the form where necessary. Each word can be used only once.

prime, dismantle, install, temporary, synonymous, controversy

(1) The old villa was ________ piece by piece and will be reconstructed in the new site.
(2) The hotel chain has recently ________ a new booking system.
(3) With their house being burned, they had to move into ________ accommodation.

(4) Wealth is not necessarily ________ with happiness.

(5) There has been ________ surrounding his latest design of the modern skyscraper.

(6) As a member of the SPAB (Ancient Building Protection Association), his ________ concern is to protect the architecture with whatever he has to do.

Summary

Fill in the blanks with words or phrases from Reading Passage 1.

Wall Street is an eight-block-long street running roughly northwest to southeast in Manhattan, New York City. Over time, the term has become a metonym for the (1)________ of the United States. New York City has been called the most economically powerful city and the leading financial center of the world, and is home to the world's two largest stock exchanges, (2) ________ and (3)________. The name of the street originates from an actual wall that was built in the 17th century by the (4) ________, who were living in what was then called (5)________. The wall was built to protect the Dutch against attacks from pirates and various (6)________ tribes.

Listening

Scan the code and listen to a microlecture about Wall Street. Please choose the best answer to each of the following questions.

(1) Which of the following stock exchange is not located on Wall Street?

A. New York Stock Exchange. B. NASDAQ.

C. American Stock Exchange. D. London Stock Exchange.

(2) Which of the following is the Chinese meaning of "from scratch"?

A. 从零开始. B. 回到起点.

C. 退出比赛. D. 受到重创.

(3) Wall Street is the leading ________ center of the world.

A. theatrical B. financial

C. car D. technological

Speaking

The Charging Bull on Wall Street is a symbol of aggressive financial optimism and prosperity. What does bull market mean? What is bear market? Refer to the following words and expressions if necessary.

go up / greed / stock market / investment / strong economy / optimistic / opposite of a bull market / move down / scared

Writing

1. Example Sentence

Charging Bull, sometimes referred to as the *Wall Street Bull* or the *Bowling Green Bull*, is a bronze sculpture that stands on Broadway just north of Bowling Green in the Financial District of Manhattan, New York City.

2. Analysis

(1) 本句使用分词短语"referred to..."以及定语从句"that stands on..."的形式提供了更多关于华尔街铜牛的详细信息。本句可译为:华尔街铜牛,又被称为 Wall Street Bull 或者 Bowling Green Bull,位于美国纽约曼哈顿区鲍林格林公园以北,是一座坐落于华尔街的铜质公牛塑像。

(2) 在英文表达中,许多信息可以放在一个长句中表达;汉语则正好相反,不同的信息往往通过短句表达出来。

3. Practice

试着找出下列句子的主干,并将英语中的长句翻译为汉语的短句。

Interest in historical methods had arisen less through external challenge to the validity of history as an intellectual discipline and more from internal quarrels among historians themselves.

第三节　波士顿邮路

1792 年,在当时的美国宾夕法尼亚州首府费城,乔治·华盛顿总统签署了 1792 年的《邮政服务法》。虽然基本的殖民地邮件服务已经存在了近一个半世纪,但这项新法律完全改变了邮政规则。正如该法所描述的,它赋予了联邦政府建立官方邮路的能力。它还允许报纸以较低的价格被包括在邮件投递中。这样做是为了确保信息可以从城市中心传播到这个正在成长的国家最遥远的边境。此后,在纽约和波士顿之间建立了每月一次的邮递路线,它被称为旧波士顿邮路,今天它仍然是美国 1 号公路的一部分。

Culture Express

1926 年,美国规划国道系统,这条以波士顿邮路为雏形发展而来的东海岸大动脉,因为其独特的地理位置和历史贡献,荣获 1 号公路的编号。1938 年,连接迈阿密和基韦斯特岛的长达 180 千米的跨海高速路修通,成为 1 号公路的最后一块拼图。如今,波士顿邮路这个名称已经淡出了人们的记忆,但由它发展出的 1 号公路仍旧是美国东部最重要的交通运输要道。

Reading Passage 1

导读

美国国道系统中有一些非常有名的成员，其中包括 1 号公路。这条路北启缅因州美加边界，南到佛罗里达州最南端的基韦斯特岛，和大西洋海岸相伴而行，全程约 3850 千米，沿途串起了波士顿、纽约、费城、巴尔的摩、华盛顿、里士满、迈阿密等重要城市。这条公路因其地理位置而荣获 NO.1 的编号，它对美国历史的贡献也完全担得起这个名号。谈到这里，就不得不提它的前世——波士顿邮路(the Boston Post Road)了。对波士顿邮路做出突出贡献的人物有小约翰·温特莱普(John Winthrop Jr.)和弗朗西斯·洛夫莱斯(Francis Lovelace)。

The Boston Post Road was a system of mail-delivery routes between New York City and Boston, Massachusetts, that evolved into one of the first major **highways** in the United States.

Since it became America's first mail route back in 1673, the Boston Post Road has connected Boston to New York City, delivering messages, guiding travelers, and tying the Northeast together. In that time, some legs of the route have shifted, and most of it is now known by other names—Washington Street, Route 20, Main Street, or Mass. Route 9. But if you know how to **follow the thread**, you can still trace the Post Road beneath our modern streets and highways.

John Winthrop Jr.

In November 1645, John Winthrop Jr., son of the Massachusetts Bay Colony Governor, embarked on a **grueling**, unprecedented 26-day tour of southern New England. In choosing his route, he relied on Indian trails. Three decades after his trip, when Winthrop Jr. was Governor of Connecticut, he was asked to **chart** the Colonial mail route between Boston and Manhattan. He used those Indian paths as his blueprint for what would become the Post Road.

Francis Lovelace

Francis Lovelace had been the royal governor of New York, and he had sent the first official **postrider** to Boston. Sometime in February 1673, the first mail ever arrived in Boston from New York City via the Boston Post Road. The first postrider started out, swearing to obey Lovelace's instructions to behave **civilly**, to ask the governor of Connecticut, John Winthrop Jr., how to form the best post road, and to mark the trees for the direction of passengers. Thus Francis Lovelace initiated both the U.S. Postal Service and the Boston Post Road.

On Dec. 27, 1672, Lovelace wrote to Connecticut Governor John Winthrop the Younger, presenting him with two "**rarities,**" "a pacquet of the latest intelligence I could meet withal, and a post."

In some towns, the area near the Boston Post Road has been placed on the ***National Register of Historic Places***, since it was often the first road in the area, and some buildings of historical significance were built along it. The Boston Post Road Historic District has been designated a **National Historic Landmark.** The Post Road is also famous for **milestones** that date from the 18th century, many of which survive to this day.

(Adapted from *https://www.newenglandhistoricalsociety.com/francis-lovelace-founds-boston-post-road*-1673/)

注释:

1.highway 高速公路
2.follow the thread 顺着……的线索，摸清……的来龙去脉
3.grueling 艰辛的,使人筋疲力尽的
4.chart 绘制
5.postrider 驿传者,骑马的邮差
6.civilly 恭谦地
7.rarity 稀世珍品
8.*National Register of Historic Places*《美国国家历史遗迹名录》
9.National Historic Landmark 国家历史地标
10.milestone 里程碑

Reading Passage 2

导读

美国是一个车轮上的国家,有非常发达的公路网络。其中,成立于1926年的美国国道系统(US Routes,也叫编号公路系统)及其下辖的道路联通了美国本土48个州几乎每一个重要城镇,总长度超过了25万千米,在美国的交通运输方面有不可替代的作用。在美国国家高速公路系统(National Highway System, NHS)中主要的成员有四位。

Highways in the United States are split into at least four different types of systems: **Interstate Highways, U.S. Highways, state highways,** and **county highways.** Highways are generally organized by a route number or letter. These designations are generally displayed along the route by means of a highway shield. Each system has its own unique shield design that will allow quick identification to which system the route belongs. Below is a list of the different highway shields used throughout the United States.

The Interstate Highway System is a federally funded and administered (but state-maintained) system of freeways that forms the transportation backbone of the U.S., with millions of Americans relying on it for commutes, long-distance travel, and **freight transport** daily. Interstate highways are all constructed to precise standards, designed to maximize high-speed travel safety and efficiency. All Interstate Highways are part of the

National Highway System, a network of highways deemed essential to the defense, economy, and mobility of the country.

The United States Numbered Highway System is an older system consisting mostly of surface-level trunk roads, coordinated by the American Association of State Highway and Transportation Officials and maintained by state and local governments. U. S. Highways have been relegated to regional and **intrastate** traffic, as they have been largely **supplanted** by the Interstate system for long-distance travel except in areas (especially in the west) where the Interstate system is absent or underdeveloped. This has led to the **decommissioning** and **truncation** of U.S. Highways that were formerly vital **long-haul routes**, such as U.S. Route 21 and U.S. Route 66.

Each state also has a state highway system. State highways are of varying standards, capacity, and quality. Some state highways become so heavily traveled that they are built to Interstate Highway standards. Others are more lightly traveled and have low capacity.

Many state highway markers are designed to suggest the geographic shape of the state or some other state symbol such as its flag. Most of the others are generically rectangular or some other neutral shape. The default design for state highway markers is the circular highway shield, which is how state highways are designated on most maps and atlases.

The final administrative level in some states is the county highway. As the name suggests, this type of road is maintained by a county. County roads vary widely from well-traveled **multilane** highways to **dirt roads** into remote parts of the county. In Louisiana, parish roads exist in place of county highways, as counties in that state are called parishes. Alaska also has no counties, and all roads are maintained at the national, state or municipal level. In some states, such as Massachusetts, county roads are now administered by regional entities.

(Adapted from *https://intertropolisandrouteville.fandom.com/wiki/United_States_Numbered_Highway_System*)

注释:

1.Interstate Highway 州际高速公路
2.U.S. Highway 美国国道
3.state highway 州内高速公路
4.county highway 县内高速公路
5.freight transport 货物运输
6.intrastate 州内的
7.supplant 代替,排挤掉
8.decommission 关闭,拆除
9.truncation 截断,截尾

10.long-haul routes 远程航线

11.multilane 多车道

12.dirt road 泥土路

Word Power

Fill in the blanks with the words or phrases given below. Change the form where necessary. Each word can be used only once.

embark on, blueprint, initiate, milestone, rectangular

(1) The architectural designer offered the officer a ________ of the whole place, complete with heating ducts and wiring.

(2) I'm not suggesting you never invest in technology, but make sure you take expert advice, and ________ such a move only when the time is right.

(3) They wanted to ________ a discussion on economics.

(4) He said the launch of the party represented a ________ in Zambian history.

(5) The football coach said that the perfect playing field should be in the ________ shape.

Summary

Fill in the blanks with words or phrases from Reading Passage 1.

The Boston Post Road was a system of mail-delivery routes between (1) ________ City and (2) ________, Massachusetts, that evolved into one of the first major highways in the United States. People who have contributed to the construction of the road include the then Connecticut Governor (3) ________, New York Governor (4) ________. The Post Road is also famous for (5) ________ that date from the 18th century, many of which survive to this day.

Listening

Scan the code and listen to a microlecture about The Boston Post Road. Please choose the best answer to each of the following questions.

(1) Which of the following does not belong to American road net?

A. Interstate Highway. B. U.S. Highway.

C. State Highway. D. U.S. Railway.

(2) Who did the most contributions to the Boston Post Road?

A. Thomas Jefferson. B. Benjamin Franklin.

C. Abraham Lincoln. D. Joseph Smith.

(3) Boston Post Road literally changed American history because it contributed to and helped win the ________.

A. American Revolutionary War　　B. American Civil War
C. World War One　　D. World War Two

Speaking

From U.S. Routes and Interstate Highways to state and county roads (each with different signage and numbering systems), highways in the United States can be daunting. If you are driving in America, how would you identify the different kinds of roads? Refer to the following expressions if necessary.

The United States Numbered Highway System / U. S. Highway shield / U. S. Highway marker / U.S. Road signs Designing and Numbering system

Writing

1. Example Sentence

In that time, some legs of the route have shifted, and most of it is now known **by other names**—Washington Street, Route 20, Main Street, or Mass. Route 9.

2. Analysis

(1)句中的"be known by other names"在汉语中意思为"还有其他的名字",不能翻译为被动。

(2)英语比较喜欢用被动语态,科技英语尤其如此。汉语虽然也有"被""由"之类的词来表示句中的动作是被动的,但这种表达远没有英语的被动语态那么常见。

(3)英语中很多习惯表达也惯用被动,如:

It must be pointed out that... 必须指出……,

It must be admitted that... 必须承认……,

It is imagined that... 人们认为……,

It can not be denied that... 不可否认……。

3. Practice

翻译下面的句子,注意汉语与英语语态的不同。

许多人认为,普通人的思维活动根本无法与科学家的思维活动相比,认为这些思维活动必须经过某种专门训练才能掌握。

第四节　东公园路

曾经有人说:"没有奥姆斯特德,美国不会是现在的这个样子。"美国景观设计师弗雷德里克·劳·奥姆斯特德的景观设计哲学引发了人们对居住环境的更多思考。纽约的中央公园是美国和全世界最著名的城市公园之一,它给居住在纽约、处于紧张忙碌生活中的人们提供了放松身心的环境。中央公园的意义不仅在于它是全美第一个城市公园,更重要的是,在其规划建设中,诞生了一个新的学科——景观设计学。

Culture Express

位于纽约曼哈顿区的中央公园建成之后，别的区也不甘落后，为了与中央公园媲美，布鲁克林区居民聘请了同一团队，为他们设计了布鲁克林的城市绿洲——展望公园(Prospect Park)。而后又设计了东公园路，将散落在布鲁克林的城市公园串连在一起，使人们在行走中宛若置身自然公园一般惬意舒畅。

Reading Passage 1

导读

美国最初的园林大道，是由美国现代园林之父弗雷德里克·劳·奥姆斯特德(Frederick Law Olmsted)和卡尔弗特·沃克斯(Calvert Vaux)在19世纪后期设计的，这两位设计师提出："规划道路，将市区与郊区公园连接起来"，并将其定义为"园林大道"(parkway)。

Eastern Parkway is a major **boulevard** that runs through a portion of the New York City borough of Brooklyn. Conceived by Frederick Law Olmsted and Calvert Vaux, it was the world's first parkway, having been built between 1870 and 1874. At the time of its construction, Eastern Parkway went to the eastern edge of Brooklyn, hence its name.

The term parkway was coined by these designers as a landscaped road built **expressly** for "pleasure-riding and driving" or scenic access to Prospect Park (also designed by Olmsted and Vaux). The parkway was **constructed** from Grand Army Plaza to Ralph Avenue (the boundary of Brooklyn). Olmsted and Vaux intended Eastern Parkway to be the Brooklyn nucleus of an interconnected park and parkway system for the New York area. The plan was never completed but their idea of bringing the countryside into the city influenced the construction of major parks and parkways in cities throughout the United States.

The original design called for a 55-foot wide carriage drive centered between two pedestrian malls with four rows of trees extending 2.2 miles. There were also side roads for delivery wagons. Adorned almost exclusively with **American Elms**, this landscape of over 1100 trees is now mixed with twenty-four other species. Varieties of maple, linden, oak, and ash trees were introduced to discourage the spread of **infestations** such as **Dutch Elm Disease**. Eastern Parkway Extension, which proceeds northeast to Bushwick Avenue, continues the landscape for another two miles.

Eastern Parkway hosts many special events, including the springtime "Welcome Back to Brooklyn," which celebrates the borough's famous sons and daughters, and the early September Caribbean Day Parade. Community members along Eastern Parkway celebrated a remarkable milestone in August 1978. At that time, the United States Secretary of the Interior designated Eastern Parkway a National Scenic Landmark in order to preserve the legacy of the world's first parkway.

(Adapted from *https://tclf.org/landscapes/eastern－parkway*)

注释：

1.boulevard 林荫大道
2.expressly 特别地
3.American Elms 美国榆树
4.infestation 感染，侵扰
5.Dutch Elm Disease 荷兰榆树病

Reading Passage 2

导读

在纽约，每当人们想在城中找个地方放空一下时，中央公园(Central Park)就会第一个浮现在他们的脑海中。寸土寸金的纽约不仅有声名在外的中央公园，更有布鲁克林的城中绿洲——展望公园。与中央公园一样，展望公园也是建筑师费雷德里克·劳·奥姆斯特德和卡尔弗特·沃克斯的杰作。下面让我们跟随本文一起来欣赏公园夏日的美景吧！

As most people know, space is a prized commodity in New York City, and that includes green space. When people think about places in the city to relax, Central Park often comes to mind. But where does Prospect Park, the 585-acre recreational oasis in Brooklyn, fit in?

Like Central Park, Prospect Park was designed by the architectural team of Frederick Law Olmsted and Calvert Vaux. But Prospect Park, which opened in 1867, is remarkable in its own right. The park is accessible **year-round**, but truly shines in the summer.

David P. Colley, the author of *Prospect Park: Olmsted and Vaux's Brooklyn Masterpiece*, wrote that "Olmsted and Vaux understood that the natural world seldom displays itself in the ideal, and they set out to construct an impression of nature at its most harmonious and sublime."

Here is a guide, from West Drive to Prospect Park Lake to the Boathouse, with paths, meadows and trails in between.

Grand Army Plaza

Like the **Arc de Triomphe** in Paris, the Soldiers' and Sailors' Memorial Arch, in the middle of a busy traffic circle at Grand Army Plaza, is a **testament** to the architectural aspirations of the 19th century. The arch, which was built to honor soldiers who fought for the Union during the Civil War, was dedicated in 1892 and dominates the surrounding area leading to Prospect Park.

West Drive

After passing four eagle-topped columns at the main Prospect Park entrance, the convergence of bikers, joggers and pedestrians at West Drive comes into view. West Drive has been car-free since 2015 and the entire park became car-free earlier this year, which creates a less hurried environment throughout the park. The **tree canopy** over much of West Drive, with sunlight filtering through the leaves, makes this a favorite part of the park.

Prospect Park West

Veer west and walk slightly outside of the park grounds to reach Prospect Park West, one of the most **sought-after** residential streets in the city, and a gateway to the **Park Slope** neighborhood of Brooklyn. With a mix of brownstones, **co-op buildings**, neo-Italian Renaissance homes and **rowhouses**, the street offers a range of architecture reflective of its development in the early 20th century.

Long Meadow

Back on the main grounds, the expansive Long Meadow cuts through much of the northern end of the park. On any given summer day, there are people sunbathing on the lawn, enjoying a picnic or participating in a yoga session.

(Adapted from *https://www.nytimes.com* / 2018/06/19 / *travel* / *prospect-park-brooklyn-new-york.html*)

注释:

1.year-round 全年
2.Arc de Triomphe 凯旋门
3.testament 证明
4.tree canopy 树冠
5.veer 转向
6.sought-after 受欢迎的,吃香的
7.Park Slope 公园坡
8.co-op building 复式公寓
9.rowhouse 联排别墅

Word Power

Match the words given below with their meanings.

conceive, adorn, construct, dedicate, filter

(1)________ to make something / somebody look more attractive by decorating it or them with something

(2)________ to build or make something such as a road, building or machine

(3) ________ to pass liquid, light, etc. through a special device, especially to remove something that is not wanted

(4) ________ to form an idea, a plan, etc. in your mind; to imagine something

(5) ________ to give a lot of your time and effort to a particular activity or purpose because you think it is important

Summary

Fill in the blanks with words or phrases from Reading Passage 1.

Eastern Parkway is a major (1) ________ that runs through a portion of the New York City borough of Brooklyn which was designed by Frederick Law Olmsted and Calvert Vaux. It was the world's first (2) ________, having been built between 1870 and 1874.

The term parkway was coined by these designers as a landscaped road built **expressly** for " (3) ________ and (4) ________." It has access to many parks, including the one designed by Frederick Law Olmsted in Brooklyn, (5) ________. Olmsted and Vaux intended Eastern Parkway to be the Brooklyn nucleus of an interconnected park and parkway system for the New York area. The plan was never completed but their idea of bringing the countryside into the city influenced the construction of major parks and parkways in cities throughout the United States.

Listening

Scan the code and listen to a microlecture about Eastern Parkway. Please choose the best answer to each of the following questions.

(1) Which of the following is not the urban park of America?

A. Prospect Park.　　B. The Yellowstone.

C. Necklace Chain Park.　　D. Central park.

(2) Eastern Parkway is in ________.

A. Manhattan　　B. Brooklyn

C. The Bronx　　D. The Queen

(3) The term "parkway" was coined by designers as a landscaped road built expressly for many reasons except ________.

A. pleasure-riding　　B. relaxing

C. releasing driving pressure　　D. access to parks

Speaking

When you think about somewhere that is tranquil, what do you imagine? Whether it's a wide open meadow, a deserted beach, or a river as it lazily flows along on a warm summer's afternoon. Research shows that tranquillity is mainly found in natural outdoor environments. But in industrial society, citizens find it hard to expose themselves to the outdoor environment.

What can you learn from Olmsted's design of parkways? Share your ideas with your classmates. Refer to the following words and expressions if necessary.

urban parks / leafy roads / pleasure-riding and driving / tranquil space pedestrian / parkway

Writing

1. Example Sentence

Eastern Parkway is a major boulevard that.... **Conceived** by..., it was the world's first parkway... was **coined** by these designers as a landscaped road **built** ....

2. Analysis

(1)本句话中使用了不同的动词(conceive、coin、build)来表达“设计”这个概念。

(2)在英语中,表达相同的概念时往往会变换表达方式。而汉语对变换表达方式的要求相对较低,可以使用重复的表述表达前文的某个概念。

3. Practice

试译下面的句子并找出对相同概念(拖拉机)的不同表达方式。

The monkey's most extraordinary accomplishment was learning to operate a tractor. By the age of nine, the monkey had learned to solo on the vehicle.

第五节　国家之路

美国独立战争(1775～1783 年)结束后,美国资本主义经济有了大幅发展,美国东部市场已经无法满足大资本家对于财富的追求。为方便贸易、获得更多的土地和栖息地,议会颁布了关于修路的法案,并由托马斯·杰弗逊总统于 1806 年签署执行,由此开始了国家之路的建设。之后美国开始了大规模的西进运动,也为其后来在国际上取得霸主地位奠定了基础。

Culture Express

1803 年的路易斯安那置地案使美国的领土面积扩张了一倍。既然该地区如此辽阔,那么法国为什么甘愿将其出售给美国呢?

当时的法国在美洲刚刚经历了一次挫败,拿破仑军队在中美洲海地镇压奴隶起义的军事行动中遭遇了惨败,法军的损失很大。这次失利对拿破仑的刺激很大,他发现法国与美洲远隔重洋,无法远距离殖民美洲。当时的世界海上霸权掌握在法国的对手英国人手里。更为重要的是,当时法国正处于和英国开战的边缘,如果英国海军将法国和美洲殖民地阻隔开来,那么即便拿破仑的军事天分再高也将无能为力。正当此时,美国人介入进来了,并以极低的价格从拿破仑手里购买了路易斯安那地区大片的土地,由此拉开了美国西进运动的大幕。

Reading Passage 1

导读

1803 年,美国乘拿破仑忙于应付欧洲战争之际,从法国手中以极低的价格购买了路易斯安那的广大地区。为了开发广袤的西部领土、加强中西部的联系,杰弗逊总统签署法案,由联邦政府出资修建这条打通中西部的国家之路(National Road)。

The Louisiana Purchase was the acquisition of the territory of Louisiana by the United States from France in 1803. In return for fifteen million dollars, or approximately eighteen dollars per square mile, the United States **nominally** acquired a total of 828,000 square miles. However, France only controlled a small fraction of this area, with most of it inhabited by Native Americans; for the majority of the area, what the United States bought was the "**preemptive**" right to obtain Native American lands by treaty or by conquest, **to the exclusion of** other colonial powers. The Louisiana Purchase extended United States sovereignty across the Mississippi River, nearly doubling the nominal size of the country. The purchase included land from fifteen present U.S. states and two Canadian provinces.

The Louisiana Purchase was by far the largest territorial gain in U. S. history. Stretching from the **Mississippi River** to the **Rocky Mountains**, the purchase doubled the size of the United States. Before 1803, Louisiana had been under Spanish control for forty years. Although Spain aided the rebels in the American Revolutionary War, the Spanish didn't want the Americans to settle in their territory.

Although the purchase was thought of by some as unjust and **unconstitutional**, Jefferson determined that his constitutional power to negotiate treaties allowed the purchase of what became fifteen states. **In hindsight**, the Louisiana Purchase could be considered one of his greatest contributions to the United States. On April 18, 1802, Jefferson penned a letter to United States Ambassador to France Robert Livingston. It was an intentional **exhortation** to make this supposedly mild diplomat strongly warn the French of their **perilous** course.

(Adapted from *https://www.history.com/topics/westward-expansion/louisiana-purchase*)

注释:

1.nominally 名义上地
2.preemptive 优先购买的,有先买权的
3.to the exclusion of 排除掉,排斥,不计
4.Mississippi River 密西西比河
5.Rocky Mountains 落基山脉
6.unconstitutional 违宪的

7.in hindsight 事后看来
8.exhortation 讲道词，训词；劝告
9.perilous 危险的

Reading Passage 2

导读

路易斯安那置地案后，议会颁布了修路的法案，并由托马斯·杰弗逊总统于1806年签署执行。这是一个“传奇”的项目，因为这既是美国第一个联邦公共项目（由联邦政府出资），也为其他道路的修建提供了样板。并且美国的经济、东西方贸易也因此繁荣起来。如今，国家之路被并入了美国40号国道，沿途的建筑和桥梁向过往的人们诉说着西进之路的历史。

The National Road (also known as the Cumberland Road) was the first major improved highway in the United States built by the federal government. Built between 1811 and 1837, the 620-mile (1,000 km) road connected the **Potomac** and **Ohio Rivers** and was a main transport path to the West for thousands of settlers.When rebuilt in the 1830s, it became the second U.S. road surfaced with the **macadam** process pioneered by Scotsman **John Loudon McAdam.**

In 1811 the first contract was awarded and the first 10 miles of road built. By 1818 the road was completed to Wheeling and mail coaches began using the road. By the 1830s the federal government conveyed part of the road's responsibility to the states through which it runs. **Tollgates** and **tollhouses** were then built by the states, with the federal government taking responsibility for road repairs.

Along the road, lots of constructions are still in use. Historic stone bridges on the National Road have their own stories to tell as well as reminding us of the craftsmanship of early engineers. The stone Casselman River Bridge still stands east of Grantsville, Maryland. A product of the early 19th century federal government improvements program along the National Road, the Casselman River Bridge was constructed in 1813-1814. Its 80-foot span, the largest of its type in America, connected Cumberland to the Ohio River.

Another remaining National Road bridge is the Wheeling Suspension Bridge at Wheeling, West Virginia. Opened in 1849 to carry the road over the Ohio River, it was the largest suspension bridge in the world until 1851, and is today the oldest vehicular suspension bridge in the United States still in use.

Mile markers have been used in Europe for more than 2,000 years and European ancestors continued that tradition in America. These markers tell travelers how far they are from their destination and were an important icon in early National Road travel.

(Adapted from *https: //www.fhwa.dot.gov / infrastructure / back*0103.*cfm*)

注释:

1.Potomac River 波托马克河
2.Ohio River 俄亥俄河
3.macadam 碎石路面
4.John Loudon McAdam 约翰·马卡丹
5.tollgate 收费关卡
6.tollhouse 通行税征收处

Word Power

Match the words given below with their meanings.

acquisition, inhabit, craftsmanship, vehicular, icon

(1)________ to live in a particular place

(2)________ intended for vehicles or consisting of vehicles

(3)________ a famous person or thing that people admire and see as a symbol of a particular idea, way of life, etc.

(4)________ the act of getting something, especially knowledge, a skill, etc.

(5)________ the level of skill shown by somebody in making something beautiful with their hands

Summary

Fill in the blanks with words or phrases from Reading Passage 1and Passage 2.

The Louisiana Purchase was the (1)________ of the territory of Louisiana by the United States from France in 1803. The Louisiana Purchase was by far the largest territorial gain in U.S. history. Stretching from the (2)________ to the (3)________, the purchase doubled the size of the United States.

After the purchase, in order to unify the nation, the then-president (4)________ signed an act for the building of this National Road. The National Road (also known as the Cumberland Road) became the first major improved highway in the United States built by the (5)________.

Listening

Scan the code and listen to a microlecture about the landmarks in Boston. Please choose the best answer to each of the following questions.

(1) The National Road was the first major improved highway funded by the ________ government.

A. municipal
B. county
C. state
D. federal

(2) The National Road is to connecting Potomac River and ________ River.

A. Mississippi River
B. Ohio River
C. Colorado River
D. Columbia River

(3) The Louisiana Purchase was the acquisition of the Louisiana territory by the United States from ________ in 1803.

A. Italy
B. France
C. Britain
D. Germany

Speaking

Roads are the arteries through which the economy pulses. By linking producers to markets, workers to jobs, students to school, and the sick to hospitals, roads are vital to any development agenda. Since 2002, the World Bank has constructed more than 260,000 km of roads. However, while roads bring economic and social benefits, they can also come with social costs such as pollution or deforestation. The Amazon rainforest is crisscrossed by almost 100,000 km of roads—enough to circle the Earth two and a half times. Please share your ideas on road construction. Refer to the following expressions if necessary.

transport policies / infrastructure / economic development / carbon dioxide emission / local particle pollution

Writing

1. Example Sentence

The Louisiana Purchase was the acquisition of the territory of Louisiana by the United States from France in 1803.

2. Analysis

(1)本句翻译为:路易斯安那置地案是指美国在1803年从法国人手中购买了路易斯安那地区的购买案。

(2)本句中使用了acquisition这个名词,但在汉语句子中翻译为动词"购买"。

(3)在写作中,中文多用动词,而英文多用名词。

3. Practice

试译下面两句话并比较中英文的用词区别。

(1) 吃一堑,长一智。

(2) 未经许可,禁止入内。

第十章　好莱坞电影中的明星大桥

概　述

在本章中，你将欣赏到好莱坞电影中的明星大桥。好莱坞电影的魅力众人皆知：新颖的题材、精美的制作、壮观的场景、浪漫的剧情、动听的音乐等。在关注情节的同时你是否仔细观察过电影的选址？好莱坞电影中出镜率最高的大桥是哪一座？连接曼哈顿和布鲁克林的大桥为何被戏称为“宝马桥”？七英里桥为何能成为散落在大西洋上最耀眼的明珠？这些问题的答案都将在本章中一一被揭晓。本章所包含的大桥包括：灾难片的最爱——金门大桥、旧金山的新地标——海湾大桥、曼哈顿和布鲁克林的纽带——布鲁克林大桥和曼哈顿大桥以及佛罗里达的明珠——七英里桥。

第一节　金门大桥

加利福尼亚州的旧金山面积不足 130 平方千米，却是世界上最伟大的城市之一。旧金山拥有宏伟的维多利亚之家、充满活力的多元化社会、高耸的红色大桥以及风景优美的海滨，是一座名副其实的海湾城市。从米其林星级餐厅到生意红火的街边小吃，旧金山引领着餐饮潮流；此外它拥有世界知名的交响乐、芭蕾舞、戏剧、歌剧，这些都使其成为当之无愧的旅游胜地。

Culture Express

金门大桥作为美国旧金山的标志性建筑，每年吸引世界各地的游客前来参观。大桥横跨旧金山湾湾口，全桥呈火红色，风光迷人。既然全桥都是红色的，那么为何它叫“金门”大桥呢？人们普遍认为，探险家 John C. Fremont 最早发现了旧金山湾湾口海峡（金门大桥所跨水域）并将其命名为 Chrysopylae（希腊语“金门”之意），金门大桥由此得名。那为何桥是深红色的呢？其实这完全是意外惊喜。大桥初建好时，桥身上的钢铁仅涂了一层红色底漆。一位顾问工程师喜欢桥这时的状态，建议保留红色，并协助确定了大桥最后的油漆颜色。

Reading Passage 1

导读

金门大桥可谓是好莱坞电影中的明星桥了，出镜率极高，经常一言不合就被毁灭。现实中更多人是通过电影认识它的。

The Bridge Hollywood Loves to Hate

The Golden Gate Bridge is a suspension bridge spanning the Golden Gate, the one-mile-wide (1.6 km) strait connecting San Francisco Bay and the Pacific Ocean. Though very few people have the chances to see it themselves, large amount of the visitors can get a glimpse of its splendid appearance through Hollywood screens.

Hollywood hates a popular landmark. The Eiffel Tower, Big Ben and the Statue of Liberty have all perished by the hand of **super-villains**, natural disasters and alien invasions. But nothing has fallen so frequently, and so spectacularly, as the Golden Gate Bridge. The film industry has destroyed the bridge so many times—nine in the past 10 years! —and with such loving detail, while using so much slow motion, that it probably qualifies clinically as a **fetish**.

For the 80th anniversary of the opening of the Golden Gate Bridge this weekend, Curbed SF looked at the never-ending **grandeur** of the sparkling span in the eyes of photographers and at the most colorful highlights of its eight-decade history.

But that's only part of the story. For billions of people, the Golden Gate Bridge exists not as structure of steel and concrete but as a shining vision on a movie screen. As one of the most **telegenic** of all human-made expanses—"a perfect **amalgam** of delicacy and power," as Herb Caen called it—the bridge has a special place in film history.

Hollywood loves to wreck the bridge, particularly in recent years. Still, there's no such as bad publicity. Here are some of the angelic arch's best silver screen memories.

1. *Dark Passage* (1947)
2. *It Came from Beneath the Sea* (1955)
3. *Vertigo* (1958)
4. *Superman: The Movie* (1978)
5. *A View to a Kill* (1985)
6. *Star Trek IV: The Voyage Home* (1986)
7. *Interview with the Vampire* (1994)
8. *X-Men: The Last Stand* (2006)
9. *Zodiac* (2007)
10. *Big Hero* 6 (2014)

11. *Godzilla* (2014)

12. *Terminator*: *Genisys* (2015)

(Adapted from *https://sf.curbed.com*/2017/5/26/15693300/*golden-gate-bridge-movies-sf*)

注释:

1.super-villain 超级大反派
2.fetish 偶像
3.grandeur 壮丽,庄严,宏伟
4.telegenic 适用于电视广播的
5.amalgam 汞合金,混合物

Reading Passage 2

导读

金门大桥长期以来不仅是旧金山最著名的景点,也被认为是建筑和美学史上的壮举。通体红色的大桥横跨旧金山湾,湾里经常升起氤氲的薄雾,笼罩其中的红色大桥仿佛通往彼岸的仙境。但这里"全球自杀圣地"的称呼也为金门大桥蒙上了一丝阴影。人们不禁发问:"为何这里深受自杀者的欢迎?"下面让我们倾听一位自杀幸存者的讲述。

Since it was erected in 1937, more than 1,700 people are estimated to have jumped off the Golden Gate Bridge, and just 25 are known to have survived, according to Robert Olson of The Centre for Suicide Prevention in Calgary, Canada.

Depression, **delusions**, **paranoia**—these conditions drove Kevin Hines to attempt suicide, but he survived. Today Kevin is on a mission to help others, starting with a new documentary and a plan to create a Golden Gate Bridge **suicide barrier net.**

"Jump now," said the voice in Kevin Hines's head, "And I did. I was compelled to die."

Hines leaped over a rail on the Golden Gate Bridge in September of 2000 and began a freefall that would reach 75 miles per hour on impact. The moment his fingers left the railing, he felt instant regret.

"I thought it was too late, I said to myself, 'What have I done, I don't want to die.'" says Hines, now 38, "I realized I made the greatest mistake of my life."

Hines fell about 240 feet in just four seconds. He crashed feet first into the waters below, crushing **spinal vertebrae** and breaking an ankle. But he survived.

Now, Hines travels the world to speak about suicide prevention and mental health, telling his story to help others stay alive.

Hines details his story in the new documentary that he produced, *Suicide: The Ripple Effect*, which opened across the United States in March 2018. He has also authored a memoir, *Cracked Not Broken, Surviving and Thriving after a Suicide Attempt*. Hines' story is definitely **resonating**—he has over 18,000 followers on Twitter.

"My goal is to try to instill hope in at least one individual," Hines says, "so that one individual says, 'Maybe I can stay here, maybe there are tools to fight this.'" Hines helps suicidal people he has met in one-on-one situations—through social media and at his speeches. He has helped save numerous lives.

(Adapted from *https://www.psycom.net / kevin-hines-survived-golden-gate-bridge-suicide /*)

注释:

1.delusion 幻觉,错觉
2.paranoia 偏执狂
3.suicide barrier net 防自杀屏障网
4.spinal vertebrae 脊柱
5.resonating 产生共鸣的

Word Power

Fill in the blanks with the words given below. Change the form where necessary. Each word can be used only once.

delicacy, span, grandeur, landmark, erect

(1) She searched around for a ________ that could be seen over the trees, but nothing was tall enough.

(2) The centre arch has a ________ of 152 ft., and rises 29 ft.

(3) The guest house was ________ in 1988.

(4) The power and ________ of these concerts is inconceivably striking and pleasing to the hunter's ear.

(5) Thus the restoration and interpretation of the historic architecture is one of peculiar ________ and difficulty.

Summary

Fill in the blanks with words or phrases from Reading Passage 1.

The Golden Gate Bridge is a (1)________ spanning the Golden Gate, the one-mile-wide (1.6 km) strait connecting San Francisco Bay and (2) ________. Like the Eiffel Tower, Big Ben and the Statue of Liberty, Golden Gate Bridge has been chosen as the choice to be destroyed by the hand of (3)________, (4)________and alien invasions. For billions of people, the Golden Gate Bridge exists not as structure of (5) ________but as a shining vision on a movie screen.

Listening

Scan the code and listen to a microlecture on Golden Gate Bridge. Please choose the best answer to each of the following questions.

(1)The Golden Gate connects the San Francisco Bay to ________.

A.the Atlantic Ocean　　B.the Indian Ocean

C.the Pacific Ocean　　D.the Arctic Ocean

(2)The color of the Golden Gate Bridge is called ________.

A.International Red　　B.International Orange

C.International Grey　　D.International White

(3) Although the Golden Gate Bridge is painted in reddish color, there is dark side about the bridge because it's the world's leading ________ spot.

A. suicide　　B. love

C. tourist　　D. filming

Speaking

Less than three months after the iconic Golden Gate Bridge opened in 1937, *a man named Harold Wobber walked to its halfway point. "This is where I get off." Wobber said, and suddenly leaped from the four-foot-high railing. He became the first known person to die by suicide at the international orange feat of engineering. Then more than one thousand followed. If you are to make a speech to people seeking suicide on Golden Gate Bridge, what will you say to them? Refer to the following words / phrases if necessary.*

suicide site / hitting the water / landing on concrete / bones break / float / unable to move / drown crisis counseling / suicide barrier net / positive mindset / optimistic attitude

Writing

1. Example Sentence

Though very few people have the chances to see it themselves, large amount of the visitors can get a glimpse of its splendid appearance through Hollywood screens.

2. Analysis

(1)本句意思是:虽然亲临金门大桥参观的观赏者很少,但很多人都能从好莱坞电影中一睹其壮丽的外观。

(2)本句中有一个前置的修饰语:though 引导的让步状语从句。

(3)修饰语(状语)的位置相对灵活,可以在句首、句中或句尾,可以由从句、不定式、副词或者分词短语来担当。

3. Practice

通过改变句子成分的顺序，修改以下病句，注意把修饰语放在合理位置。

Maria, went to sleep, quickly and quietly, a young girl, hoping to please her mom.

第二节　海湾大桥

旧金山三面环水，东面的旧金山湾（San Francisco Bay）经金门海峡与西边的太平洋相连。旧金山与周边连通的桥有两座：北面横跨金门海峡连接旧金山与北加利福尼亚的是金门大桥，向东横跨旧金山湾连接旧金山与奥克兰市的叫海湾大桥（the Bay Bridge）。有趣的是，虽然两座大桥都将旧金山与周边连接，但它们的知名度有着天壤之别。

在上一节中，我们可以感受到金门大桥受到的万千宠爱。在人们心目中，她像是旧金山的形象代言人、一个地标、一座丰碑。相比之下，默默无闻的海湾大桥虽然开通时间早其半年，长度是其 5 倍，车流量约是其 3 倍，但鲜少被关注。海湾大桥更像一个埋头苦干的暖男，有担当又不张扬。

Culture Express

旧金山-奥克兰海湾大桥的历史要从 1933 年开始说起。受美国南北淘金热影响，美国城市发展迅速，单纯依靠水路运输已严重影响了旧金山的发展，人们迫切希望建一座大桥来连接旧金山和奥克兰。于是，海湾大桥于 1933 年动工，1936 年底即竣工并投入使用。

事实上，早在 19 世纪 70 年代早期就有人提议建造一座连接旧金山和奥克兰的大桥。不过旧金山海域又深又宽，美国当时的技术根本无法实现这一“天方夜谭”的想法。尽管技术上不能实现，但相关人士依旧不愿放弃，直到 1933 年各方面条件成熟后，美国才决定建造海湾大桥。为了配合大桥的顺利建造，当年的耶尔巴布埃纳岛（美国海军基地）也不得不搬走，另觅他处。

Reading Passage 1

导读

当你行驶在海湾大桥上时，一定会被眼前的壮观景色震撼到：设计大气的双侧悬索、一眼望不到头的桥面（海湾大桥是世界跨度最大的桥梁之一）、川流不息的车辆长龙（日通行量达 26 万辆）等。皇冠加身，它却沉稳平实，不与人争。

The San Francisco-Oakland Bay Bridge, known locally as the Bay Bridge, is a complex of bridges spanning San Francisco Bay in California. As part of **Interstate 80**and the direct road between San Francisco and Oakland, it carries about 260,000 vehicles a day on its two decks. It has one of the longest spans in the United States.

The toll bridge was conceived as early as the **California Gold Rush days**, but construction did not begin until 1933. Designed by Charles H. Purcell, and built by American Bridge Company, it opened on Thursday, November 12, 1936, six months before the Golden Gate Bridge. It originally carried automobile traffic on its upper deck, with trucks, cars, buses and commuter trains on the lower, but after the Key System abandoned rail service, the lower deck was converted to all-road traffic as well. In 1986, the bridge was unofficially **dedicated** to James Rolph.

The bridge has two sections of roughly equal length; the older western section, officially known as the Willie L. Brown Jr. Bridge (after former San Francisco Mayor and California State Assembly Speaker Willie L. Brown Jr.), connects downtown San Francisco to Yerba Buena Island, and the newer unnamed eastern section connects the island to Oakland. The western section is a **double suspension bridge** with two decks, westbound traffic being carried on the upper deck while eastbound is carried on the lower one. The largest span of the original eastern section was a **cantilever bridge.** During the 1989 earthquake, a portion of the eastern section's upper deck collapsed onto the lower deck and the bridge was closed for a month. Reconstruction of the eastern section of the bridge began in 2002; the new eastern section opened on September 2, 2013, at a reported cost of over $6.5 billion, a 2,500% cost overrun from the original estimate of $250 million (for a **seismic retrofit** of the existing span). Unlike the western section and the original eastern section of the bridge, the new eastern section is a single deck with the eastbound and westbound lanes on each side making it the world's widest bridge, according to *Guinness World Records*, as of 2014.**Demolition** of the old east span was completed on September 8, 2018.

(Adapted from *https://baybridgeinfo.org/history*)

注释：

1.Interstate 80 80号州际公路
2.California Gold Rush days 加州淘金热
3.be dedicated to 将……献给
4.double suspension bridge 双悬索桥
5.cantilever bridge 悬臂桥
6.seismic retrofit 抗震加固
7.demolition 拆除

Reading Passage 2

导读

1989年旧金山发生特大地震，海湾大桥在这场地震中受到重创，美国决定在老桥旁建造一座崭新的海湾大桥。为了提高其抗震能力，当时美国投入了史上最高金额——72亿美元来建造新大桥，而大桥最为核心的地段是由中国团队完成的。令美国人感到意外的是，中国团队不仅出色地完成了大桥核心地段的建造，还节省了4亿多美元。

California is spending more than $7 billion building what it says will be an

architectural marvel: the new San Francisco-Oakland Bay Bridge. But the state saved a lot of money sending some of the construction work overseas.

The new eastern span of the Bay Bridge will have a distinctive design to rival its more famous cousin, the Golden Gate Bridge.

Bart Ney, a spokesman for the project, recently stood near the top of a **gleaming** white tower, more than 500 feet above the San Francisco Bay. "What we're standing on will be the world's largest **self-anchored** suspension bridge." he says. A typical suspension bridge is held up by **cables** strung between two towers like a hammock. This bridge features a single tower and a single mile-long cable that drapes up and over the tower and supports the deck like a **sling**. The cable is made up of 137 strands of steel. "We will pull those strands across the bay to make this cable," says Ney, "And we keep doing that until we have all of them in place, and then we can start hanging up the suspender wires that hold up the deck."

This assembly will be performed early next year by American labor. But the massive cable, key sections of the iconic tower and deck were all made in China, which is emerging as an **infrastructure powerhouse** in more places than San Francisco. For example, Chinese companies have contracted with New York City for a bridge, the subway system and a commuter train platform.

"The decision to **outsource** the fabrication of key sections of the Bay Bridge was made about five years ago, when a contractor offered alternate bids on the project." says Tony Anziano, a manager at the California Department of Transportation. "One proposing to do work domestically, one proposing to do the work internationally: There was a $400 million **differential** in that bid, and in that case it would have required the work to go international." he says.

California avoided legal requirements to use domestic steel by not using federal funds for the job. The steel contract went to a state-owned Chinese company, **Shanghai Zhenhua Heavy Industries**, which had several advantages: modern production facilities, ships to deliver the steel and, of course, low-cost labor. A Chinese steel polisher makes about $12 a day.

Bob LaVenture, a district director for the United Steelworkers Union, has opposed outsourcing this job. "There is no way that American workers will be able to ever compete with $12 a day," he says, "It's just not right, and it's not right for America."

"It wasn't just the cost of labor that made Chinese steel more attractive." Anziano says. He says American steel fabricators don't have the capacity for a job like the Bay Bridge. When union and industry groups questioned the quality of the Chinese steel, Anziano says, "The state and the contractor sent more than 200 people to China to watch over the fabrication process."

"In this particular case, we had **full-time staff** on site over in China—24/7—that monitored all aspects of fabrication work and performed their own quality-assurance testing," he says, "so we have a very high level of assurance about what we are getting."

California Assemblyman Luis Alejo says that even at a savings of hundreds of millions of dollars, the decision to outsource has done more damage to California than it was worth. "When you have a project of that size here in California, it has a **multiplier effect**," he says, "It gives thousands of families those jobs, and then those paychecks and their subsequent spending ends up going back into our economy. And so now all that money has permanently disappeared from California."

California's unemployment rate is 12 percent, well above the national average. Yet when the deal was made for the Chinese steel, unemployment ran at just under 5 percent. If it were still that low now, this debate would likely have less punch.

(Adapted from *https://www.publicradiotulsa.org/post/california—turns—china—new—bay—bridge*)

注释：

1.architectural marvel 建筑奇迹
2.gleaming 闪闪发光的
3.self-anchored 自锚式的
4.cable 缆绳
5.sling 吊索
6.infrastructure powerhouse 基建强国
7.outsource 外包
8.differential 差别
9.Shanghai Zhenhua Heavy Industries 上海振华重工
10.full-time staff 专职人员
11.multiplier effect 乘数效应

Word Power

Match the word with its appropriate meaning in English.

toll, complex, span, westbound, deck

(1)________ lead to the west or are travelling toward the west
(2)________ the charge for using a specific road or for making a telephone call
(3)________ group of buildings designed for a particular purpose
(4)________ the total width of something from one end to the other
(5)________ a lower or upper area of something, such as a ship or a building

Summary

Fill in the blanks with words or phrases from Reading Passage 1.

The San Francisco-Oakland Bay Bridge, known locally as the (1) ________, is a complex of bridges spanning San Francisco Bay in California. It has one of the longest (2)________ in the United States.

The bridge has two sections of roughly equal length; the older (3)________, which connects downtown San Francisco to Yerba Buena Island, and the newer unnamed (4) ________which connects the island to Oakland. The western section is a double (5) ________ with two decks. The largest span of the original eastern section was a (6)________.

During the 1989 earthquake, a portion of the eastern section's upper deck collapsed onto the lower deck and (7)________ of the eastern section of the bridge began in 2002 and opened on September 2, 2013. Demolition of the old east span was completed on September 8, 2018.

Listening

Scan the code and listen to a microlecture on Bay Bridge. Please choose the best answer to each of the following questions.

(1)Bay Bridge is to connect San Francisco with ________.

A. Oakland B. California C. Los Angeles D. Hollywood

(2) Which section of the Bay Bridge was damaged in the 1989 earthquake?

A. Eastern section. B. Western section. C. Both sections. D. Neither.

(3) The western section of the Bay Bridge is ________ bridge.

A. double suspension B. cantilever C. stone D. arch

Speaking

In the previous sections, we have learned China's dedication to the reconstruction of the new Eastern section of the Bay Bridge. Having completed many dozens of infrastructure projects at home, China is now also offering her services to other countries in the world. Some say it's a reflection of China's economic power, some say it's China's tool to influence the world. What do you think of China's infrastructural capacity? Refer to the following words and expressions if necessary.

domestic and international relation / economic power / boost economy / civil engineering skills / infrastructure project / uphold the welfare of Chinese citizens

Writing

1. Example Sentence

Allowing his men to make important decisions in a democratic manner, Lewis fostered a spirit of togetherness and commitment among his fellow explorers.

2. Analysis

(1)英文善用长句,汉语善用短句。

(2)英文写作中,除了可以以并列句的形式连接两句话之外,还可以将其中一句处理为短语的形式,作为主句的修饰成分。如本句中的现在分词短语"allowing his men to make important decisions in a democratic manner"。"allow"的逻辑主语与主句主语一致,故可以省略。

(3)作修饰成分的短语除了分词短语外,还可以是不定式、介词短语、形容词等。

3. Practice

请使用介词短语作修饰语的形式,将以下两句合并。

(1)The expeditionary force was completely out of touch with their families for over two years.

(2)They put their faith entirely in Lewis and Clark's leadership and never once rebelled against their authority.

第三节　布鲁克林大桥

纽约市共有五个区,分别为曼哈顿、布朗克斯、布鲁克林、皇后区和斯塔滕岛。布鲁克林区位于美国东北部,纽约曼哈顿岛的东南边,是纽约市五大区中人口最多的一个。如果该区是一座城市,将是美国第四大城。虽然现在它是纽约市人口最多的区,但布鲁克林区一开始只包括 6 个建在东河边上的荷兰移民小村庄,因此在当时有"小荷兰"的称号。1664 年,它成为纽约属地的一部分,1898 年被正式划入纽约市,成为五大区之一。

Culture Express

在纽约,横跨纽约东河连接曼哈顿区和布鲁克林区的大桥有三座。到纽约旅游,人们通常都能观赏到并排凌驾于东河之上的这三座大桥:布鲁克林大桥(the Brooklyn Bridge)、曼哈顿大桥(the Manhattan Bridge)和威廉斯堡大桥(Williamsburg Bridge)。

布鲁克林大桥 1883 年 5 月 24 日正式交付使用。大桥全长 1834 米,桥身由上万根钢索吊离水面 41 米,是当年世界上最长的悬索桥,也是世界上首次以钢材建造的大桥,落成时被认为是继世界古代七大奇迹之后的第八大奇迹,被誉为工业革命时代全世界七个划时代的建筑工程奇迹之一。

Reading Passage 1

导读

几乎所有关于纽约的电影，都会从布鲁克林大桥掠过，仿佛从这里进入纽约才有电影般的仪式感。蜘蛛侠在大桥上变身，《我是传奇》里大桥被炸毁，《欲望都市》里米兰达和丈夫在桥上重逢，还有《闻香识女人》《纽约我爱你》《教父》《美国往事》等无一不选择布鲁克林大桥为拍摄背景。

The Brooklyn Bridge is a **hybrid cable-stayed / suspension bridge** in New York City, spanning the East River between the boroughs of Manhattan and Brooklyn. Opened on May 24, 1883, the Brooklyn Bridge was the first **fixed crossing** across the East River. It was also the longest suspension bridge in the world at the time, with a main span of 1,595.5 feet (486.3 m) and a deck height of 127 ft (38.7 m) above mean high water. The span was originally called the New York and Brooklyn Bridge or the East River Bridge but was officially renamed the Brooklyn Bridge in 1915.

The Brooklyn Bridge is the southernmost of four toll-free **vehicular bridges** connecting Manhattan Island and Long Island, with the Manhattan, Williamsburg, and Queensboro bridges to the north. Only **passenger vehicles** and pedestrian and bicycle traffic are permitted. A major tourist attraction since its opening, the Brooklyn Bridge has become an icon of New York City. Over the years, the bridge has been used as the location of various stunts and performances, as well as several crimes and attacks. The Brooklyn Bridge has been designated a National Historic Landmark, a New York City landmark, and a National Historic Civil Engineering Landmark.

The bridge is often featured in wide shots of the New York City skyline in television and film, and has been depicted in numerous works of art.

Films that feature the Brooklyn Bridge include: *I am Legend*, *Scent of Woman*, *Godfather and Once Upon a Time in America*.

(Adapted from *https://www.history.com/topics/landmarks/brooklyn—bridge*)

注释：

1.hybrid 混合
2.cable-stayed 斜拉桥
3.suspension bridge 悬索桥
4.fixed crossing 固定通道
5.vehicular bridge 行车桥，公路桥
6.passenger vehicle 载客汽车

Reading Passage 2

导读

“按照我的设计完成作品的话，（它）将不仅仅是现存最伟大的桥，也是这个州、这个时代最伟大的工程。它最显著的特点是伟大的塔楼，其将是连接两座城市的地标，将被评为国家历史遗址。一件伟大的艺术品、一个先进桥梁工程的标本，这个结构将永远证明这个社会的活力、财富和进取心。”约翰·罗布林（John Roebling）在1867年用他一贯“好像没有什么不可能”的语气写下这些话。但是大桥的建设并不顺利，约翰·罗布林也没能见证大桥的竣工。布鲁克林大桥最终耗时13年才建成，让我们一起来探究大桥背后这一可歌可泣的设计故事吧！

The Brooklyn Bridge was initially designed by German immigrant John Augustus Roebling, who had previously designed and constructed shorter suspension bridges, such as Roebling's Delaware Aqueduct in Lackawaxen, Pennsylvania, Waco Suspension Bridge in Waco, Texas, and the John A. Roebling Suspension Bridge in Cincinnati, Ohio. While conducting surveys for the bridge project, Roebling sustained a crush injury to his foot when a ferry pinned it against a **piling**. After **amputation** of his crushed toes he developed a **tetanus** infection which left him **incapacitated** and soon resulted in his death, not long after he had placed his 32-year-old son Washington Roebling in charge of the project. Washington Roebling also suffered a **paralyzing** injury as a result of **decompression sickness** shortly after the beginning of construction on January 3, 1870.

Washington Roebling conducted the entire construction from his apartment with a view of the work, designing and redesigning **caissons** and other equipment. He was aided by his wife Emily Warren Roebling who provided the critical written link between her husband and the engineers on site. Under her husband's guidance, Emily studied higher mathematics, the calculations of catenary curves, the strengths of materials, bridge specifications, and the intricacies of cable construction. She spent the next 11 years assisting Washington Roebling, helping to supervise the bridge's construction. When iron probes underneath the caisson found the bedrock to be even deeper than expected, Roebling halted construction due to the increased risk of decompression sickness. He later deemed the aggregate overlying the bedrock 30 feet (9 m) below it to be firm enough to support the tower base, and construction continued. Harbour pilot Joseph Henderson was called upon as an expert seaman to determine the height of the water span of the Brooklyn Bridge.

The Brooklyn Bridge was opened for use on May 24, 1883. The opening ceremony was attended by several thousand people and many ships were present in the East Bay for the occasion. President Chester A. Arthur and New York Mayor Franklin Edson crossed the bridge to celebratory cannon fire and were greeted by Brooklyn Mayor Seth Low when they reached the Brooklyn-side tower. Arthur shook hands with Washington Roebling at the latter's home, after the ceremony. Roebling was unable to attend the ceremony (and in fact rarely visited the site again), but held a celebratory banquet at his house on the day of the bridge opening.

(Adapted from *http://onthesetofnewyork.com / mostpopularbrooklynbridge.html*)

注释:

1.piling 地桩
2.amputation 截肢
3.tetanus 破伤风
4.incapacitated 丧失能力的
5.paralyzing 瘫痪
6.decompression sickness 减压病
7.caissons 沉箱

Word Power

Match the word with its appropriate meaning in English.

borough, toll-free, icon, in charge of, specification

(1)________ a requirement which is clearly stated
(2)________ something as important as a symbol
(3)________ without having to pay
(4)________ take the responsibility of, in attendance
(5)________ a town, or a district within a large city

Summary

Fill in the blanks with words or phrases from Reading Passage 1.

The Brooklyn Bridge is a hybrid cable-stayed and suspension bridge in New York City, spanning the East River between the boroughs of (1)________ and (2)________. When it was finished, it was also the longest ________ in the world at the time. It is the southernmost of four ________ vehicular bridges connecting Manhattan Island and Long Island, with the Manhattan, Williamsburg, and Queensboro bridges to the north. The Brooklyn Bridge has been designated a ________, a New York City landmark, and a National Historic Civil Engineering Landmark and is often featured in television and film, and has been depicted in numerous works of art.

Listening

Scan the code and listen to a microlecture on Brooklyn Bridge. Please choose the best answer to each of the following questions.

(1)The idiom, "If you believe that, then I have a bridge I want to sell you." is used to describe someone who is ________.

A.intelligent　　B. beautiful

C. gullible　　D. conservative

(2)All of the following made great contributions to the construction of the Brooklyn Bridge except ________.

A.John Roebling　　B. Washington Roebling

C. Emily Roebling　　D. Joseph Strauss

(3) The architect of the Brooklyn Bridge, Washington Roebling was paralyzed because of ________.

A.heart attack　　B. infection

C. decompression disease　　D. high pressure

Speaking

As one of the greatest cities in the world, New York is always a whirlwind of activity, with famous sites at every turn and never enough time to see them all. If you have the chance to visit New York, which site would you choose to visit first and explain the reasons. Refer to the following expressions if necessary.

Brooklyn Bridge / Statue of Liberty / Central Park / Time Square / Metropolitan Museum of Art / Broadway and the Theater District

Writing

1. Example Sentence

A major tourist attraction since its opening, the Brooklyn Bridge has become an icon of New York City.

2. Analysis

(1)本句中,"A major tourist attraction since its opening"是句子主语 Brooklyn Bridge 的同位语。

(2)同位语相当于定语从句省略了关系词。本句也可改写为:The Brooklyn Bridge which is a major tourist attraction since opening, has become an icon of New York City.

(3)使用同位语作修饰成分时,通常用逗号将其与主句分割。

3. Practice

将下面句子中的定语从句转换成同位语的形式。

Sacagawea, who was one of the Indian wives of Charbonneau, who was a French fur-trader, accompanied the expedition as a translator.

第四节 曼哈顿大桥

曼哈顿区在纽约市的五个区中面积最小，仅有57.91平方千米，为东西窄、南北长的小岛。纽约市有60多座桥梁，乘巡航游船绕曼哈顿岛航行56千米要经过20座桥，越过4条隧道和73个地铁分站。由于曼哈顿岛四周环水，因此桥梁及隧道数量众多，这是其一大特色。这些桥梁及隧道对曼哈顿的发展贡献巨大，因为它们是民众往来曼哈顿及郊区的必经通道。

Culture Express

纽约各区如同小积木一样工整地拼在一起，根据地理位置而得名："上东""中城""下城"等。上东区(Upper East Side)是纽约市曼哈顿所有社区中最富裕的区域之一，它是"老钱区"的代名词，有史以来纽约绝大多数的上流社会家族都居住于此，如石油大亨洛克菲勒家族、美国总统罗斯福家族和肯尼迪家族、企业家惠特尼家族和烟草大王杜克家族等。

Reading Passage 1

导读

曼哈顿大桥(the Manhattan Bridge)是一条悬索桥，跨越东河连接曼哈顿与布鲁克林。本文介绍了大桥的相关信息。

The Manhattan Bridge, suspension bridge over the East River connecting southeastern Manhattan with western Brooklyn in New York City. The bridge first opened to traffic in 1909, eight years after construction started.

The bridge is newer than the Brooklyn Bridge and the Williamsburg Bridge, the other two suspension bridges that span the East River, and often acts as an alternate route due to its **proximity** to the Brooklyn Bridge. The Manhattan Bridge, which is 6,855 feet (2,089 metres) long, consists of a double-deck motorway with four lanes on top and three lanes on the bottom that are designed to change direction when necessary to assist traffic flow. In addition to cars, the bridge carries four subway lines, a pedestrian lane, and a separate bikeway. Nearly 80,000 vehicles and more than 320,000 people use it (via public transportation) each day.

The bridge was designed by Leon Moisseiff, built by The Phoenix Bridge Company, and opened to traffic on December 31, 1909. Its design being innovative, this was the first suspension bridge to employ Josef Melan's **deflection theory** for deck stiffening, resulting in the first use of a lightly-webbed weight-saving **Warren truss** for its construction. This design saved in cost, material, and construction time. Renovations in 1940 revealed significant **wear** on the structure, with the subway trains partly responsible for the wear. Those trains, upon entering the bridge at the same time from opposite sides, would cause the bridge to shift up to 8 feet (approximately 2.5 metres). Additional renovations were undertaken in 1978. Since then the Manhattan Bridge has been featured in movies and undergone regular repairs and **retrofitting**, and now remains one of the most graceful bridges in New York City.

Considered the forerunner of modern suspension bridges, it served as the model for many of the record-breaking spans built in the first half of the twentieth century.

(Adapted from *https://www.britannica.com / topic / Manhattan-Bridge*)

注释:

1.proximity 接近
2.deflection theory 挠曲理论
3.Warren truss 瓦伦大梁,[建] 华伦式桁架
4.wear 耗损
5.retrofitting 改装,翻新

Reading Passage 2

导读

生活在纽约曼哈顿的中央商务区,意味着要支付昂贵的租金。但其实纽约市几乎每一个地方的房租都是昂贵的。所以那些低收入人群,几乎不可能生活在这个地区。有人发现曼哈顿桥不仅有交通运输的用途,还被人用作了其他用途。下面是来自《纽约邮报》的报道。

A homeless man living within **beams** of the Manhattan Bridge claims he was forced to build that **precarious** nest because cops have torn down his **shanty** on more stable ground.

The Post first reported on Sunday that at least two men now make their home in this dangerous spot, high above the East River between Manhattan and Brooklyn.

One of the residents—a 40-something Asian immigrant, who would only identify himself as "Joe"—said he used to live in **encampments** that he built on a grassy patch, just off the **bike on-ramp** to the Manhattan Bridge.

But over the past 13 years of homelessness in New York, cops have always torn down those quarters, he said. "Five times they take down. Five times!" Joe said of what had been his more stable shanties. Joe then pointed at his current home—a **crevice** above the bike path and subway tracks and below cars on the span's upper deck. It's about 150 feet east into the bridge's Brooklyn-bound side. "I build here." Joe said, pointing at his **death-defying** spot, "Not take down."

The man gets a mini-workout every day, climbing up and down a chain-link fence that separates subway tracks from the bike path on the Manhattan Bridge's lower level. That fence is Joe's **impromptu** stairway to the coffin-size space he calls home.

When *The Post* found Joe this week, he was plucking his eyebrows, using a broken mirror **wedged** into the bridge ledge. He appears to be in his late 40s, with rotten and missing lower teeth. Joe was remarkably well dressed, given his lot in life, in a striped men's dress shirt, a light blue and black striped sweater vest and jeans. He was wearing open sandals with socks.

In his broken English, Joe explained that his last steady job was in a kitchen. He told *The Daily Mail* newspaper that he's been living in the bridge for the last year and that he's lost a lot of money gambling. The man **fortifies** his bridge **abode** with discarded wood he finds nearby.

(Adapted from *https://nypost.com* / 2014/04/15/*cops-forced-me-to-live-in-the-manhattan-bridge* /)

注释：

1.beam 横梁
2.precarious 危险的
3.shanty 简陋的小屋，棚屋
4.encampments 营地，露营
5.bike on-ramp 自行车道入口
6.crevice 裂缝
7.death-defying 生死攸关的，视死如归的
8.impromptu 即兴的
9.wedge 楔入，挤进
10. fortify 加固
11. abode 住所

Word Power

Match the word with its appropriate meaning in English.

alternate, lane, pedestrian, renovation, record-breaking

(1)________ used to describe one that beats the previous best success, result, or performance

(2)________ the process of repair and improve an old building and get it back into good condition

(3)________ a plan, idea, or system which can be used to replace the previous one

(4)________ a part of a main road which is marked by the edge of the road and a painted line

(5)________ person who is walking, rather than travelling in a vehicle

Summary

Fill in the blanks with words or phrases from Reading Passage 1.

The Manhattan Bridge is a (1) ________ over the East River connecting southeastern Manhattan with western Brooklyn in New York City. This bridge, together with other two suspension bridges, (2) ________ and (3) ________, span the East River, work as the main route for transportation between the boroughs.

An innovative design, it was the first suspension bridge to employ Josef Melan's (4) ________ for deck stiffening, resulting in the first use of a lightly-webbed weight-saving (5) ________ for its construction

Listening

Scan the code and listen to a microlecture on Manhattan Bridge. Please choose the best answer to each of the following questions.

(1) Which of the following bridges does not cross the East River in New York?

A. The Manhattan Bridge.　　B. The Brooklyn Bridge.

C. The Williamsburg Bridge.　　D. The Golden Gate Bridge.

(2) In the Hollywood movie, *Once Upon A Time in America*, the image of Robert De Niro staring over Brooklyn warehouse under the background of the ________ became the poster(海报) often used in the movie's publicity.

A. Manhattan Bridge　　B. Brooklyn Bridge

C. Williamsburg Bridge　　D. Bay Bridge

(3) How many decks does the Manhattan bridge have?

A. One.　　B. Two.

C. Three.　　D. Four.

Speaking

Three bridges span the East River in connecting different boroughs. We have introduced Manhattan Bridge and Brooklyn Bridge. Will you please search for more information about Williamsburg Bridge and try to introduce the third bridge and its distinctive features to your classmates? Refer to the following words and phrases if necessary.

Manhattan Island and Long Island / suspension bridge / toll-free vehicular bridge / caisson

Writing

1. Example Sentence

Its design being innovative, this was the first suspension bridge to employ Josef

Melan's deflection theory for deck stiffening.

2. Analysis

(1)本句中"Its design being innovative"为独立主格结构。

(2)独立主格结构通常放在句首,由一个名词(独立主格的逻辑主语)加分词结构组成。

(3)独立主格结构可以使英文表达更加简洁、句型多变,值得我们学习。

3. Practice

使用独立主格的形式将下列句子组合成一句。

(1) Lewis's fame and fortune was virtually guaranteed by his exploits.

(2) Lewis disappointed the entire world by inexplicably failing to publish his journals.

第五节 七英里桥

佛罗里达礁岛群(Florida Keys)在迈阿密的南部,属于列岛,东临大西洋,西邻墨西哥湾,是由约 1700 个小岛组成的一丛岛屿。群岛从佛罗里达半岛东南角靠近迈阿密处,一路往南渐渐弯曲向西,直到最底端的基韦斯特(Key West,礁岛群最西)。基韦斯特是 Key West 的官方译名,作为美国本土的极南端,Key West 离古巴只有约 145 千米的距离,这里宜人的气候、湛蓝的海面、充满南美风情的景色吸引了众多游客。

Culture Express

海明威故居博物馆就坐落于基韦斯特主岛的老城区,是一幢西班牙殖民地建筑风格的小楼。1931～1939 年海明威和他的家人生活在这里,并在此创作了关于 Key West 经济萧条时期的小说《有钱人和没钱人》和著名短篇小说《乞力马扎罗的雪》等作品。

Reading Passage 1

导读

七英里大桥(the Seven Mile Bridge)旧桥,本来是一座通行火车的铁路桥(Old Seven Mile Bridge)。它的建设者是一位名叫佛莱哥(Henry Flagler)的石油大亨。1905～1912 年,他将铁路从佛罗里达一路向南修到了群岛的最南端。1935 年的一场毁灭性的飓风终止了 23 年的跨海铁路经营;损毁的轨道未再重建,跨海公路(Overseas Highway,即在群岛上的美国 1 号公路,U.S. Highway 1)由此取代了铁路,成为从迈阿密到西礁岛的主要交通路线。

The Seven Mile Bridge is a bridge in the Florida Keys, in Monroe County, Florida. It connects Knight's Key in the Middle Keys to Little Duck Key in the Lower Keys. Among the longest bridges in existence when it was built, it is part of the Overseas Highway in the Keys, which is part of the 2,369-mile (3,813 km) U.S. Route 1.

There are two bridges (the old and the new) in this location. Completed in 1912, the old structure, initially a railroad bridge, was known as the "Eighth Wonder of the World" because even attempting to build something so ambitious over miles of open water and a soft bottom in a harsh tropical climate seemed a bit **nutty** . Henry Morrison Flagler, a **craggy**, white-haired business genius who made his fortune in the oil business, hadn't gotten rich by being cautious. In the 19th century he came to Florida, built a hotel in St. Augustine and founded the Florida East Coast Railway. By 1896, his train was going all the way to Miami. That wasn't good enough. He wanted his railroad to go another 100 miles or so south to Key West.

"Flagler's **Folly.**" That's what a lot of folks called it. "Just watch me." was Flagler's **credo.**

Starting in 1905, he spent ＄30 million of his own money to lay track and build dozens of bridges, hiring 4,000 workers for the small fortune of ＄1.50 a day. They had to **wade through** swamps where boots sank into the mud as crocodiles slipped off the banks. Some workers died of heatstroke and snakebite. Everybody was bitten by mosquitoes. Folks were chronically hungry and thirsty. In 1908, the workers reached Marathon Key where about seven miles of open water lay ahead. Flagler's civil engineers had to invent new technology as they went along. At their disposal were two steamships, **tugboats**, **paddle wheelers**, **dredges**, **launches** and a **catamaran.** Flagler sent away to England for a kind of cement capable of drying underwater. Divers wearing helmets positioned underwater structures. Barges swung in the current as workers tried to keep their balance. They slept in tents and in **bunkhouses** Flagler built on Pigeon Key, about two miles from shore. The bunkhouses are still there. A ferry will take you to the island and a guide will show you around. You'll learn that on Jan. 28, 1916, the train rumbled to a stop in Key West. Flagler, 82, stepped out of his private car with his young wife. "Now I can die happy." Flagler whispered to a friend, "My dream is fulfilled."

(Adapted from *https://en.wikipedia.org / wiki / Seven_Mile_Bridge*, *https://www.visitflorida.com / en-us / cities / florida-keys / the-keys-seven-mile-bridge.html*)

注释：

1.nutty 奇怪的，愚蠢的

2.craggy 崎岖的，多峭壁的

3.Folly 愚蠢，荒唐事

4.credo 信条，教义

5.wade through 涉水，艰难地完成

6.tugboat 拖船

7.paddle wheeler 用桨轮推进的船
8.dredge 挖泥船
9.launch 汽艇
10.catamaran 双体船
11.bunkhouse 简易住屋

Reading Passage 2

导读

佛莱哥生前散尽千金而矢志不渝，不料几十年后的一场飓风摧毁了他生前的杰作。1935 年跨海铁路被劳工节飓风摧毁，1960 年又遭遇堂娜飓风。如今老桥已是观光桥。安全起见，有关单位拆卸了老桥的旋转桥段(swing span)，使之成为断桥。

The death of Flagler's railroad happened on Labor Day in 1935. It began when the **barometer** started dropping. Nobody knew that the most powerful hurricane ever hitting the United States was on its way. It swept across Matecumbe Key, in the Central Keys, that evening. Officials from the railroad had **dispatched** a train to **evacuate** residents and 800 World War I veterans who were living in tents and working on a new road near the railroad tracks.

The current road bridge was constructed from 1978 to 1982. It's certainly breathtaking and it has a fearsome reputation. The bridge itself doesn't seem that scary. But its position in the Florida Keys makes it a prime target for the region's many hurricanes. In fact, the current bridge is the second **iteration**. The newer bridge **scrapped** the **swing span** concept of the original **in lieu of** a sturdier 65-foot-high arch to allow boats to pass by. While it may be sturdier, we still wouldn't want to be on it during a storm. It's one of the most spectacular bridges in the world. As for the design, the new bridge is a **box-girder segmental structure** built from **precast**, prestressed concrete sections, comprising 440 spans. Near the center, the bridge rises in an arc to provide 65-foot-high clearance for boat passage. The remainder of the bridge is considerably closer to the water surface.

It's quite a famous bridge having appeared in a lot of movies, with a starring role in action thrillers ***Licence to Kill***, ***True Lies***, ***The Haunted Mansion*** , ***Mission Impossible III***, ***I Am Number Four*** and ***Leverage***, the Florida Keys' Seven Mile Bridge looks as impressive on film as it does in real life.

(Adapted from *https://www.visitflorida.com / en-us / cities / florida-keys / the-keys-seven-mile-bridge.html*)

注释：

1.barometer 气压计
2.dispatch 派遣

3.evacuate 疏散,撤退
4.iteration 反复,重复
5.scrap 废弃
6.swing span 旋转桥段
7.in lieu of 代替
8.box-girder segmental structure 箱梁抗损结构
9.precast 预制的,预先浇筑的
10.*Licence to Kill*《杀人执照》(007 系列电影)
11.*True Lies*《真实的谎言》
12.*The Haunted Mansion*《幽灵鬼屋》
13.*Mission Impossible* Ⅲ《碟中谍 3》
14.*I Am Number Four*《猎杀第四行者》
15.*Leverage*《都市侠盗》

Word Power

Fill in the blanks with the words given below. Change the form where necessary. Each word can be used only once.

dispatch, track, construct, sturdy, segmental

(1) He had been continually ________ scouts (侦察兵) ahead.

(2) The floods carried away everything—houses, cars, bridges, railway ________ and swirled it around before flushing it back down the valley and out to sea.

(3) His company recently ________ an office building in downtown Denver.

(4) This bridge is ________, meaning it's constructed with several parts.

(5) This building was constructed with high strength cement and was very ________.

Summary

Fill in the blanks with words or phrases from Reading Passage 1and Passage 2.

The Seven Mile Bridge is a bridge in the (1)________, in Florida, United States. It connects Knight's Key to Little Duck Key. When built, it is among the longest bridges in existence and part of the (2)________ in the Keys.

The old Seven Mile Bridge was completed in 1912, and was known as the "Eighth Wonder of the World." As for the design, the new bridge is a (3) ________ structure built from (4)________, prestressed concrete sections, comprising 440 spans. Near the center, the bridge rises in an (5)________ to provide 65-foot (20 m)-high clearance for boat passage. The remainder of the bridge is considerably closer to the water surface.

Listening

Scan the code and listen to a microlecture on Seven Mile Bridge. Please choose the best answer to each of the following questions.

(1) The old Seven Mile Bridge is originally used as ________.

A. railroad　　B. highway

C. pedestrian lane　　D. motor lane

(2) The Seven Mile Bridge is used to connect islands in ________.

A.Florida Keys　　B. Mexico Keys

C. Miami Keys　　D. California Keys

(3) The Seven Mile Bridge is a ________ bridge.

A.suspension　　B. cantilever

C. segmental　　D. cable-strayed

Speaking

Have you ever been watching a movie while thinking "Why does this setting look so familiar?" As it turns out, many of the most popular Hollywood movies aren't just filmed in their studios. The movie industry loves to film in some of the biggest cities across the world. Until now we have introduced five bridges in the U.S. Can you think of one Hollywood movie and introduce its filming location or the architecture in it? The followings are some of the popular film locations Hollywood loves to use. Refer to them if necessary.

Popular Film Location / Times Square, New York / UCLA, California / Williamsburg, New York / Greenwich Village, New York / Central Park, New York

Writing

1. Example Sentence

Completed in 1912, the old structure, initially a railroad bridge, was known as the "Eighth Wonder of the World" because even attempting to build something so ambitious over miles of open water and a soft bottom in a harsh tropical climate seemed a bit nutty.

2. Analysis

(1)本句中"completed in 1912"为分词短语作状语,动词"complete"的逻辑主语与主句主语一致,故可省略。并且"complete"与逻辑主语是被动关系,所以使用过去分词短语,置于句首。

(2)主句和从句之间用连词 because 连接。"because even attempting..."在句中作原因状语。

(3)英语是形合的语言,要善于使用连词表明句与句之间的逻辑关系。汉语是意合的语言，逻辑词的使用相对宽松。英语主从句之间一般有因果、先后、让步、转折等关系。

3. Practice

(1)使用让步状语从句将下列句子组合成一句。

① William Clark was not officially granted the rank of captain prior to the expedition's departure.

②Captain Lewis more or less ignored this technicality and treated Clark as his equal in authority and rank.

(2)使用时间状语从句将下列句子组合成一句。

①The explorers approached the headwaters of the Missouri.

②They discovered, to their horror, that the Rocky Mountain range stood between them and their goal, a passage to the Pacific.

第十一章　名校殿堂

概　述

作为拥有世界名校最多的国家，美国以其全球领先的教育资源和多元开放的教育理念，吸引着世界各地无数学子前往求学。这一章我们将开启校园之旅，一起走进梦想中的学府殿堂，去探寻校园特色建筑背后的故事与内涵，领略世界顶尖学府的文化魅力。本章所选的老牌名校包括美国最古老的高等学府哈佛大学、被誉为“硅谷心脏”的斯坦福大学以及有“美国总统摇篮”之称的耶鲁大学。

第一节　哈佛大学

哈佛大学位于美国马萨诸塞州大波士顿都会区的剑桥市，是一所享誉世界的私立研究型大学、著名的常春藤盟校成员，也是美国本土历史最为悠久的高等学府。学校创建于1636年，比美国独立早140年，因此有“先有哈佛，后有美国”的说法。它最初名为“新市民学院”，后为了纪念最重要的捐赠者约翰·哈佛，更名为哈佛大学。

Culture Express

绯红色（crimson）是哈佛校报的名称，也是校队的名字，还是哈佛的代表色。从校徽到校服，从报纸到横幅，哈佛绯红在校园里随处可见。令人印象更为深刻的是，满园的褐石建筑也与绯红色协调一致，看起来雄伟壮观、庄重典雅。

Reading Passage 1

导读

建成于1878年的哈佛纪念堂，是哈佛最具标志性的建筑之一，也是美国国家历史地标。其建筑风格属于维多利亚全盛时期哥特式。在哈佛众多建筑物中，哈佛纪念堂的彩色屋顶和圆花窗（rose window）格外耀眼夺目。

Memorial Hall, located in the triangle-shaped area between Cambridge, Kirkland, and Quincy streets in Cambridge, Massachusetts, is an **imposing** High Victorian Gothic building in memory of Harvard men in defense of the Union during the American Civil War, particularly the 136 dead—a "Hall of Alumni in which students and graduates might be inspired by the pictured and **sculpted** presence of her founders, benefactors, faculty, presidents, and most **distinguished** sons."

It was designed by architects William Robert Ware, A.B. 1852 and Henry Van Brunt, A.B. 1854. The **cornerstone** for the building was laid in 1870, and construction was completed in several stages over the next eight years. A 1907 publication gives **dimensions** of 305 by 113 feet, with a height of 190 feet at the tower; a 2012 source gave a height of 195 feet, making it the ninth-tallest building in Cambridge at that time. Its 1970 National Historic Landmark **designation** recognized it one of the nation's most dramatic examples of High Victorian Gothic architecture.

Memorial Hall was described as consisting of three main divisions: one of them a theater, for academic ceremonies; another a vast **refectory**, covered with a **timbered** roof, hung about with portraits and lighted by **stained** windows, like the halls of the colleges of Oxford; and the third, the most interesting, a chamber high, dim and severe, **consecrated** to the sons of the university who fell in the long Civil War.

The "three divisions" are known today as respectively Sanders Theatre, Annenberg Hall (formerly Alumni Hall or the Great Hall), and Memorial **Transept**. The opening of Loker Commons in 1996 added more student space in the lower level, including food service areas. The Queen's Head Pub opened there in 2007.

(Adapted from *https://guides.library.harvard.edu / hua / MemorialHall*)

注释:

1.imposing 雄伟壮观的
2.sculpt 雕刻,雕塑
3.distinguished 杰出的
4.cornerstone 奠基石
5.dimension 尺寸,规模
6.designation 称号
7.refectory 食堂,餐厅
8.timbered 木结构的
9.stained 彩色的
10.consecrate 祝圣,圣化
11.transept (十字形教堂的)耳堂

Reading Passage 2

导读

图书馆是一所大学的灵魂，像哈佛这样的世界名校，图书馆多达近百所。哈佛大学拥有美国最大的学术图书馆，规模位列全球第五。在哈佛庞大的图书馆系统中，处于中央领航位置的怀德纳图书馆，是世界上规模最大的大学图书馆，又因其地下六层的巨大藏书库以及与泰坦尼克号邮轮相关的故事而声名远播。

The Harry Elkins Widener Memorial Library, **housing** some 3.5 million books in its vast and **cavernous** stacks, is the center-piece of the Harvard College Libraries and, more broadly, of the entire Harvard Library system. It honors 1907 Harvard College graduate and book collector Harry Elkins Widener, and was constructed by his mother Eleanor Elkins Widener after his death in the sinking of the **RMS** Titanic in 1912.

The library's holdings, which include works in more than one hundred languages, **comprise** one of the world's most comprehensive research collections in the humanities and social sciences. Its 57 miles of shelves, along five miles of aisles on ten levels, comprise a **labyrinth** which one student could not enter without feeling that he ought to carry a compass, a sandwich, and a whistle.

At Harvard's geographical and intellectual heart directly across **Tercentenary** Theatre from Memorial Church, Widener Library is a hollow **rectangle** of Harvard brick with Indiana **limestone traceries**, 250 by 200 by 80 feet high and enclosing 320,000 square feet, **colonnaded** on its front by immense pillars with elaborate **Corinthian capitals**, all of which stand at the head of a flight of stairs that would not disgrace the capitol in Washington. Sources describe the building's style as variously **Beaux-Arts**, Georgian, **Hellenistic**, or the **austere**, formalistic Imperial or "Imperial and Classical" style displayed in the Law School's Langdell Hall and the Medical School Quadrangle.

The east, south, and west wings house the stacks, while the north contains administrative offices and various reading rooms, including the Main Reading Room (now the Loker Reading Room)—which, spanning the entire front of the building and some 42 feet in both depth and height, was termed by architectural historian Bainbridge Bunting "the most **ostentatious** interior space at Harvard." Topmost floor, supported by the stacks framework itself, contains thirty-two rooms for special collections, studies, offices, and seminars.

At the building's heart are the Widener Memorial Rooms, displaying papers and **mementos** recalling the life and death of Harry Widener, as well as the Harry Elkins Widener Collection, the precious group of rare and wonderfully interesting books brought together by Mr. Widener, to which was later added one of the few perfect Gutenberg Bibles—the object of a 1969 burglary attempt **conjectured** by Harvard's police chief inspired by the heist film *Topkapi*.

(Adapted from *https://www.librarianshipstudies.com/2020/04/widener-library-harvard-university.html*)

注释：

1.house 收藏
2.cavernous 大而深的
3.RMS 皇家邮轮(Royal Mail Ship)
4.comprise 构成
5.labyrinth 迷宫
6.tercentenary 三百周年纪念
7.rectangle 长方形
8.limestone 石灰岩
9.tracery 窗花格
10.colonnade 柱廊
11.Corinthian capital 科林斯式柱头
12.Beaux-Arts 布杂艺术，学院派
13.Hellenistic 希腊风格的
14.austere 朴素的，简朴的
15.ostentatious 浮华的，惹人注目的
16.memento 纪念品
17.conjecture 推测

Word Power

Match the word with its appropriate meaning in English.

comprise, conjecture, distinguished, imposing

(1)________ very successful and admired by other people
(2)________ impressive to look at
(3)________ to form part of a larger group of people or things
(4)________ form an opinion or reach a conclusion on the basis of information that is not certain or complete

Summary

Fill in the blanks with words or phrases from Reading Passage 2.

As the center-piece of the entire Harvard Library system, Widener Library (1)________ some 3.5 million books in more than one hundred languages, (2)________ one of the world's most comprehensive research collections in the humanities and social sciences. It was (3) ________ in memory of Harry Elkins Widener, 1907 Harvard College graduate and book collector, by his mother Eleanor Elkins Widener after his death in the (4) ________ of the RMS Titanic in 1912. Widener Library is a (5) ________ rectangle of Harvard brick with Indiana limestone traceries, colonnaded on its front by (6) ________ pillars with elaborate Corinthian capitals.

Listening

Scan the code and listen to a microlecture about Harvard University. Please choose the best answer to each of the following questions.

(1) John Harvard was the ________ of Harvard University.

A. founder　　B. benefactor

C. principal　　D. professor

(2) What is the official color of Harvard University?

A. Brown.　　B. Red.

C. Crimson.　　D. Jacinth.

(3) Which of the following is not true?

A. Harvard was originally called the New College.

B. Sherman Hoar sat as a model for the head of the statute of John Harvard.

C. Harvard University was established in 1636.

D. The statute of John Harvard was nicknamed the "statue of three truths."

Speaking

Can you briefly introduce Memorial Hall at Harvard University? Please refer to the following words and expressions if necessary.

is located in / dramatic example of / High Victorian Gothic building / in memory of / consisting of three main divisions

Writing

1. Example Sentence

Memorial Hall was described as consisting of three main divisions: one of them a theater, for academic ceremonies; another a vast refectory, covered with a timbered roof, hung about with portraits and lighted by stained windows, like the halls of the colleges of Oxford; and the third, the most interesting, a chamber high, dim and severe, consecrated to the sons of the university who fell in the long Civil War.

2. Analysis

(1)这一句描写纪念堂的构成,使用了非常简洁的总分结构,后面的每一部分都省略了系动词 was。

(2)consist of 意思是“由……构成”,前面是整体,后面是部分。

(3)covered with…, hung about…, lighted by…, consecrated to…都是过去分词作后置定语。

(4)the most interesting 形容词词组用作评注性状语,表示看法或评价,常用逗号与前后文隔开。

在写作中需要使用分词作后置定语时,首先判断该动词与被修饰名词的主被动关系,主动用现在分词,被动用过去分词。

3. Practice

参照例文格式,使用后置定语合并下列句子。

(1) Tower cranes in general are composed of three main parts.

(2) The base is connected to a large concrete foundation that carries the entire weight.

(3) The mast gives the crane its height.

(4) The slewing unit is attached to the top of the mast, allowing the crane to rotate along its axis.

第二节　斯坦福大学

斯坦福大学坐落于美国加州旧金山湾区南部的帕罗奥多市(Palo Alto),是一所私立研究型大学,紧邻硅谷,培养了众多高科技知名品牌创始人,因其学术声誉和创业氛围而享誉全球。它与旧金山北湾的加州大学伯克利分校(University of California, Berkeley)共同构成了美国西部学术中心。

Culture Express

斯坦福校园整体的建筑概念由当时著名景观设计师弗雷德里克·奥姆斯特德(Frederick Law Olmsted)负责,他拒绝使用山地而建议多加利用平地。校园建筑布局方正、四平八稳,黄砖红瓦、拱廊相接,给人以厚重的历史感,加上西海岸的阳光、草地、棕榈大道,古朴典雅的建筑与美国西部地域特色相映成趣,使得斯坦福大学获评全球最美大学之一。

Reading Passage 1

导读

斯坦福大学的创建,始于一个悲伤的故事。创始人斯坦福夫妇为纪念因伤寒离世的15岁独子,选择建立一所大学及博物馆。因此,校园的规划设计处处有斯坦福家族的印记。校园选址在他们自家的大农场,这也是斯坦福常被称为“大农场”的原因之一。

Stanford University, officially Leland Stanford Junior University, is a private research institution of higher learning at Stanford, California, U.S., one of the most

prestigious in the country. The university was founded in 1885 by railroad **magnate** Leland Stanford and his wife, Jane, and was **dedicated** to their deceased only child, Leland, Jr.; it opened in 1891.

The university campus largely occupies Stanford's former Palo Alto farm. In 1876, Leland Stanford purchased 650 acres of what had been Rancho San Francisquito for a country home and began the development of his Palo Alto **Stock Farm** for trotting horses. In 1885, a year and a half after the death of their only child, Jane and Leland Stanford executed **a deed of trust** conveying the farm, along with several other parcels of land, to the trustees for the founding of the Leland Stanford Junior University. He later bought the **adjoining** properties totaling more than 8,000 acres. The size and varied **topography** of the 8,180 acres of foothills and plains that Stanford has today in the center of the San Francisco **Peninsula** provide a rare opportunity for comprehensive land use and resource management.

The Stanfords traveled widely before founding Stanford and wanted the Main Quadrangle and the Palm Drive main entrance to reflect European Beaux Arts formalism. The Stanfords' collaboration with Olmsted, the **foremost** landscape architect of the time, and the architectural firm of Shepley, Rutan and Coolidge resulted in **California Mission-inspired buildings** of local sandstone with **red-tiled** roofs, surrounding a **cloistered** quadrangle with Memorial Church as its focus. The rectangular plan of the Main Quadrangle was designed to provide for expansion through a series of quadrangles developed laterally. The campus sustained heavy damage from earthquakes in 1906 and 1989 but was rebuilt each time.

(Adapted from *https://www.britannica.com/topic/Stanford-University*, *http://facts.stanford.edu/about/lands/*)

注释:

1. prestigious 久负盛名
2. magnate 产业大亨
3. dedicate 献给
4. stock farm 畜牧场
5. a deed of trust 信托契约
6. adjoining 毗邻的
7. topography 地形
8. peninsula 半岛
9. foremost 最好的
10. California Mission-inspired building 加州使命(复兴)式建筑
11. red-tiled 红瓦
12. cloistered 有回廊的,修道院的

Reading Passage 2

导读

斯坦福校园的著名地标有胡佛塔(Hoover Tower)、罗丹雕塑园(the Rodin sculpture garden)、主方院(Main Quadrangle)和纪念教堂(Memorial Church)等。其中一座建筑被誉为“皇冠上的明珠”,外部镶嵌美轮美奂,室内装潢富丽堂皇,这就是著名的纪念教堂。它就像一颗耀眼的宝石,作为核心统领着校园的建筑。

Stanford Memorial Church is located at the center of Stanford University, sitting the middle of the long southern range of the school's Main Quad rangle. The church was **commissioned** by Jane Stanford as a memorial to her husband, Leland Stanford.

The Church is part of a linked, complex system of **arcades** that make up the Quad rangle, which serves to unify the entire complex. The church's heavy red tile roofs, round **turrets**, low **arches**, and **rough-hewn** stonework matches the design of other buildings in the Quad rangle. The building is **Romanesque** in form and **Byzantine** in its details, inspired by churches in the region of Venice, especially, Ravenna. Its stained glass windows and extensive **mosaics** are based on religious paintings the Stanfords admired in Europe. The church has been called "the University's architectural crown jewel."

Built during the American **Renaissance** period, the church was described as a perfect example of the movement, with elements of the Renaissance, Byzantine and **Medieval** art, the Romanesque period, and the **Pre-Raphaelites.** The original designs for Memorial Church were made in 1886 by prominent American architect Henry Hobson Richardson; when he died that same year, his student Charles A. Coolidge completed them. Coolidge loosely based his design of Memorial Church on Richardson's design of **Trinity Church** in Boston.

The church has five **pipe organs**, which allow musicians to produce many styles of organ music. Stanford Memorial Church has **withstood** two major earthquakes, in 1906 and 1989, and was extensively **renovated** after each.

(Adapted form *https://infogalactic.com/info/Stanford_Memorial_Church*)

注释:

1. commission 委托
2. arcade 拱廊
3. turret 角楼,塔楼
4. arch 拱形
5. rough-hewn 粗制的
6. Romanesque 罗马式的
7. Byzantine 拜占庭式的(尤指有高穹顶和马赛克装饰的教堂)

8. mosaic 马赛克
9. Renaissance 文艺复兴
10. medieval 中世纪的
11. Pre-Raphaelites 拉斐尔前派
12. Trinity Church 三一教堂
13. pipe organ 管风琴
14. withstand 经受住
15. renovate 修复

Word Power

Match the word with its appropriate meaning in English.

prestigious, commission, withstand, renovate

(1) ________ to be strong enough not to be hurt or damaged by extreme conditions
(2) ________ respected and admired as very important or of very high quality
(3) ________ restore to a previous or better condition
(4) ________ formally arrange for someone to do a task for you

Summary

Fill in the blanks with words or phrases from Reading Passage 1.

The Palo Alto farm, formerly purchased by the Stanfords for trotting horses, is largely (1) ________ by Stanford campus. In 1885, a year and a half after the death of their only child, a deed of trust was (2) ________ by the Stanfords to (3) ________ the farm as well as several other parcels of land to the trustees for the (4) ________ of the Leland Stanford Junior University. He later bought the adjoining properties (5) ________ more than 8,000 acres. In the center of the San Francisco Peninsula, the size and varied topography of the 8,180 acres of foothills and plains that Stanford has today provide a rare opportunity for (6) ________ land use and resource management.

Listening

Scan the code and listen to a microlecture about Stanford University. Please choose the best answer to each of the following questions.

(1) The primary building materials of The Main Quad were local ________ sandstone.

A. brown　　B. red
C. yellow　　D. grey

(2) ________ has been called "Stanford University's architectural crown jewel."

A. The Main Quad
B. Hoover Tower
C. The Rodin sculptures
D. Stanford Memorial Church

(3) Who is the designer of the New York Central Park?

A. Herbert Hoover.
B. Leland Stanford.
C. Frederick Law Olmsted.
D. Jane Stanford.

Speaking

Can you briefly introduce Stanford Memorial Church? Please refer to the following words and expressions if necessary.

is located at / sitting the middle of / is part of / unify / match / is Romanesque in form / is Byzantine in details

Writing

1. Example Sentence

The church's heavy red tile roofs, round turrets, low arches, and rough-hewn stonework matches the design of other buildings in the Quad rangle. The building is Romanesque in form and Byzantine in its details, inspired by churches in the region of Venice, especially, Ravenna. Its stained glass windows and extensive mosaics are based on religious paintings the Stanfords admired in Europe.

2. Analysis

(1) 这一句通过细节描写突出斯坦福纪念教堂的建筑特色和内外风格。

(2) red、round、low 和 rough-hewn 四个形容词与所修饰名词的并列使用，给读者以生动的画面感，颜色、形状、结构高矮、质地粗细，一目了然。

(3) inspired by...是过去分词作后置定语。

(4) the Stanfords admired in Europe 是省略了 that 的定语从句，修饰前面的 paintings。

对于建筑物的精细描写，用形容词作前置定语比较简洁明快，在写作中可与后置定语搭配使用。

3. Practice

下面句子介绍了斯坦福主方院建筑的细节特色，请选择合适的形容词与名词搭配。

sturdy, simple, low, massive

This group of architects are noted for the Richardsonian Romanesque style, and features of that style including "round (1) ________ arches, (2) ________ piers, (3) ________ walls, (4) ________ silhouettes and sheltering roofs" are prominent in the Quadrangle.

第三节 耶鲁大学

耶鲁大学是位于美国康涅狄格州纽黑文市（New Haven，Connecticut）的著名私立研究型大学，常春藤盟校成员。耶鲁大学创建于1701年，是美国第三古老的高等学府。它初名为"大学学院"(Collegiate School)，后为感谢英国东印度公司总裁伊利胡·耶鲁(Elihu Yale)的捐助，改名为"耶鲁学院"(Yale College)，并逐渐由学院发展为大学。

Culture Express

耶鲁流传着这样一句玩笑："一不小心，你就会教出一个总统来。"这是因为耶鲁大学著名校友中包括5位美国总统以及众多政界名人，耶鲁因此赢得了"美国总统摇篮"的美称。此外，耶鲁毕业生还包括许多著名大学的创始人或第一任校长，如普林斯顿大学、哥伦比亚大学、芝加哥大学、康奈尔大学等。因此，耶鲁又被誉为"美国学院之母"。这些应归功于耶鲁关心社会和重视"领导者教育"的传统。

Reading Passage 1

导读

耶鲁大学享有"美国最美丽的城市校园"的美誉。建筑多以哥特式为主，兼有佐治亚风格(Georgian style)，整个校园弥漫着古典与浪漫的气息。建筑师为了凸显校园建筑庄重典雅的气质，故意以硫酸泼溅的方式将楼宇做旧，再用中世纪的方式进行修复，辅以壁龛，看起来就像是完美的全石质结构，当然事实并非如此。

Yale's central campus in downtown New Haven covers 260 acres (1.1 km^2) and comprises its main, historic campus and a medical campus **adjacent** to the Yale-New Haven Hospital. In western New Haven, the university holds 500 acres (2.0 km^2) of athletic facilities, including the Yale Golf Course. In 2008, Yale purchased the 136-acre (0.6 km^2) former **Bayer Pharmaceutical** campus in West Haven, Connecticut, the buildings of which are now used as laboratory and research space. Yale also owns seven forests in Connecticut, Vermont, and New Hampshire—the largest of which is the 7,840-acre (31.7 km^2) Yale-Myers Forest in Connecticut's Quiet Corner—and **nature preserves** including Horse Island.

Yale is noted for its largely **Collegiate Gothic** campus as well as several iconic modern buildings commonly discussed in architectural history survey courses. Yale also owns and has restored many **noteworthy** 19th-century **mansions** along Hillhouse Avenue, which was considered the most beautiful street in America by Charles Dickens when he visited the United States in the 1840s. In 2011, *Travel+Leisure* listed the Yale campus as one of the most beautiful in the United States.

Many of Yale's buildings were constructed in the Collegiate Gothic architecture style from 1917 to 1931, financed largely by Edward S. Harkness, including the Yale Drama School. Stone sculptures built into the walls of the buildings **portray** contemporary college personalities such as a writer, an athlete, a tea-drinking **socialite**, and a student who has fallen asleep while reading. Similarly, the decorative **friezes** on the buildings **depict** contemporary scenes such as policemen chasing a robber (on the wall of the Law School), or a student relaxing with a mug of beer. The architect, James Gamble Rogers, **faux-aged** these buildings by **splashing** the walls with acid, deliberately breaking their **leaded** glass windows and repairing them in the style of the Middle Ages, and creating **niches** for decorative **statuary** but leaving them empty to **simulate** loss or theft over the ages. In fact, the buildings merely simulate Middle Ages architecture, for though they appear to be constructed of solid stone blocks in the **authentic** manner, most actually have steel framing as was commonly used in 1930. One exception is **Harkness Tower**, 216 feet (65.8 m) tall, which was originally a free-standing stone structure.

(Adapted from *https://infogalactic.com/info/Yale_University*)

注释：

1. km^2 = square kilometre 平方千米
2. adjacent 毗连的，邻近的
3. Bayer Pharmaceutical 拜耳制药
4. nature preserve 自然保护区
5. Collegiate Gothic 学院哥特式
6. noteworthy 重要的，值得关注的
7. mansion 公馆，宅第
8. portray 描绘，描画
9. socialite 社交名流
10. frieze (柱顶过梁和挑檐间的)雕带
11. depict 描绘，描画
12. faux-age 做旧
13. splash 泼洒
14. leaded (窗户)有花饰铅条的
15. niche 凹进去的地方，壁龛
16. statuary 雕像，雕塑
17. simulate 模仿，冒充
18. authentic 真实的，逼真的
19. Harkness Tower 哈克尼斯塔(耶鲁地标)

Reading Passage 2

导读

始于1792年的线性建筑规划(linear building plan)被称为“老砖排”(Old Brick Row),是美国第一个校园规划,并成为19世纪建造的许多美国大学校园的典范。耶鲁大学唯一留存下来的一栋老砖楼,同时也是保存下来的迄今为止最古老的建筑,就是康涅狄格大会堂(Connecticut Hall),采用的是佐治亚建筑风格。它在施行线性建筑规划时期也曾被“乔装改扮”,如今它已历经二百多年风雨沧桑,依然矗立在耶鲁老校区,继续见证这所世界名校的发展变化。

Connecticut Hall, built in 1750-52, was the first of Yale's brick buildings. It is an altered example of a **conservatively** designed Georgian structure. It is also Yale's oldest **extant** building and only surviving example of an eighteenth century structure. It was **designated** a National Historic Landmark in 1965.

In size and arrangement, Connecticut Hall is a close **parallel** to Massachusetts Hall at Harvard, which was built in the Early Georgian style in 1718-20. Connecticut Hall's simple and functional style made it **adaptable** down through the years to the changing conditions. Its exterior was altered at least three times, its interior more times than are recorded. Apparently it changed color with the changing tastes of the world around it—from red-and-white to **cream** to **allover-drab** and back to red-and-white.

By 1790 it was already old-fashioned, and when John Trumbull, **exponent** of the new classical style of the post-Revolutionary generation, learned that he would have to **incorporate** the old building into his modern plan for a new Yale campus, he complained that it would have to go.

Instead Connecticut Hall was given an additional story and a new roof and took its place as part of Trumbull's classical Brick Row, **fronting the Green** along College Street, completed by 1820. But by the middle of the century the Brick Row was out of style and Connecticut Hall was being described as "**dilapidated**, **scabby** and **malodorous**." After the Civil War Yale decided to **raze** all its old Georgian architecture and redevelop the West side of the Green with larger and more modern buildings. But by the 90's the **Colonial Revival** was beginning and before Connecticut Hall could be **demolished**, a group of alumni organized to save and restore it.

Once again Connecticut Hall received a new roof and became part of a new campus plan. The dark paint was **scraped** off the window frames and the **gambrel roof** that Trumbull had removed was replaced. Another major operation followed fifty years later in 1952-54, when the interior was entirely **gutted** and a new set of modern rooms was built inside the brick shell. The building remains in that form today, housing faculty, seminars and freshman reading rooms.

(Adapted from *http://nhpt.org / connecticut-hall*)

注释：

1. conservative 保守的，守旧的
2. extant 现存的，存世的
3. designate 选定，命名
4. parallel（尤指不同地点或时间的）极其相似的人（或情况、事件等）
5. adaptable 能适应的
6. cream 奶油色，米色
7. allover-drab 整体单调的，土褐色的
8. exponent 拥护者，倡导者
9. incorporate 并入，包含
10. front 面向，朝向
11. the Green 纽黑文绿地(New Haven Green)
12. dilapidated 破旧的
13. scabby 肮脏的
14. malodorous 恶臭的
15. raze 彻底摧毁
16. Colonial Revival 殖民复兴风格
17. demolish 拆除
18. scrape 刮掉，除去
19. gambrel roof 斜折线屋顶，复折式屋顶
20. gut 损毁（建筑物）的内部

Word Power

Fill in the blanks with the words given below. Change the form where necessary. Each word can be used only once.

extant, authentic, incorporate, noteworthy

(1) ________ deserving to be noticed or to receive attention because it is unusual, or important

(2) ________ still in existence

(3) ________ almost the same as or as good as the original

(4) ________ to include something so that it forms a part of something

Summary

Fill in the blanks with words or phrases from Reading Passage 2

As a close (1) ________ to Massachusetts Hall at Harvard, Connecticut Hall is an (2)________ example of a conservatively designed Georgian structure. It is also Yale's oldest (3) ________ building and was designated a National Historic Landmark in 1965. Due to its simple and functional style, Connecticut Hall has been (4) ________ down through the years to the changing conditions. Its interior was altered more times than are recorded and the (5) ________ at least three times. With the changing (6) ________ of the world around it, it changed color obviously—from red-and-white to cream to allover-drab and back to red-and-white.

Listening

Scan the code and listen to a microlecture about Yale University. Please choose the best answer to each of the following questions.

(1) Which of the following is reckoned as the oldest and most beautiful of Yale residential colleges?

A. Branford College.　　B. Morse College.

C. Berkeley College.　　D. Pierson College.

(2) When was Connecticut Hall declared a National Historic Landmark?

A. 1917.　　B. 1931.

C. 1965.　　D. 1950.

(3) Who did not graduate from Yale University?

A. Bill Clinton.　　B. Dick Cheney.

C. George W. Bush.　　D. Hillary Clinton.

Speaking

Can you briefly introduce Yale's central campus in downtown New Haven? Please refer to the following words and expressions if necessary.

covers / comprises / Collegiate Gothic / stone sculpture / faux-aged / simulate

Writing

1. Example Sentence

Stone sculptures built into the walls of the buildings portray contemporary college personalities such as a writer, an athlete, a tea-drinking socialite, and a student who has fallen asleep while reading. Similarly, the decorative friezes on the buildings depict contemporary scenes such as policemen chasing a robber (on the wall of the Law School), or a student relaxing with a mug of beer.

2. Analysis

(1) 这两句描写的是耶鲁校园建筑中的细节——嵌入墙体的石像和装饰性雕带，采用列举的方式呈现刻画的主题和内容。

(2) similarly 意为"同样地"，在这里作为衔接词，表示两句之间的比较关系，用于描述相似点，同时具有增补的效果。

(3) built into、chasing 和 relaxing 都是分词作后置定语。

(4) 两句都用 such as 来进行不完全列举，后面无须出现 and so on、ect.、and others 这样的表达。

文章中的衔接词(或短语)表明段落、句子或句子成分之间的关系，在阅读理解中准确定位衔接词，有助于快速高效把握文章的整体框架和主旨脉络。同理，在写作中正确使用衔接词有助于整合文章观点，阐明前后的逻辑关系，起到画龙点睛的作用。

3. Practice

选择合适的衔接词(或短语)填空。

namely, otherwise, similarly, while, in brief, such as

In some schools, students may learn that behaviors (1) ________ following the rules, acting in expected ways, and not questioning adults are rewarded. (2) ________ in other schools students learn that personal expression, taking initiative, or questioning authority are rewarded behaviors. (3) ________, if biased or prejudicial behaviors and statements are tolerated in a school, students may embrace the values that are accepted or modeled by adults and other students.

参考答案

第一章　美国城市地标建筑

第一节

Word Power

1. (1)N　(2)N　(3)P　(4)E　(5)P

2. (1)audacious　(2)unparalleled　(3)prominent　(4)stubborn　(5)inefficient　(6)clueless　(7)stubborn

Summary

(1)inscribed　(2)designer　(3)chosen　(4)submissions　(5)misjudged

Listening

(1)D　(2)A　(3)A

Writing

Lin, a graduate from Yale University and a designer of the Vietnam Veterans Memorial, entered the competition and won again.

第二节

Word Power

(1)ornament　(2)rivet　(3)revamps　(4)radiates　(5)hoist

Summary

(1) Art Deco　(2) automobile　(3) machine　(4) ornamented　(5) radiator　(6) Empire State　(7) iconic　(8) contemporary

Listening

(1)D　(2)A　(3)A

Writing

(1)Happy are those who are contented.

(2)So sudden was the attack that he had no time to escape.

第三节

Word Power

(1)flourishing　(2)ephemeral　(3)groundbreaking　(4)radical

Summary

(1) curved (2) images (3) distortion (4) landscape (5) perception (6)proximity

Listening

(1)D (2)B (3)A

Writing

He, in hope for winning the contest of designing eco-friendly homes, worked day and night for nearly three months and even consulted the professor working at his college.

第四节

Word Power

(1)abhor (2)erupts (3)evicted (4)quirky (5)sturdy

Summary

(1)boom (2)urbane (3)threatened (4)shadow (5)location (6)restoration (7)preserved

Listening

(1)D (2)D (3)A

Writing

Built in the 1860s, Doc Maynard's house near Alki Point is an example of an earlier Victorian style known as Gothic Revival, whose architectural character is almost unrecognizable today.

第五节

Word Power

(1)wither (2)blight (3)obsolete (4)reinvigorate

Summary

(1)redevelopment (2)urban (3)envisioned (4)reinvigorate (5)coordinated (6)eliminate (7)liberate (8)clutter

Listening

(1)C (2)A (3)C

Writing

The 1250-foot (381 m) steel-framed Empire State Building was the tallest building in the world until 1971.

第六节

Word Power

(1)on (2)out (3)By (4)to (5)for

Summary

(1)pyramid-shaped (2)beacon (3) Adjacent (4)skyscraper (5)reflects (6) interfere (7)reflections

Listening

(1)A (2)A (3)C

Writing

In the heated debate, this professor proposes to protect the shopping center instead of demolishing it because of its value in research, a contrast with most people' opinion.

第二章 美国国家公园建筑

第一节

Word Power

(1)integrity (2)segregation (3)fragile (4)trample (5)commissioned

Summary

(1)integrity (2)segregated (3)view (4)scenic (5)fragile (6)pristine (7)surrounding

Listening

(1)A (2)C

Writing

(1)We must preserve these endangered species, as (is) known to all.

(2)The material is elastic, as (is) shown in the figure.

第二节

Word Power

(1) Legislation (2) petition (3) preservationist (4) conservationists (5)pavement

Summary

(1)integrate (2)incomparable (3)Preservation (4)modification (5)adversely (6)Rustic (7)blend

Listening

(1)A (2)A

Writing

American opinion is divided between those who insist on the universal right to bear arms and those who advocate stricter gun controls.

第三节

Word Power

(1)monotonous (2)dominating (3)intricate (4)unparalleled (5)discordant

Summary

(1)architect (2)discordant (3)promontory (4)intricate (5)decorative (6)imbedded (7)spiritual

Listening

(1)A (2)C

Writing

In 1990, chicken was the most popular meat in this city, with about 285 grams consumed per person per week.

第四节

Word Power

(1)unobstructed (2)piqued (3)intrigued (4)booming (5)prized

Summary

(1)logging (2)swept (3)raw (4)Timber (5)discovered (6)sawmills (7)prized

Listening

(1)A (2)C

Writing

Failing in efforts to pass the entrance examination to graduate school, she turned toward looking for a job in hope of enhancing her expertise from a work.

第三章 美国先驱人物的故居

第一节

Word Power

(1)halve (2)remodel (3)elongate (4)estimate (5)typify

Summary

(1)neo-classical (2) small mountain (3) villa (4)continual (5)remodeling (6)domes

Listening

(1)C (2)C (3)C

Writing

Empire State Building imbued New York City with a deep sense of pride, desperately needed in the depths of the Great Depression, when many city residents were unemployed and prospects looked bleak.

第二节

Word Power

(1)assassination (2)consolidate (3)bustling (4)segregation (5)decaying

Summary

(1)residential (2)spiritual (3)prior to (4)birth (5)assassination (6)cherished (7)iconic

Listening

(1)C (2)A

Writing

Cold and hungry, the little girl kept crying.

第三节

Word Power

(1)renovation (2)furnishings (3)inheritance (4)oddity (5)novelty

Summary

(1)Gothic (2)fortress (3)completion (4)notable (5)renovate (6)installing (7)rented (8)returning

Listening

(1)A (2)A (3)A

Writing

(1)Some are laughing, and some crying.

(2)Sam won the first match, and John the second.

第四节

Word Power

(1)hermit (2)botanist (3)shanty (4)cart (5)ravage

Summary

(1)hermit (2)botanist (3)ornithologist (4)observer (5)use (6)delight (7)surveyor

Listening

(1)C (2)B

Writing

Courtesy is a habit, showing your attitude toward your life. Also, courtesy is a respect, sending the message of care to others.

第五节

Word Power

(1)marvel (2)extract (3)makeshift (4)superior

Summary

(1)equipped (2)superior (3)consisting (4)contained (5)perpendicular (6)complex

Listening

(1)C (2)D

Writing

Heavy fog enshrouding the earth in the evening, nobody could make out what the dark mass was from a distance.

第六节

Word Power

(1)laureate (2)stipulates (3)caustic (4)intrepid (5)eloquent

Summary

(1)influential (2)caustic (3)intrepid (4)poetic (5)honorary (6)purchased

Listening

(1)D (2)B

Writing

The southern states wanted to set up a country of their own, where they would be free to keep black slaves.

第四章 科技巨头的奇幻建筑

第一节

Word Power

(1)infuse (2)interlocks (3)excavate (4)deploy (5)tapped

Summary

(1) out-of-the-box (2) functional (3) innovation (4) reflect (5) foster (6)boom (7)infused

Listening

(1)C (2)D (3)A

Writing

Making a short movie requires many steps. First, the script needs to be written. And after that, a location must be found. Then the lines are rehearsed. Next, the movie is shot and edited. Finally, titles and credits need to be added.

第二节

Word Power

(1)transit (2)temperate (3)transparent (4)intact (5)reigns

Summary

(1)consists of (2)retail (3)transit (4)trails (5)soliciting (6)environmental

Listening

(1)A (2)D

Writing

The value of residential property in America—at around $34trn—rivals the market capitalisation of all listed American companies.

第三节

Word Power

(1)endemic (2)contempt (3)exhilarated (4)caustic (5)exacerbates

Summary

(1) impressive (2) errors (3) signature (4) serious (5) small-town (6)contempt

Listening

(1) A (2)A

Writing

Building a theater is a tremendous enterprise involving literally thousands of people.

第五章　食品生产大国

第一节

Word Power

(1)c　(2)d　(3)a　(4)b　(5)e

Summary

(1)flat　(2)agricultural　(3)Great　(4)primary　(5)230

Listening

(1)B　(2)A　(3)C

Writing

He flew away, not so that he could escape punishment, but so that he could chase the real murderer.

第二节

Word Power

(1)evicted　(2)propagandist　(3)comprise　(4)steadfast　(5)fugitive

Summary

(1)Recreation　(2)impounded　(3)hydroelectricity　(4)sacred　(5)negative　(6) comprise

Listening

(1)D　(2)C　(3)C

Writing

罗伯特·富尔顿曾经写道:"机械工程围绕杠杆、螺丝、楔、轮子等展开,就像诗人对待字母表中的每个字母一样,其用它们来展示自己的思路,其中的每一个新组合都表达一种新的思想。"

第三节

Word Power

(1)whirled　(2)reassemble　(3)dwarfed　(4)terrorize　(5)artificial

Summary

(1)dazzling　(2)transformations　(3)dwarfing　(4)dominate　(5)surrounded

Listening

(1)C　(2)A　(3)D

Writing

(1) 他正坐在窗边读书。(表示陪衬性的动作或伴随情况)

(2)按照说明,我开始使用这台洗衣机。(表示行为方式或手段)

(3) 他做出了一个选择,让全家人都陷于危险之中。(表示结果)

第四节

Word Power

(1)Undernutrition (2)infectious (3)permanent (4)requisite (5)iconic

Summary

(1)excess (2)extent (3)physical (4)primary (5)replace (6)consists

Listening

(1)D (2)D (3)A

Writing

(1)It is impossible to finish the task on time.

(2) I find it interesting that we go climbing the mountain together.

(3)It is reported that the temperature will rise in several days.

第六章 行走中的国度

第一节

Word Power

(1)assuage (2)released (3)accommodate (4)constraints (5)soaring

Summary

(1) terminal (2) complex (3) composed (4) resembles (5) integrates (6)afterthought (7)sacrifice (8)achievable

Listening

(1)D (2)D (3)B

Writing

(1) This meeting gave everyone a chance to express their own opinions.

(2) The survey results indicate that there is a direct connection between obesity and diet.

(3) The computer has solved this problem.

第二节

Word Power

(1)cohesiveness (2)consists (3)outlying (4)designated (5)heritage

Summary

(1)major (2)remaining (3)commuter (4)handles (5)reflecting (6)historic (7)replaced (8)footprint

Listening

(1)A (2)B (3)C

Writing

The commuter plane that connected the bigger city with smaller communities connected the remote areas with the rest of the world.

第三节

Word Power

(1)c (2)d (3)a (4)e (5)b

Summary

(1)direct (2)inhabited (3)hub (4)award (5)inspiring (6)centerpiece

Listening

(1)B (2)C (3)A

Writing

(1) I saw his arrival.

(2) The occurrence of the accident was at Fifth Avenue.

(3) The police conducted an investigation into the case.

第四节

Word Power

(1)c (2)d (3)e (4)a (5)f (6)b

Summary

(1)designed (2)stacked (3)exclusively (4)residential (5)separate (6)adjacent (7)architectural (8)considerable

Listening

(1)D (2)A (3)C

Writing

(1) The old building was pulled down.

(2) She felt she was being followed.

(3) These buses are required to transport tourists.

第七章 用电大国

第一节

Word Power

(1)c (2)f (3)d (4)a (5)g (6)e (7)b (8)h

Summary

(1)luminaire (2)functional (3)aesthetic (4)integrated (5)conservation (6)appeal (7)blended (8)encompass

Listening

(1)B (2)B (3)D

Writing

(1) With passion and care for the career, he tried to become an outstanding doctor.

(2) With the money run out, I had to find a job.

(3) With the children grown, the old couple began to travel around the world.

第二节

Word Power

(1)e (2)c (3)g (4)d (5)h (6)a (7)f (8)b

Summary

(1)distribute (2)reject (3)active (4)involve (5)mechanical (6)convert (7)sources (8)ventilation

Listening

(1)C (2)D (3)B

Writing

(1) 如果大坝倒塌,那么多亩良田将消失。

(2) 如果这一切被及时阻止,那么大坝就不会倒塌了。

(3) 如果没有了音乐,世界就将变成一个沉闷的世界。

第三节

Word Power

(1)c (2)e (3)a (4)g (5)b (6)d (7)h (8)f

Summary

(1)range (2)sustainability (3)lessen (4)sacrificing (5)orientation

Listening

(1)C (2)B (3)B

Writing

(1) The teacher doesn't know when they are going to hand in the homework.

(2) My mother asked me if I was hungry.

(3) Peter asked me where the girl lives.

第八章 改变美国的建筑

第一节

Word Power

(1)passionate (2)self-taught (3)monumental (4)neoclassical (5)vista

Summary

(1)Thomas Jefferson (2)state government (3)Maison Carrée

(4)independence (5)the White House (6) United States Capitol

Listening

(1)A (2)A (3)D

Writing

It has always been my dream that I would be a diplomat after graduating from university.

第二节

Word Power

(1)b (2)a (3)c (4)e (5)d

Summary

(1)oldest (2) puritans (3) clay roof (4) arches (5) rough stones (6) towers

Listening

(1)C (2)A (3)C

Writing

Love is a battlefield.

Love is a red, red rose.

第三节

Word Power

(1)surges (2)suspect (3)accommodate (4)atop (5)get underway

Summary

(1) Chicago (2) metal (3) iron skeleton (4) the Great Chicago Fire (5)economy

Listening

(1)D (2)D (3)A

Writing

一些书可以浅尝辄止，一些书可以狼吞虎咽，而极少数的书则需要细嚼慢咽、好好消化。

第四节

Word Power

(1) Venue (2) resort to (3) revolutionary (4) accessible (5) diminishes

Summary

(1) fully enclosed (2) climate-controlled (3) revolutionary (4) Dayton Company (5) inefficient

Listening

(1) A (2) B (3)A

Writing

Basically, only a few high school players will make it to the NBA.

第九章 改变美国的街道

第一节

Word Power

(1) thoroughfare (2) musical (3) metonym (4) district (5) parade (6) convert

Summary

(1) New York (2) theatrical (3) Manhattan (4) Canyon of Heroes (5) The Great White Way (6) ticker-tape parades (7) illuminated

Listening

(1)D (2)A (3)C

Writing

总的来说,得出这样一个结论是有一定把握的,但是必须具备两个条件:一是能够假定这个孩子和与之相对比的另一个孩子对待测试的态度相同;二是他没有因缺乏别的孩子已掌握的有关知识而被扣分。

原文中两个 only if 引导的从句显然使整个句子变得很复杂,可是由于有并列连词 but 和 and,整句话的逻辑关系十分清楚:"……能够得出结论……但是只要……而且只要……"。

第二节

Word Power

(1) dismantled (2) installed (3) temporary (4) synonymous (5) controversy (6) prime

Summary

(1) financial markets (2) the New York Stock Exchange (3) NASDAQ (4)Dutch (5) New Amsterdam (6) Native American

Listening

(1)D (2)A (3)B

Writing

人们对历史研究方法产生了兴趣,这与其说是因为外部对历史作为一门知识学科的有效性提出了挑战,还不如说是因为历史学家内部发生了争吵。

英文原句是个典型的长句,由 27 个词组成,中间没有使用任何标点符号,完全靠结构使整个句子的意思化零为整:less through...and more from...构成一个复杂的状语,修饰动词 arisen。在中文翻译中,"产生兴趣"这一重要内容由一个独立的句子表达,两个不同的原因则分别由不同的句子表达,整个句子被化整为零。

第三节

Word Power

(1) blueprint (2)embark on (3)initiate (4)milestone (5)rectangular

Summary

(1)New York (2) Boston (3) John Winthrop Jr. (4) Francis Lovelace (5)milestones

Listening

(1)D (2)B (3)A

Writing

And it is imagined by many that the operations of the common mind can by no means be compared with these processes in scientists'minds, and that they have to be required by a sort of special training.

原文中有三个主动词"认为"、"相比"和"掌握",在英文表达中都变成了被动,即 "is imagined"、"be compared"和 "be required"。

第四节

Word Power

(1) adorn (2) construct (3) filter (4) conceive (5) dedicate

Summary

(1)boulevard (2) parkway (3) pleasure-riding (4) driving (5)Prospect Park

Listening

(1) B (2) B (3)C

Writing

这只猴子最了不起的成就是学习驾驶拖拉机。到九岁的时候,这只猴子已经学会单独表演驾驶拖拉机了。

(tractor 和 vehicle 在句中显然都表示"拖拉机",英语表达方式有变化,而在汉语中则可以使用重复表达法。)

第五节

Word Power

(1) inhabit (2) vehicular (3) icon (4) acquisition (5) craftsmanship

Summary

(1)acquisition (2)Mississippi River (3)Rocky Mountains (4)Thomas Jefferson (5)federal government

Listening

(1) D (2) B (3)B

Writing

1.A fall into a pit, a gain in your wit.(钱锺书译)

"吃""长",都是非常"强势"的动词,钱钟书先生把握住了英文的精髓:喜静不喜动。fall(掉落)、pit(坑)、gain(获得)、wit(智慧) 都是名词,形式对仗,朗朗上口。

2.No admittance without authorization.

admittance(进入)、authorization(授权),都是名词。这个表达方式很明显是偏重用名词的。

在英文写作中,我们要摒弃中式思维,在中英文之间自由切换。从中文切换到的英文的时候,我们要"由动入静";从英文倒翻回中文的时候,要"由静入动"。

第十章　好莱坞电影中的明星大桥

第一节

Word Power

(1) landmark (2) span (3) erected (4) grandeur (5) delicacy

Summary

(1) suspension bridge (2) the Pacific Ocean (3) super-villains (4) natural disasters (5) steel and concrete

Listening

(1)C (2)B (3)A

Writing

Quickly and quietly, Maria, a young girl, went to sleep hoping to please her mom.

第二节

Word Power

(1) westbound (2)toll (3) complex (4) span (5) deck

Summary

(1)Bay Bridge (2) spans (3)western section (4)eastern section

(5) suspension bridge (6)cantilever bridge (7) reconstruction

Listening

(1)A (2)A (3)A

Writing

Completely out of touch with their families for over two years, the men of the expedition put their faith entirely in Lewis and Clark's leadership and never once rebelled against their authority.

第三节

Word Power

(1)specification (2)icon (3)toll-free (4)in charge of (5)borough

Summary

(1) Manhattan (2) Brooklyn (3) suspension bridge (4) toll-free

(5)National Historic Landmark

Listening

(1)C (2)D (3)C

Writing

Sacagawea, one of the wives of the French fur-trader Charbonneau, accompanied the expedition as a translator.

第四节

Word Power

(1)record—breaking (2)renovation (3)alternate (4) lane (5)pedestrian

Summary

(1) suspension bridge (2) Brooklyn Bridge (3) Williamsburg Bridge (4) deflection theory (5) Warren truss

Listening

(1) D (2) A (3) B

Writing

His fame and fortune virtually guaranteed by his exploits, Lewis disappointed the entire world by inexplicably failing to publish his journals.

第五节

Word Power

(1) dispatching (2) tracks (3) constructed (4) segmental (5) sturdy

Summary

(1) Florida Keys (2) Overseas Highway (3) segmental (4) precast (5) arc

Listening

(1) A (2)A (3) C

Writing

(1)Although William Clark was not officially granted the rank of captain prior to the expedition's departure, Captain Lewis more or less ignored this technicality and treated Clark as his equal in authority and rank.

(2)As the explorers approached the headwaters of the Missouri, they discovered, to their horror, that the Rocky Mountain range stood between them and their goal, a passage to the Pacific.

第十一章 名校殿堂

第一节

Word Power

(1)distinguished (2)imposing (3)comprise (4)conjecture

Summary

(1) houses (2) comprising (3) constructed (4) sinking (5) hollow (6)immense

Listening

(1)B (2)C (3)D

Writing

Tower cranes in general are composed of three main parts: one of them the base, connected to a large concrete foundation that carries the entire weight; another a mast, giving the crane its height; and the third, the slewing unit, attached to the top of the mast, allowing the crane to rotate along its axis.

第二节

Word Power

(1)withstand (2)prestigious (3)renovate (4)commission

Summary

(1) occupied (2) executed (3) convey (4) founding (5) totaling (6) comprehensive

Listening

(1)C (2)D (3)C

Writing

(1)low (2)sturdy (3)massive (4)simple

第三节

Word Power

(1)noteworthy (2)extant (3)authentic (4)incorporate

Summary

(1)parallel (2)altered (3)extant (4)adaptable (5)exterior (6) tastes

Listening

(1)A (2)C (3)B

Writing

(1)such as (2)While (3)Similarly